Praise for *The Community Engagement and Service Mission of Universities*

Universities have traditionally approached local communities from the elitist view that they are places filled with 'needs'. This book is an excellent guide to a new era of community-university relationships. It demonstrates in theory and practice that productive relationships depend upon understanding the assets of local communities and connecting them with the supportive assets of universities.

John McKnight, Co-Director, Asset-Based Community
Development Institute, Northwestern University, Illinois, USA

This is a timely and important book by two internationally acknowledged experts in the field. The strength of the book lies in its breadth of subject matter and the diversity of practice under discussion. The book rightly argues for flexible partnerships between universities and their communities, the creation of new community-relevant knowledge and the pivotal role that universities can, and should, play in tackling local and regional issues. Highly recommended for anyone concerned with making universities more effective as agents of change.

Rod Purcell, Director of Community Engagement,
University of Glasgow, UK

Cities and regions change when leaders from government, business and civil society – embodying local diversity as far as possible without losing the capacity to compromise and act based on common interests – build action partnerships with sufficient clout to institute policies based on research and best practices. As one engaged in this effort in post-Katrina New Orleans, it has been my experience that there are two roles for universities within this action-oriented mix: As citizen-leaders in the consensus-building process and as 'guidance systems' for those who are participating by giving ready access to research and best practices. The essays in this timely volume shed light on both roles.

Michael A. Cowan, Executive Director of Common Good, Loyola University, New Orleans and Assistant to the President of Loyola

Periods of economic stagnation or recession provide excellent opportunities for university agencies to apply their research and knowledge in ways that generate lasting benefits to society. PASCAL is unique in its ability to bring together scholars and practitioners from around the world to address local concerns. This book is an outstanding example of approaches used by university agencies in working with practitioners to promote regional enrichment and should be read by those interested in trying new and innovative approaches.

Norm Walzer, Ph.D., Senior Research Scholar Center for Governmental Studies, Regional Development Institute, Northern Illinois University, USA

From different – often competing – perspectives, concepts such as the 'learning city', 'knowledge region', and 'third mission' seek to encapsulate complex social, economic and political dynamics. All too frequently neglected, however, is an investigation of the nature of the knowledge which lies at the heart of these relationships: the ways in which it is generated, valued and disseminated. This volume makes a truly distinctive contribution by exploring new forms of knowledge generation based on engagement, along with critical evaluation of challenges encountered in attempts to develop genuine partnership between institutions of higher education and a wide variety of public, private and voluntary community based organisations. Leading international experts from Europe, Australia and North America add to our conceptual understanding, while fascinating case studies of innovative developments in Canada and the United States illustrate the issues involved in practice. I highly recommend this book to all with an interest in exploring the relationship between universities and the communities in which they are located – policy-makers, university leaders, researchers and representatives of public, private and voluntary sectors.

Professor Maria Slowey, Director of Higher Education Research and Development, Dublin City University, Ireland

The Community Engagement and Service Mission of Universities

Edited by
Patricia Inman
Hans G. Schuetze

Maxine Adam
publication coordinator

niace

promoting adult learning

Published by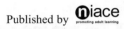

© 2010 National Institute of Adult Continuing Education
(England and Wales)

21 De Montfort Street
Leicester
LE1 7GE

Company registration no. 2603322
Charity registration no. 1002775

NIACE has a broad remit to promote lifelong learning opportunities for adults.
NIACE works to develop increased participation in education and training,
particularly for those who do not have easy access because of class, gender,
age, race, language and culture, learning difficulties or disabilities,
or insufficient financial resources.

You can find NIACE online at www.niace.org.uk

Cataloguing in Publication Data
A CIP record of this title is available from the British Library

ISBN 978-1-86201-457-2

Typeset by Avon DataSet Ltd, Bidford-on-Avon, Warwickshire
Printed and bound in the UK by Ashford Colour Press, Gosport

Contents

Acknowledgements

The editors wish to thank the following PASCAL Associates for their blind review of one or several of the chapters in this book.

German Alvarez-Mendiola
Professor, Department of Eucational Reseaerch (Departamento de Investigaciones Educativas - DIE), Centre of Research and Advanced Studies (Centro de Investigacion y Estudios Avanzados), Mexico City, Mexico

Eugenia Arvanitis
Associate, Department of Educational Planning and Intercultural Education, Ministry of Education, Lifelong Learning and Religious Affairs, Greece

Ana Correia
Professora Catedrática Convidada ISEGI (Instituto Superior de Estatística e Gestão de Informação) – UNL -Universidade Nova de Lisboa, Portugal and Senior Researcher, LNEG – Laboratório Nacional de Energia e Geologia, Portugal

Pat Davies
Project Director, European Universities Continuing Education Network (EUCEN), Spain

Katie Davison
Research Associates with Center for Governmental Studies, Northern Illinois University, USA

John Field
Professor, Centre for Research in Lifelong Learning, University of Stirling, Scotland, United Kingdom

Ralph Godsall
Priest Vicar of Westminster Abbey and Canon Emeritus of Rochester Cathedral, UK

Ivan Grdesic
Professor of Political Science, Faculty of Political Science, University of Zagreb, Croatia

Garnet Grosjean
Senior Research Fellow and Lecturer, University of British Columbia, Canada

Melissa Henriksen
Research Associates with Center for Governmental Studies, Northern Illinois University, USA

Peter Jarvis
Professor Emeritus, University of Surrey, UK; Founder and Editor of the International Journal of Lifelong Learning

Wolfgang Juette
Professor of Lifelong Learning, University of Bielefeld, Germany

Peter Kearns
Director, Global Learning Services, Australia

Fumi Kitagawa
Research Associate, University of Bristol, UK

Norman Longworth
Honorary Professor, Longlearn, France

Indra Odina
Associate Professor, Faculty of Education, Psychology and Art, University of Latvia, Latvia

Acknowledgements

Roberta Piazza
Professor of Education, University of Catania, Italy

Glen Postle
Professor Emeritus, University of Southern Queensland, Australia

Mireille Pouget
Honorary Senior Research Fellow, University of Glasgow, UK

Julia Preece
Professor, Department of Adult Education, National University of Lesotho, Lesotho

John Storan
Director of Continuum, University of East London, UK

Sonia Thompson
Director, Transformations Ltd., UK

Nestor Torres
Professor of Biochemistry and Molecular Biology, University of La Laguna, Spain

Aune Valk
Director of the Open University Centre University of Tartu, Estonia

Shirley Walters
Director of Division for Lifelong Learning (DLL) and Professor of Adult and Continuing Education, University of Western Cape (UWC), South Africa

Norm Walzer
Ph.D., Senior Research Scholar Center for Governmental Studies, Regional Development Institute, Northern Illinois University, USA

Henrik Zipsane
Director, Jämtli Museum, and The Nordic Center for Heritage Learning, Östersund, Sweden

The community engagement and service mission of universities: An introduction by the editors

Patricia Inman and Hans G. Schuetze

This book is a collection of papers from the conference hosted by PASCAL International Observatory and the Centre for Policy Studies in Higher Education and Training at the University of British Columbia in May 2009. The title of the conference was 'Community Engagement and Service: The Third Mission of Universities'. As the majority of the people attending were from North America it was considered most representative to follow this focus in the volume.

PASCAL

The PASCAL International Observatory is a non-governmental, not-for-profit network of local and regional government officials and elected leaders, policy researchers, faculty members, and university administrators from Europe, the Pacific Rim, South and North America, and Africa. The term 'PASCAL' is an acronym for three concepts that unite the network's members: place management, social capital formation, and learning regions. The PASCAL members come from both two-year and four-year higher education institutions, and from local and regional authorities, bodies and non-governmental organizations (NGOs). The network is administered jointly by the Royal Melbourne Institute of Technology (RMIT) in Australia, the University of Glasgow in Scotland, Northern Illinois University in the United States, and the University of South Africa. PASCAL grew out of a series of international conferences and a related study about learning cities and learning regions led by the Paris-based Organization for Economic

Cooperation and Development (OECD). Although several PASCAL experts were involved in this earlier work of the OECD, PASCAL has no formal links to OECD.

Universities' 'third' mission and 'learning regions'

One of the activities of PASCAL is the PURE Project (PASCAL Universities and Region Engagement). The purpose of PURE is to arrive at a better understanding of the 'third mission' of the universities operating within a regional context and to promote the concept that universities must be engaged with their region and, conversely, regions should consider universities and other higher education institutions one of their greatest assets for the development of regional culture as well as social and economic development. Since teaching and research have always been seen as the primary mandate of universities, i.e. their first and second mission, interaction with the community and regional setting has often been considered the 'third mission'. The title of the PASCAL conference followed this understanding and terminology and was in part intended to showcase the different ways in which the 15 regions participating in the PURE project are linked to and engaged with their universities or institutions of higher education.

It was assumed that the title of the conference would serve as the title of the publication with the conference proceedings. However, from the inception of the conference and even more importantly, by the end of the conference, this title was in dispute. Participants argued that while regional and community engagement is often regarded as, and called, a 'third mission', this term would suggest in fact a marginalized status of university engagement and university–region partnership. Rather, all research and teaching should be framed around this regional focus and rather than a 'third' mission, this relationship and these activities should be an inherent part of the first and second mission. The title of this publication reflects this argument.

As environmental sustainability becomes a major concern of society, people are increasingly looking for a connection to place. Consequently, there is a growing demand from cities, regional governments, universities and NGOs for expertise to support initiatives related to 'place' by developing communities of practice and groups of learners addressing regional and environmental issues. This priority is often in stark contrast with the mission and rationale of (research) universities, namely scientific inquiry as 'pure'

2

(as opposed to 'applied'), that is 'placeless' and abstract. In fact, institutions of higher education typically articulate mission statements that strive for universalism transcending and abstracting from actual locations.

Therefore, grounded, collective scholarship that takes place in, or is focused on an actual place has been somewhat of a foreign concept. For the same reason, the 'learning region' is a somewhat new concept, since learning was previously understood to occur at the individual and, more recently, at the organizational level. However, regional stakeholders with diverse viewpoints and agendas are much more difficult to bring into a discussion than a classroom of individuals following a defined curriculum or abstract research agenda. So, how does one set the table for such regional learning, i.e. develop curricula for, and assess learning impact and progress within such an unwieldy classroom? How can regional learning, a collective process with individual and institutional learners, be organized? What role do universities and other institutions of higher education play in this process? What do higher education institutions have to contribute to this learning process, and what must they first learn themselves?

Also, 'regions' must often define themselves. In the absence of clear and accepted boundaries, political or geographical, cultural or historical, what defines them? Defining a region strictly in terms of 'proximity' gives little attention to the primary feature of regions. Meaningful regions are ones largely defined by a wide range of mutual interdependencies that exist among people, businesses, governments, and institutions that operate within certain common geographic bounds. These are the 'ties that bind' a region together and give it meaning. And they are the ties upon which a foundation of inter-cooperation between people, businesses, governments, and institutions within the region can be built.

Regional policy must take account of a region's diversity and focus future actions on problems, priorities, practices, and assets which enable people to dwell together in a defined place. This means that cities and rural areas are understood as basic political units depending on each other. Regional policy becomes all the more elusive when we consider the political barriers that defeat government and institutional representatives as they attempt to find common ground. Utilizing educational resources not only to research innovative solutions, but to educate the public in their application is a priority for PASCAL as is obvious in the PURE project, where institutions of higher education and governmental bodies work together in their own 'place'.

This book

The contributors to this book discuss these issues in greater detail and present tools to 'set the table' for collective learning and collaboration. Since North American universities are world leaders in community engagement and regional service, the editors are confident that readers will find new perspectives and frames of reference for university engagement.

Different concepts and missions

Part 1 addresses basic concepts in regional engagement. While the importance of the service or 'third' mission of universities has been widely acknowledged, universities have embraced it with very different levels of engagement. In the US, land-grant universities and other universities with an explicit regional service mission support an active role in this area and see regional development as part of this mission. Research universities, however, are much more likely to insist that their mandate of service is to the 'global' aggregation of knowledge rather than local application. In the opening chapter, Hans G. Schuetze distinguishes and discusses various notions and manifestations of regional engagement. While some universities follow the older model of service *to* the community, others stress a more participatory model of engagement *with* the community or region. Not all of them however 'walk the talk' and, as several chapters in Part 2 of the book show, there are multiple barriers in the structure and traditions of universities as well as the habitat of university professors and administrators which make such an engagement difficult.

Chris Duke asks why, in spite of ample evidence for the benefits of engagement both for the university and the region, engagement is often frustrated. He looks at the intensification of work, and mission spread, and reflects on political and deeper cultural forces, values and assumptions on both sides. He points out that, often overlooked in studies that merely focus on the perspective of higher education, regions, too, suffer from constraints and pressures – of resources, politics and attitude – that inhibit full engagement. He argues that, at a time of global fiscal-economic crisis, we need to ask how the two parties perceive their world and work together. He warns that there is a danger that the partners will pursue business as usual despite the contemporary wider struggle to rebalance the economic with the social and societal, after the Reagan–Thatcher reforms and the ensuing emergence of unfettered neo-liberalism.

Exploring difficulties in understanding the significance and character of

4

social processes in different regional or national settings, Bruce Wilson discusses one of the most important but least obvious hindrances to engagement – clarity of purpose. He argues that in engaging multiple stakeholders various social dimensions must be understood and considered, and proposes that a more rigorous framing is critical to understanding why an emphasis on economic development alone will only have partial benefits. Implications for policy-makers, researchers and programme officers complete this chapter.

The following two chapters are concerned with different methods and approaches to measure and evaluate university engagement with the community. David Charles and Paul Benneworth, renowned experts in this field and the authors of the Higher Education – Business and Community Survey in the UK, examine major qualitative and qualitative indicators and other methods to gauge university engagement. Together with their co-authors, Cheryl Conway and Lynne Humphrey, they stress the difficulties of measuring highly complex relationships and processes and describe and analyse the benchmarking tool that they have developed for the partners who are cooperating in PASCAL's PURE project.

Nirmala Lall, a doctoral student, also provides a critical literature review of evaluation methods for engagement activities and a look at implications for the future. Who better to do this than a doctoral student who will carry engagement into the future? She suggests current programme assessment may not address the scholarship of relationships. She looks at innovative hybrid tools that can better represent and assess engaged scholarship and makes the point that while the stage appears to be set for university– community partnerships there are few evaluative frameworks to measure engagement and provide continuous programme improvement.

We close the first section with suggestions for institutionalizing engagement. Most universities offer engagement opportunities by establishing a separate entity to serve as a linchpin for civic initiatives. The key challenge presented to such centres is that of looking at a wide range of strategic relationships rather than linear progression of a plan. This complexity is not easily managed. In the past stakeholders in university-community partnerships have not always had a voice in defining issues. As communities are situated, connection to place requires a university to look at its regional resources and interdependencies. Patricia Inman provides a methodology to set the table for such collaborative projects with an example of its use in a local food initiative.

Forms of engagement

Part 2 extends the discussion with examples of engaged research and learning. We start with a foundational discussion of the history of university engagement in North America. Robert Gleeson makes the point that engaged relationships led by academics are often devoid of self-questioning controversies. Several hypotheses regarding the controversy are presented and recommendations for defusing this sense of conflict are covered.

Chapters 9 to 14 discuss the development of various joint community–university partnerships and make several generalizations regarding guidelines for successful engagement. The case studies presented allow the reader to experience the various stages as collaborative projects evolve. The authors do not only showcase successful examples of community service and engagement but the whole spectrum of the 'good, the bad and the ugly'.

Kathryn Mohrman suggests that while context and practices vary with location institutions of higher education can learn a great deal from experience elsewhere. The University Design Institute, a joint project of Arizona State University and Sichuan University in China, has collected 15 case studies from seven countries of university-community collaboration. This chapter compares these case studies to generalize on successful strategies for community engagement.

The University of British Columbia Learning Exchange is a community–university engagement initiative based in Vancouver's Downtown Eastside, a neighbourhood that is well known as Canada's poorest. For the past ten years the Learning Exchange has offered free educational resources to hundreds of Downtown Eastside residents. Margo Fryer, the initiator and now the director of the Learning Exchange, outlines the developmental stages that have occurred as the Learning Exchange has evolved from being an initiative that was viewed with suspicion to being a valued part of the community.

Community-based research, one of the fields of university-community interaction that has more recently come to the fore, follows particular rules: No longer is the community just object of academic research; the community defines both focus and methodology and is a partner in the research effort. Such participatory research is, as Seth A. Agbo argues in his chapter, of particular importance for research on and with indigenous communities. The author examines how participatory research can be utilized as a dialogue in redefining indigenous 'other' cultures and how university-based research in indigenous communities can and must be removed from its current Euro-centric and methodological constraints to a collaborative, differentiated, and specialized referent, partly based on *praxis* and dialogue.

The Office of Community-Based Research (OCBR) at the University of Victoria in British Columbia is another example of a community-university partnership that supports research to create vibrant, sustainable and inclusive communities. As founder, Budd L. Hall has used the principles of transformational learning and asset-based development to connect and develop new synergies and opportunities to enhance economic, environmental and social well being of communities. Together with his co-author, Lise Bérubé, he discusses organization and support systems of community-based research.

Mexico's Constitution requires that for any college student to graduate, he or she must first complete 480 hours of professional service to the community. The motivation of such a law was the need to rebuild the country during the post-revolutionary era. Hugo Gutierrez and Nora Guzman discuss integral strategies some universities have adopted that result in a more participatory and committed civil society. A problem identified in this chapter is the failure on the part of many private universities to concern themselves with issues of community engagement. Suggestions for future integration of community service for all universities as well as a case study of the successful Mexico Rural Program are presented.

In Chapter 13, two researchers from the University of British Columbia, one from education and the other from regional and community planning, discuss their involvement and approach to community engagement through community-based research. Central to their discussion is an exploration of the conditions that support or, conversely, impede the creation of mutually beneficial and respectful collaborations, recognizing that universities and communities often have differing resources and issues. Shauna Butterwick and Penny Gurstein argue for a feminist and critical orientation to such collaborative activity. The authors suggest framing partnerships in this way can lessen polarization and social inequality.

Paul Crawford, Anne Kaplan and Diana Robinson of Northern Illinois University describe how this large public regional university in America's heartland (100 km west of Chicago) has been adapting its practice of engagement to fundamental shifts in demography, economics and public policy. Serving increasing numbers of students articulating from two-year institutions as well as non-traditional populations provides challenges in balancing tradition and innovation. This chapter discusses the need for units within institutions to adopt complex, boundary-spanning practices of engagement.

The following two chapters address the difficulties in institutionalizing engagement practices. Melvin Hill and LaVerne Williamson Hill suggest that, while colleges and universities frequently promote 'service' as a mission equal to teaching and research, this is not always reflected in faculty reward systems. Even faculty members who might prefer to be involved in service or applied scholarship may not pursue this work since this will ultimately not advance their careers. The Hills not only discuss specific difficulties inherent in the current faculty reward systems of most universities but, more importantly, suggest ways in which faculty reward systems can be modified to encourage applied scholarship research to the benefit of faculty, institution and community.

James E. Randall discusses the denial of place in many established university mission statements. He raises the argument that modern research universities, striving for universalism and reflecting a scientific truth that transcends time and place, have established missions that deny their groundedness and so offer no path to engagement. In his analysis of collective agreements of Canadian universities, he searches for 'engaged' language. The author echoes the theme of the previous chapter regarding the relatively minor role community engagement plays in the faculty evaluative process, even though community involvement if encouraged by most institutions of higher education.

Harley d'Entremont presents an interesting case study of how a group of Canadian higher education institutions have developed institutional structures to respond to the demands and needs of specific communities – the French-language communities outside Quebec. The author describes how many of these organized themselves in a loosely-structured organization of thirteen French-language or bilingual universities. The development of these inter-institutional relationships is described as a result of a number of factors, notably a general commitment to community engagement on the part of the universities in question as well as the active participation of senior leadership. Further, the policies of the Canadian government in relation to these minority-language communities are also described as contributing to the success of these partnerships, often through financial support.

One of the most innovative chapters in this volume argues that 'translational science' (TS) is the key component of community engagement and service.

The term describes the conversation between the university and the communities it serves. Janet Atkinson-Grosjean and Conor Douglas of the University of British Columbia see TS as a dialectical process through which basic academic research (discovery) moves into different spheres of application and use (utility) and is, in turn, informed by the needs and expectations of those who use it. This chapter is the result of the authors' studies of large-scale networks of biological studies through which they have identified three critical ways in which translational science helps fulfill the university's service to the community. Three forms of translational science are identified – commercial, clinical and civic. As might be expected, civic translational science is found to be the least well developed in spite of its comprehensive contributions.

The untapped potential of universities and other institutions of higher education to address regional issues seems endless. Issues less defined by political boundaries and increasingly defined by place call for a new type of engagement. This book discusses the challenges of engagement but also the possibilities. Clearly, in spite of many positive examples, in this volume and elsewhere, university engagement with the community is, on the whole, an under-developed mission of universities. The 'third' or the service mission is therefore still the 'poor cousin' of the two other missions, teaching and research. Through its ongoing work with regions and universities PASCAL is trying to eventually help to change that status. We trust that this volume will contribute to this work.

PART 1

UNIVERSITIES' ROLE IN REGIONAL DEVELOPMENT AND THEIR 'THIRD MISSION'

Chapter 1

The 'third mission' of universities: Community engagement and service

Hans G. Schuetze

Introduction: Problem and context

Universities engage with society in various and complex ways, influenced by their historical mandate and role, tradition and culture, and geographical location. Often it is not the institution as a whole but subunits like schools or faculties, institutes, centres, and programmes, and individuals within the university that interact with and serve the community in various ways. So-called 'third mission' activities include for example courses and lectures for the public, consulting by individual faculty members, contributions to learned societies and other associations as well as the many ways in which academics participate in public matters as speakers, discussants, and critics. University hospitals are important part of the regional health care system, art schools produce exhibitions, stage concerts, theatre plays, and other cultural events. As these examples show, the (third) mission of providing service to the community is not limited to assistance with matters related to economic development, although this is an important part of it. Technology transfer, joint research projects with industry partners, science parks, spin-off companies by academic researchers and university graduates are typical examples of the latter.

The 'third mission' of universities or, termed alternatively, community engagement and partnership as part of the first two missions, teaching and research, is not an entirely new theme, yet it seems more recently to have come (again) to the fore of policy discussions (OECD, 1983; 1999; 2001). There are a number of questions that need to be clarified: When we talk about 'third mission' activities or 'community service', what is meant? What type of activities are included? Who are the communities? How does community engagement fit into the academic tradition of universities, their value and merit systems, and the way universities are organized and operate? What are the incentives and what the barriers against greater engagement for and partnership with communities? How is community engagement supported? How can it be assessed in a meaningful way? These are questions this chapter seeks to address.

Before trying to answer these questions, the context in which contemporary universities operate needs to be summarized briefly. Discussions about what exactly the mandate and mission of a university are, or should be, are almost as old as universities themselves. In modern times, John Henry Newman, the nineteenth century English theologian, philosopher, and sometime Rector of the Catholic University of Dublin, postulated a university should be a place of education, religion, the training of the mind, and the development of the whole person. The academic, diplomat and Minister of Education, Wilhelm von Humboldt, who laid the foundations for a modern education system in Prussia and founded a reform university at Berlin, saw education likewise as the principal mandate of a university. Education was, however, to be linked closely with another function, scientific research, an idea at the heart of the modern 'research university'. 'Community' in a geographical sense did not figure prominently in either one of these two concepts.

This was different in the New World. The American land-grant universities and most of the newly established universities in the West of the US and of Canada, had an explicit further mission, that of service to the community, denoting primarily research and teaching that would assist with the economic, social and cultural development of the city or the region where the university was located.

Opening up universities to other than privileged young men from the ruling (elite) class led to what Trow (1973) has called a system of 'mass' higher education. This broadening of access reflected both the need for educated citizens in democratic societies and the demand for better-educated workers. As a consequence, student bodies of many universities are quite different today compared to a generation ago. Many students are older and more interested and enrolled in 'applied' rather than classical academic pro-grammes. The majority of these students, many of whom lack the traditional academic admission credentials, are looking for employment skills and preparation for work and careers rather than a traditional liberal education (Schuetze and Slowey, 2000). And the rationale for the creation in the 1960s of new non-university types of higher education, for example community colleges in the US and Canada, polytechnics in the UK and *Fachhochschulen* in Germany was a clear and often explicit mandate for these institutions to cater to local and regional needs and to contribute to their regions' economic and social development.

Over the last decade or two, some major trends have emerged which have an impact on this regional development and community service mission:

- Modern communication technologies make learning at a distance a real alternative to classroom-based learning and have begun to change profoundly the way universities teach and students learn. This entails a de-emphasis of local learning contexts as distance programmes must be relevant for a much more geographically dispersed audience.
- A global market for higher education and strong demand from countries with insufficient capacity are moving many universities towards more internationalization. Increased trans-border flows of students and academic staff mean a greater emphasis on international students and programmes and, eventually, an internationalization of the curriculum.
- Marketization, for example through competition and advertising, looks for new resources and tries to enrol more students from outside the region. This trend is enhanced through recent reforms aiming at making universities more competitive both nationally and internationally.
- World-wide ranking of universities and the attempts by university managers to secure a prominent place in these league tables for their own institution tends to reinforce the focus on traditional functions, especially research, and on global rather than local impact.
- The commercialization of knowledge, the raw material of universities, has consequences for the nature of the research being conducted (more applicable and relevant research vs. basic research) as well as the dissemination of research results (patent-ing and licensing of 'intellectual property' vs. public accessi-bility). Although this development potentially benefits the local or regional economy, for example through research parks and spin-off companies, it often does not as most research intensive-universities operate in national and international markets.
- New governance 'models' of universities, for example 'managerial' and 'entrepreneurial' models. The former has led to the rise of the importance of 'managing' and managers who

introduce management instruments and methods from the private sector that stress competition, efficiency, narrowly defined cost-benefit rationales, and revenue diversification (see for example Birnbaum, 2001). While this new model does not prevent managerial universities to engage with their community, these institutions tend to focus primarily on larger markets. In contrast, the latter model has, as Clark (1998) has shown with a number of case studies, a strong regional component and commitment.

While it is not always clear what these trends mean for universities' regional engagement and community service, it appears that most of them would have institutions emphasize larger audiences and markets rather than local ones. However, some of these trends are ambivalent and there is ample evidence (some documented in this volume) that there is also, at least in North America, a strong trend towards university programmes and activities that are regionally relevant. Although this evidence comes primarily from traditional 'regional universities' (even if they have different labels) this is not limited to them.

In the following, I shall first discuss further the notions of mission and community engagement, and secondly, three major types of engagement activities: knowledge transfer, continuing education and two more recent forms of community engagement, service teaching and community-based research. In the final section I discuss the problems of assessment of engagement activities and their sustainability.

'Third' mission, regional mandate, and service to the community

'Universities' are not a single species and have proliferated into a number of different institutional types. In North America, three basic models can be distinguished, each offering different programmes, catering to different students, and having different mandates and missions, including the 'third mission': research universities, (university) colleges which specialize in undergraduate teaching, and regional universities.

It is apparent that regional universities whose emphasis is primarily local or regional, have close links with the environment and contribute to the development of their region. However, universities, because of their quest to be recognized as research institutions, normally do not like the 'regional' label as it is understood to signal 'poor standing, low recognition, and limited appeal' (Duke, 2009, 181).

Major research universities are also serving their community (or several communities) although these are defined in different ways. Their community is primarily the 'community of scholars', world-wide and national, i.e. fellow researchers in other research organizations, both public and private including those working in corporations with their own research and development departments. This peer-group can include researchers in the same geographical region, but research universities' networks are typically national and international.

Specialized institutions such as technical universities and research institutions with an emphasis on natural sciences and engineering, normally have close links to industry in the form of cooperative research and 'technology transfer', industry-focused student research projects, co-operative education programmes, and graduate placement. Similarly, medical universities serve their communities by operating local and regional teaching hospitals which are an important part of the local and regional healthcare system as well as of the continuing education and specialty training of practitioners.

'Regional' or not, most North American universities see the 'third mission' as their mandate, not only as an addendum to their core missions, research and education, but as an integral mission in its own right, for some of them the constituting factor of why they were established. However, this recognition in principle does not always translate in active engagement and serious commitment.

The rationale for the third mission (or leg) has been explained in the following way:

> *Higher education is built on a theory . . . (H)igher education is a stool, and the stool has three legs: research, teaching, and service. There is a reason it has three legs. The service is there because it keeps the teaching and research honest. It keeps them connected to everyday problems that people have to address. And that is part of what the role of an institution of higher education ought to be* (Mason cited by Maurrasse, 2001, p. 22).

Although this metaphor of a stable stools or platform with three legs of the same strength (and length) suggests that the third mission is of equal standing as the other two, some authors have begun to question the notion of the 'third mission', taking issue with what they believe is an outdated model or notion. They argue that universities should embrace 'community engagement and community-academic partnership' and do not see such close relationship as a 'third' and separate mission, but integral to all of the university's purposes. Their rationale is that community engagement and community-academic partnerships cannot really be separated from teaching and research and will strengthen these when done in a community context.

Part of this change of emphasis is owed to different perspectives of what universities should do, and part to linguistics:

> *The language has evolved, from community service to outreach – reaching out to the community, or often to industry and business. Partnership has also grown up as a better term, . . . Another much stronger term has recently been widely adopted, . . . engagement. It . . . conveys the idea of reciprocity of relationship . . . – the shared and joint conceiving, creating, owning and using of research . . .* (Duke, 2009, p. 179).

While 'community' is an ambiguous term with respect to geography, 'region' seems not. 'Region' connotes the geographical area of which the university, through its research and teaching, is the main centre of producing and disseminating scientific knowledge.

'Region' (and also the geographical meaning of 'community') indicates proximity to the university, i.e. the distance which allows people to get together and personally interact easily. Although this geographical proximity seems to have lost some of its importance because of modern telecommunication technologies (see above), it is still considered significant for any form of close cooperation. But Charles (2005) points out that 'region' is also not unambiguous, making the point that university–region relationships are not one-dimensional and static but '(u)niversities do not just have one region but many, overlapping and nested, used at different times and for different purposes according to historical contingency and evolving patterns of interaction' (p. 153).

In his assessment of higher education reforms, Teichler (2005) finds that the regional dimension played an important role in the 1960s and 1970s when many new higher education institutions were established in Europe that had an explicit, or an implied, regional mandate and focus. He notes that this regional mandate was often not very clearly defined – with the exception that these new institutions were expected to cater primarily for students from the region in which they were located. Nor was the mandate fully implemented. Since regions did not well articulate their needs and the effects of regional outreach and engagement could not be clearly determined, especially in the short term, Teichler finds that 'the relationship between universities and regions was in many respects ambivalent, diffuse, ineffective and not free of tensions' (p. 239 – my own translation). Part of the problem, Teichler suggests, was that communication between the two partners was affected by the attitude of academics who saw regions as 'provincial' while regional representatives were confused about what universities do and can do, and how they do it.

Teichler identifies four aspects that make regional engagement unattractive for universities:

1. Outreach mechanisms and activities frequently have not met expectations – for example, technology transfer offices and science parks;
2. Policy-makers and the public are concerned about the quality of higher education, which tends to favour traditional rather than new and often untested forms of research and teaching;
3. Cutbacks in funding for higher education have led universities to focus on what they considered their core activities;
4. Higher education reforms in the 1990s in continental Europe and Japan freed universities from the detailed direction and tight control by government. These reforms had the – intended – result of enabling universities to decide their profile and mission by themselves, had the consequence – probably unintended by the reformers – of favouring concentration on 'core' activities, especially research, and traditional profiles.

While this last reason does not apply to the same extent to universities in the US and Canada, which have always enjoyed a far greater degree of institutional autonomy than universities elsewhere, the former three clearly do.

One might add to this analysis that 'academic drift', university culture, and the prevailing selection and reward system for university professors all reinforce the tendency towards basic research and traditional forms of dissemination, teaching and publishing. Other factors like increased competition and league tables have also tilted the agenda towards a more traditional agenda. It can be also assumed that resources play an important role: while plenty are available for established and recognized academic research and teaching, they are arguably scarcer for outreach and service activities, especially when there is comparatively little prestige recognition or other, more palpable benefits in return.

It is difficult to gauge the level and strength of universities' engagement with, and support of their local communities. There is no law in the US and Canada which would make community engagement or service an obligation for institutions, faculty or students (unlike in Mexico where community service is mandatory for university students – see the chapter by Guiterrez and Guzman in this volume).

Commitment and engagement do not depend just on the type of university as suggested above but also the type of community partner. Slowey (2003) makes a useful distinction between three types of connection between universities and external communities: relationships with (1) government, ministries, other public bodies and 'quangos' (semi-autonomous, non-governmental organizations), (2) the private sector, i.e. industry and business, and (3) civil society. Pointing out that 'community' is sometimes used in the sense of identifying specific groups in society such as 'disadvantaged communities', she finds that 'third arm' activities – the British terminology for the 'third' mission – with government and business are strong, since they generate prestige, political capital, and revenues. In contrast, activities serving civil society especially under-privileged communities, are much weaker, in fact they more resemble a 'withered arm'.

Main types of university engagement and partnership with the community

Although there are many forms of community outreach, engagement and partnership, only three types will be briefly discussed. The first is established in the sense that it has been much researched and discussed, especially in the 1980s and 1990, namely 'knowledge' (or, mostly, 'technology') transfer and universities' contribution to industrial innovation. The second is the classical example of university engagement with the community, at least in Britain and North America, namely university continuing education (often under different terms, for example 'extra-mural' or 'extension'). The third example is being emphasized more recently as major forms of engagement and partnership, 'community-based research' and 'service learning'.

Academic knowledge transfer

Several theories of innovation, for example cluster, endogenous growth, and innovation systems theory, are at the base of the great interest in the 1980s and 1990s in university knowledge transfer. In particular, success stories like Silicon Valley in California and Route 128 in Massachusetts fuelled interest by both researchers and policy-makers in 'university-based regional development' as many university leaders and regional policy-makers have tried to emulate these examples (Varga, 2009).

Earlier studies on industry–university relations in North America and Europe had mainly focused on the mechanisms of university–industry 'technology transfer'. Technology transfer was seen as the passing-on to industry of research results that had been developed in university laboratories. It was seen as distinct from, and unrelated to, other university activities, especially teaching and learning.

However, ever since concepts such as 'mode 2' knowledge production (Gibbons *et al.*, 1994) and 'innovation systems' (see for example Lundvall, 1995; Edquist, 1997) tried to explain the way knowledge is generated, distributed, absorbed and used, it became apparent that such a narrow view of 'transfer' is the exception rather than typical for the generation and transfer of scientific and technological knowledge which are non-linear processes requiring problem identification and analysis, communication, interaction, and learning by and among many partners. Therefore, not only (applied) research, but all learning processes which take place at or through the university are part of the contribution that the university makes to industrial innovation, for example the training of students in conjunction with industry-sponsored research projects, consulting activities by faculty members outside the university, professional continuing education, co-op education and other forms of student placement in industry, and all other kinds of formal or informal exchanges between university researchers and professionals and managers from industry (Schuetze, 2000).

Varga (2009) has suggested that for such comprehensive academic knowledge transfer three categories can be distinguished:
1. Knowledge transmission via formal or informal networks of pro-fessionals. Examples are research collaborations, employment of university graduates by local industry, faculty consulting, student internships, university continuing education, conferences and seminars, and the exchange between university researchers and industry professionals in professional associations.

2. Diffusion of technology through formalized business relations, for example through technology licensing ('technology transfer') and university 'spin-off' companies.
3. Knowledge transfer facilitated by the use of university physical facilities such as libraries, laboratories, or research parks located on university campuses (pp. 1–2).

As many empirical studies have shown, the concept of 'knowledge transfer' is, as has been explained for 'technology transfer' above, too narrow a concept as it suggests that all scientific-based and relevant knowledge originates in the university and is then passed on 'downstream' to the various communities that will absorb and put it to a practical use. Instead, more recent university-community partnership concepts like 'community-based research' and 'service learning' are based on the understanding that new knowledge is generated by a collective process, and that the universities cannot generate such knowledge alone.

University continuing education

University continuing education (UCE) is another major and established type of community outreach, including recurrent professional education, public seminars and lectures, and short-term not-for-credit courses. With the fast generation of new knowledge in many fields, for instance technology and bio sciences, especially professionals, in order to keep abreast of scientific progress, require periodical updating of their professional knowledge base.

Some twenty years ago, the organization and delivery of continuing education was the almost exclusive domain of special departments that were outside the core or mainstream organization, i.e. the faculties, departments, and institutes where research and the teaching of ordinary students took place. Increasingly however, regular faculties and departments are offering professional continuing education programmes themselves. One of the reasons for their eagerness to get involved may be the lure of financial rewards, but they profit in other ways as well. In particular, the experience of practitioners and their questions and suggestions as to the development of the field and its relationship with newly-emerging disciplines provide valuable feedback to unresolved problems and new developments. These benefit both the research and the teaching agenda.

In some countries, the mandate of university continuing education is very narrowly defined, for example in Germany, where the law requires that what is taught in university continuing education programmes must be 'scientific' in nature, i.e. research-based, mirroring what is taught in regular academic programmes (Schuetze, 2008). In contrast, in North America the field that university continuing education ploughs is much larger. Besides continuing professional education, which caters to participants who have a university degree and professional experience (Adamuti-Trache and Schuetze, 2010) UCE offers a host of other, non-academic programmes aimed at various groups as well as individual lifelong learners (Schuetze and Slowey, 2000). Not all these programmes are taught or moderated by academic researchers and regular professors, and not all are related to academic research. The mission statement of the University of British Columbia (UBC), is an example:

> *UBC Continuing Studies is an academic unit that inspires curiosity, develops ingenuity, stimulates dialogue and facilitates change among lifelong learners locally and internationally.*
>
> *We anticipate and respond to emerging learner needs and broaden access to UBC by offering innovative educational programmes that advance our students' careers, enrich their lives and inform their role in a civil and sustainable society.*
> (UBC, 2008)

Under this broad community-oriented banner UBC offers a number of programmes that would not be found in academic calendars for regular students. Central to these are learning partnerships with non-profit community groups, government organizations, businesses and industry. For the design and delivery of some of its programmes the university collaborates also with organizations of the arts community, the opera, theatres, the broadcasters, public utilities, and hospitals. For the recent Olympic Winter games in Vancouver, UBC Continuing Studies partnered with the Olympic Committee to develop a programme of learning, research and service in support of the Games. Other examples are the Life and Career Centre which offers 'life planning tools for women and men to help them identify personal goals, set priorities, develop action plans and learn about community resources' and the programme of the Centre for Intercultural Communication which offers courses and certificate programmes that 'help individuals and organizations address the cross-cultural challenges of becoming truly global citizens'.

Community-based Research and Service Learning
Two other types of activities associated with community engagement and partnership, are community-based research (CBR) and service learning,

sometimes under a different name. Characteristic of both activities is that researchers, teachers and students use the community as their research laboratory and class room, but in partnership with the community.

In other words, CBR is not research *on*, but research *with* communities, or certain groups within these. It is a form of research with community involvement and collaboration but using scientifically accepted research methods. Members of the community must be actively involved in, and understand the research process and research must yield data and information that are directly useful to the community.

Likewise, 'service learning' (SL) is different from field trips for students to enjoy some illustration of knowledge learned from books or discussed in classrooms. It is 'education that is grounded in experience as a basis for learning (Ellis, Bianchi, and Shoop, 2008) – a concept that goes back to Dewey's concept of the purpose and process of education which must be tied to social action (Dewey, 1938).

CBR and SL are thus activities in which communities become the class room and laboratory for both research and learning with the objective of increasing community capacity and social capital (Ward and Wolf-Wendel; 2000, Bringle and Hatcher, 2002). Collaboration is an interactive process among communities and universities, each with diverse knowledge and resources, working together to generate solutions for complex problems.

Using 'the community as classroom' requires more than changes of the organization of teaching, of curricula, and of teaching and assessment methods, far-reaching as they may be. Community-based learning entails a different, 'critical' pedagogy moving from a 'banking' approach of education which sees the student as a 'receptacle' of knowledge, to a 'problem-posing' model (Freire, 1989). In such a model, there is a constant interplay between consciousness-building, analysis and action, simultaneous learning by teachers and students, and a direct link to practical problems of community development. Some of these elements are also found in other forms of non-campus learning, for example co-operative education, which takes place in actual workplace settings and is also based on the learning concept of 'situated cognition', yet is not linked to community-based work.

Similarly, the concept of CBR which is based on the model of 'science shops' which originated in the 1970s in Holland (Wachelder, 2003), goes beyond the collaboration with just any partner on a joint research project.

CBR emphasizes the need for 'participatory' research in recognition of both the socially constructed nature of knowledge and the 'asymmetric relation' between the social, economic and cultural positions of the participants in traditional research projects and the resulting bias and limitations (e.g. Bourdieu, 1996). CBR is seen not only as an effective way of limiting these negative effects but also sharing process and results with the community.

Assessment and sustainability of university engagement

Of the issues concerning regional and community engagement two seem of particular interest, assessment and sustainability.

How can engagement be assessed?

Growing institutional competition and university rankings were already mentioned as putting pressure on universities to cater to larger markets. While most of the international league tables exclusively measure research excellence (e.g. the Shanghai Jiaotong University's), others also measure reputation, thereby indirectly, and the quality of teaching. None of the rankings take into account the nature and intensity of regional engagement and the quality of community service. There are two reasons for this: (1) community engagement and service do not lend themselves to easy measurement by means of quantifiable indicators (except for more marginal data such as expenditure or revenues from these activities), or (2) they are not deemed to be 'core activities'. Consequently, since community engagement never counts in rankings, it has been suggested that efforts should be made to establish categories of engagement and service and discuss the indicators by which community services could be validated and assessed (see for example Montesinos *et al.*, 2008).

Indeed, a number of instruments for assessing the range and intensity of community engagement have recently been developed. For HE institutions in the US, the Carnegie Foundation for the Advancement of Teaching has, starting in 2006, developed a system for classifying 'institutions of community engagement' (Carnegie Foundation, 2010). Community engagement is defined broadly, namely as the collaboration between institutions of higher education and their larger communities (local, regional/state, national, global) for the mutually beneficial exchange of knowledge and resources in a context of partnership and reciprocity. Unlike other Carnegie classifications, the one on community engagement is voluntary and relies on documentation provided by the institution themselves. This self-initiated, self-reported and self-assessed review takes into account various indicators ranging from 'Institutional Identity and Culture' and 'Institutional Commitment' to engagement activities such as 'Curricular Engagement' and 'Outreach and Partnership' (for other instruments, especially the one developed for PASCAL's PURE programme, see the chapter by Charles *et al.* in this volume).

How sustainable is it?

The need for support and recognition of engagement activities were already mentioned. There exist a number of sources for external support of certain outreach activities. For example in the US Higher Education institutions can obtain grants from the Community Outreach Partnerships Centers Programme (COPC) which operates under the auspices of the Department of Housing and Urban Development. These grants are narrowly targeted, focusing on activities by universities or colleges which aim at revitalizing distressed urban communities and require matching funding from other public or private sponsors (US Dept. of Housing and Urban Development, 2010). In Canada, regional development agencies often use a similar approach.

The Canadian Social Sciences and Humanities Research Council, the main funding body for social research, has a Community-University Research Alliances (CURA) programme which supports alliances between community organizations and Higher Education institutions. Unlike the COPS grants, the thematic focus of the alliances are not prescribed. The specific objectives of the CURA programme are broader, namely to: (1) promote sharing of knowledge, resources and expertise between postsecondary institutions and organizations in the community; (2) enrich research, teaching methods and curricula in postsecondary institutions; (3) reinforce community decision-making and problem-solving capacity; and (4) enhance students' education and employability by means of diverse opportunities to build their knowledge, expertise and work skills through hands-on research and related experience (SSHRC, 2009). The other two major Canadian Research Councils have adopted similar programmes, and there is support available from several government agencies, philanthropic foundations and various civil society organizations (University of Victoria, 2009).

There can be no doubt that these programmes are useful and in many cases instrumental as incentives and opportunities for faculty, students and community leaders to work on joint projects with the community. However, funding is short term only and the question must be asked about the sustainability of these alliances and the university's long-term commitment once the funding comes to an end:

> *A course lasts three or four months. Students are on campus for a few years. Faculty projects last for a few years. Foundation grants always come to an end. Communities, however, are permanent. How can higher education ensure that its commitment is genuine?* (Maurasse, 2001, p. 28)

There is no sure way of answering this question, yet there is evidence that some universities have started to make serious commitments towards more engagement with communities. Often community engagement is reflected in university mission statements or strategic plans. For example, the University of British Columbia's strategic statement about its mission, principles, goals and strategies, commits the university 'to collaborate with our local and regional communities to foster intellectual, social, cultural and economic development' (UBC, 2000, p 12). Many other Canadian as well as US universities have similar mission statements. However, when it comes to the implementation of this commitment, often the old barriers are still in place (see for example the chapters by Butterwick and Gurstein, and Hill and Hill in this volume.)

Summary

There are many examples (some described in this volume) that show that outreach to, and engagement and partnership with, the community is quite common in many North American and, perhaps more as of recently, Canadian universities. Yet, compared to the core missions of universities, teaching and research, community engagement seems clearly under-developed.

It is noteworthy that the discussion about universities' engagement has again come to the fore of the policy discussion at the time when are a number of new trends exercise pressure on universities to engage and compete nationally and globally rather than regionally and locally. Although engagement in such a scale might not be realistic for many institutions, the pressure is on, often reinforced by 'academic drift' which is pushing from the inside towards engaging in more prestigious and rewarding activities, academically or in terms of money.

Part of the discussion whether the 'third mission' and 'community service' models (and labels) should be abandoned and replaced by new ones such as 'community engagement and partnerships' is reflecting this renewed interest and the emphasis of an active outreach and relationship. Yet nothing is won with a change of labels alone. What is needed is a careful analysis of what enhanced engagement involves and how universities are oriented and organized to become more actively engaged with the community.

Although there is no magic bullet, some factors seem essential for the promotion of a more active embrace of the regional and local community. For example, anchoring regional engagement explicitly in the university's mission statement and strategic plan as an important signal not just for the region and potential regional partners but also, in more traditional universities of equal importance, for university management and academic staff. Although it is evident that this is not enough as mission statements rarely translate into action unless other conditions are met, it is a first step.

Funding and other incentives to university personnel to engage in partnership, outreach and community-based activities are important, including academic rewards for community service and the recognition that community-based research and service-learning are valid academic pursuits that enrich the traditional academic agendas, and not inferior to laboratory-based research and classroom-based teaching. More publicity, for instance through self-assessment and benchmarking is another important step towards stronger and sustainable engagement.

References

Adamuti-Trache, M. and Schuetze, H. G. (2010) 'Demand for university continuing education in Canada', *Canadian Journal of University Continuing Education*, 35(2) 87–108.

Altbach, P. (2003) 'The costs and benefits of world-class universities', *International Higher Education,* (33).

Birnbaum, R. (2001) *Management fads in higher education – where they come from, what they do, why they fail.* San Francisco: Jossey-Bass.

Bourdieu, P. (1996) 'Understanding', *Theory, Culture and Society*, 13(2), 17–37.

Bringle, R. G. and Hatcher, J. A. (2002) 'Campus–community partnerships: the terms of engagement', *Journal of Social Issues*, 58(3), 503–517.

Carnegie Foundation (2010) *Carnegie's community engagement classification* (retrieved 30 January 2010 from http://classifications.carnegie foundation.org/descriptions/community_engagement.php)

Charles, D. (2005) 'Universities and engagement with cities, regions and local communities', In C. Duke, M. Osborne and B. Wilson (eds.), *Rebalancing the Social and Economic: Learning, Partnership and Place*, pp. 143–157. Leicester: NIACE.

Clark, B. (1998) *Creating entrepreneurial universities – Organizational pathways of transformation*. Oxford: Pergamon Press.

Dewey, J. (1938) *Experience and education*. New York: Macmillan.

Duke, C. (2009) 'Please. No more "Business as usual" – What the harsh new world means for Adult and Higher Education', *Adult Education and Development*, 73, 171–184.

Edquist, C. (1997) *Systems of innovation – Technologies, institutions and organizations*. London: Pinter.

Ellis, A., Bianchi, G. and Shoop, K. (2008) 'Service-learning in American higher education: An analysis', *Higher Education* Forum, 5, 141–150.

Freire, P. (1989) *Pedagogy of the oppressed*. New York: Continuum.

Gibbons, M, Limoges, C., Novotny, H., Schwartzmann, S., Scott, P. and Trow, M. (1994) *The new production of knowledge – The dynamics of science and research in contemporary societies*. London: Sage.

Lundvall, B. (ed.) (1995) *National systems of innovation – Towards a theory of innovation and interactive learning*. London: Pinter.

Maurasse, D. J. (2001) *Beyond the campus – How colleges and universities form partnerships with their communities*. New York and London: Routledge.

Montesinos, P., Carot, J. M., Martinez, J. M. and Mora, F. (2008) 'Third mission ranking for world class universities: Beyond teaching and research', *Higher Education in Europe,* 33(2/3), 259–271.

OECD (Organization for Economic Cooperation and Development) (1983)

The university and the community. Paris: OECD.

OECD (Organization for Economic Cooperation and Development) (1999) *The response of higher education institutions to regional needs.* Paris: OECD.

OECD (Organization for Economic Cooperation and Development) (2001) *Cities and regions in the New Learning Economy.* Paris: OECD.

Schuetze, H. G. (2000) 'Industrial innovation and the creation and dissemination of knowledge: Implications for university–industry relationships', in Organization for Economic Cooperation and Development, *Knowledge management in the learning society* (pp. 161–174). Paris: OECD.

Schuetze, H. G. (2008) 'Producers of knowledge, centres of learning, drivers of change: Universities serving their regions', in P. Von Mitschke-Collande and R. Mark (eds.), *The university as a regional actor – Partnerships for professional development in Europe* (pp. 11–18) Hildesheim and Berlin: Tharax Verlag.

Schuetze, H. G. and Slowey, M. (eds.) (2000) *Higher education and lifelong learners: International perspectives on change.* London and New York: Routledge Falmer.

Slowey, M. (2003) 'Higher education and civil society', in M. Slowey and D. Watson (eds.), *Higher education and the life course* (pp. 135–151) Berkshire UK: SRHE and Open University Press.

SSHRC (Social Sciences and Humanities Research Council Canada) (2009), 'The Community-university Research Alliances program.' Retrieved 2 January 2009 from http://www.sshrc-crsh.gc.ca/funding-financement/ programs-programmes/cura-aruc-eng .

Teichler, U. (2005) *Hochschulstrukturen im Umbruch – Eine Bilanz der Reformdynamik seit vier Jahrzehnten (Changing higher education structures – An assessment of four decades of reform dynamics.* Frankfurt and New York: Campus Verlag.

Trow, M. (1973) *Problems in the transition from elite to mass higher education.* Carnegie Commission on Higher Education.

UBC (University of British Columbia) (2000) *Trek 2000 – A vision for the future.* Vancouver: UBC.

UBC (University of British Columbia) (2008) 'UBC Continuing Studies –

Our Mission.' Retrieved 2 January 2009 from http://www.cstudies.ubc.ca/about/mission.html.

University of Victoria, Office of Community-based Research (2009) 'The funding and development of community-university research partnerships in Canada.' Retrieved 1 January 2010 from http://web.uvic.ca/ocbr/assets/pdfs/CU%20SSHRC%20Report_Final2009.pdf.

US Department of Housing and Urban Development-HUD (2010) 'The Community Outreach Partnerships Centers Program (COPC).' Retrieved 2 January 2010 from http://portal.hud.gov/portal/page/portal/HUD/programdescription/copOur.

Varga, A. (ed.) (2009) *Universities, knowledge transfer and regional development*. Cheltenham, UK, Northampton, MA (USA): Edward Elgar.

Wachelder, J. (2003) 'Democratizing science: Various routes and visions of Dutch science shops', *Science, Technology and Human Values*, 28(2), 244–273.

Ward, K., and Wolf-Wendel, L. (2000) 'Community-centered service learning', *American Behavioral Scientist*, 43(5), 767-781.

Chapter 2

Engaging with difficulty: Universities in and with regions

Chris Duke

Introduction and overview

The PASCAL International Observatory was born in 2002 from an international OECD conference on learning city-regions in Melbourne.[1] It launched the PASCAL Universities and Regional Engagement Project (PURE) in 2008 – an action research project promoting the engagement of higher education institutions in the development of their regions. By the end of 2009 the project was extending beyond an initial 15 participating regions. It had convened three main international events, the third on the occasion of the May 2009 PASCAL Conference in Vancouver. A fourth such meeting in Ostersund in June 2010 attempted a first review of the Project across the by then 17 regions. The work builds a learning network of regions seeking to better engage higher education for development. Special interest clusters connect regions, and each region has its own unique action plan. This chapter draws on PURE to explore some of many problems endemic to region-university engagement[2]. Why does it seem such hard work for both sides?

Despite ever-changing language, the idea is old that universities' mission extends beyond teaching the young and doing research. Today the terms *engagement* and *third mission* enjoy ever-wider international currency. There are cogent reasons why this may prove more than passing fashion. The size and cost of higher education sectors, the greater transparency of what universities are and do, a wide management instinct for audit and value for money (VFM), and the urgency of global problems needing attention, all point towards a permanent shift (see also the passage cited from Wilson below) Several global trends, however, including 'globalization' itself, pull in another direction. They obstruct the path to stronger engagement between region or 'community' and university. In some cases interactions between globalization and other distinct trends, which include modern higher education's problematic 'three Ms' – massification, managerialism, and marketization – exacerbate this tension.

This chapter asks why engagement is so often frustrated. It looks beyond financial constraints, the intensification of work, and the spread of mission, to political and deeper cultural forces, values and assumptions within universities and among their many and varied potential partners. With limited space it draws selectively on OECD and PURE examples. It does however point to dynamics and issues common to countries and regions universally.

To anticipate my conclusion, let me say now that universities will need to implant engagement into their culture, *mores*, policy-making and daily life. 'Third mission' must become the all-informing 'first mission'. It must inform rather than be separated from and compete with teaching and research. On this higher education 'knowledge provider' side, part of the solution may lie with university – or rather tertiary – *systems* and not with single autonomous institutions. This is something that many both leading and working in autonomy-loving academe consider intrusive and regard as anathema.

Regions also suffer constraints and pressures – of time and other resources, of politics and attitude – that inhibit full and free engagement. Given the new global fiscal-economic crisis, and daily mounting evidence that we must learn to do more and better with less, if only for ecosystem survival, how can these two 'parties' perceive their world and work better together? Business as usual is an evident temptation. It needs resisting. My point of departure is that *a new balance between the economic and the social, communal and societal, needs to grow out of the 'crisis of neo-liberalism'*. By crisis I here mean the damage that uninhibited trust in a global free market, and diminution of the role and responsibilities of the State, has inflicted, culminating in the global financial crisis (GFC) in 2008. This predicament requires a new level of competent governance at sub-national regional as well as national levels. Higher education must be a part of this if it is to work affordably and well. Scanning the difficulties from both sides, I conclude that it will tend to fall to universities to look further ahead, making the earlier and greater effort to reach out to an ever-wider range of partners.

Engagement: self-evident need and missed opportunity?

This chapter accepts the now familiar case for regions to engage with their universities, and universities with their regions, to mutual benefit. The case hinges on what is called 'the knowledge economy', and more broadly 'the knowledge society'; the scale and significance of the knowledge and expertise represented by the whole higher education enterprise; the reality of local geographical and community anchorage, still, of the very great majority of universities. The advantages and economies of 'Mode Two' (Gibbons *et al.*, 1994) co-production, co-ownership and shared application (or exploitation) of much of the knowledge thus generated provides a rationale and a philosophical underpinning.

As Gleeson points out in another chapter in this volume, despite changing linguistic fashions referred to above, 'third mission' in the name of extension has a long, successful and essentially uncontroversial history dating from at least the mid nineteenth century in the United States. The great heartland civic universities of Britain founded at about the same time were also sponsored by and served the needs of regional communities and industry. Only more recently did national and then global competitiveness tempt them into marginalizing their regional engagement in elite Russell Group company.[3] Many century-old and older polytechnics, technical institutes and other specialized vocational institutions in many countries have become new, or people's, universities. Often these embody institutional traditions and memories naturally conducive to engagement in a generous sense. Among these are access and wider participation informed by the social values of equity. In the 1980s, during the neo-liberal Thatcher years in Britain, this came to be argued in terms of not wasting human resources, and in serving regional industrial and community needs through vocational curricula, rather than on equity grounds.[4]

Today a significant literature makes the case for engagement and the importance of the 'third mission' in modern universities, documenting evidence and giving examples of good practice. There are serious attempts to understand, to evaluate and even to measure the contribution and the benefits to both parties, if partly for defensive reasons in an audit era (Bjarnason and Coldstream, 2003; Charles, 2009; Charles and Benneworth, 2001; Gibbons, 2001; Goddard and Chatterton, 1999; OECD, 2001, 2007, 2008; OECD CERI, 1982; Watson 2007; Wissema, 2009; see also Talloires Network). Unless the benefit is reciprocal, and before long visible and tangible, prospects for sustained and systemic engagement will be poor. Universities are inherently selfish. Nowadays, perforce, self-interest takes the form of bottom-line income calculation. This has largely displaced the older indifference to immediate social wellbeing which was pilloried as 'ivory tower'. However, lobbies for unfettered blue-skies research, not tied to immediate benefit, however remain alive and well.[5] In a recent keynote paper on the subject of social inclusion, universities and regional development, Professor Bruce Wilson of RMIT began by arguing as follows:

> *Of their very nature, universities play a key role in the economic and social development of the region(s) in which they are located. At the very least, they are a significant source of employment and purchaser of goods and services. More purposefully, they provide learning pathways for young people, shape access to careers and generate a planned supply of graduates for local labour markets, if also for other regions and international enterprises. Beyond this, they can make an ongoing contribution to local knowledge generation, potentially relevant in all kinds of fields and at all levels, from local community activities to sophisticated technological innovation and production. Again, the latter might be of value far beyond the region(s) in which the university is based, but nevertheless, the very nature of the knowledge generation activity means that there is typically some constellation of research facilities and of commercial producers who are geographically contiguous, working in close cooperation.*

> *However, the typical story of university engagement with regional development is one of missed opportunity. It is not hard to find disgruntled industry representatives who register a range of stories about the difficulties of working with universities. There are regional authority representatives who are disappointed that university leadership appears more interested in the university's institutional status than the broader framework of regional interests. The lack of attention to regional development aspirations, reflected in university decisions about priorities in research appointments and funding, in areas of student recruitment, in the speed with which universities respond to emerging regional needs, all lead to frustration with the ways in which universities take their places as key regional stakeholders and drivers of appropriate development.* (Wilson, 2009)

Why the disappointment, and how to alter the situation?

Regions and the involvement of universities

I suggested above that 'it will tend to fall to universities to look further ahead, making the earlier and greater effort to reach out to an ever-wider range of partners'. On balance and in principle, and given capable confident leadership, universities have a marginally less formidable mountain to keep climbing in order to achieve, sustain and implant engagement throughout their 'core business' of teaching and research. Let us look rather at the other side of the partnership – the local region. The focus of this chapter, in keeping with work by the OECD and PASCAL, tends towards partnership developed with local/regional administrations and planning authorities. However, that engagement does in principle take in all kinds of regional 'stakeholders' across private, public and third sectors.[6] Here, I consider only region-level public sector partnership, drawing on the PASCAL PURE project work to demonstrate the complexity and difficulties for regions

The first regions to take part in the PURE project, and others that are considering joining, illuminate the diversity of difficulties that regions discover when they do try working systematically with universities in their regions. In some cases this reflects problems inherent in 'the region' itself; it may lack the identity and powers for viable partnership, even when the recognition of need and the will to do so are there.

For the OECD in its programme of work on the engagement of higher educa_ tion in regional development, the region must be a jurisdictional entity recognized by the member state. This at any rate ensures formal recognition, and whatever powers are delegated or assumed by the regional administration. In practice it may mount to rather little in centralized systems; or it may be negated by policy and practice at central government level. Not surprisingly then, many of the recommendations from OECD's recent round of studies are directed at central governments, alongside others to universities and to regional administrations (OECD, 2007). That work also illustrated the vulnerability to political change of developing engagement; centrally in the case of the Republic of Korea, at regional level in the case of Spanish regions. Similarly, regions contemplating joining the PURE project commonly find themselves awaiting the outcome of a national or regional election.

The fact that a region is recognized for political and administrative purposes does not of itself ensure its viability for development purposes, as the maps of Africa and other formerly colonial and otherwise contested territories testify. Many regions as present-day political and administrative entities do not correspond well with geographical, historical, cultural, linguistic or economic realities. People do not then identify with a region and its administration's policy objectives, however commendable; or non-negotiable economic and physical geography militate against success. PURE's wider interpretation of 'region' allows for a wider range of natural regions to take part, with the potential to learn which kinds of region best enable which forms of collaboration.

In the Puglia region of Italy, and to some extent in Melbourne and Victoria in Australia, identification is at a more local level. In Puglia the difficulty is exacerbated by scepticism about corruptness of government at province as well as national level, so social capital is found and engaged mainly or only through community networks. On the other hand, as some European Commission inter-regional projects recognize, the reality of development potential necessarily straddles state boundaries. The Swedish–Danish Oresund region was a participant in the OECD round of reviews undertaken in 2004–07. The PURE Thames Gateway region similarly represents a particular purpose development ambition straddling part of multiple regional and local jurisdictions. Some expressions of 'region' and of 'partner' from a university perspective may well fit one aspiration and enable one kind of outcome, while being unfitted to others.

Together with the reality of the powerful state goes the instability that frequent centrally induced changes to the structure and agencies of regional and local administration can engender. Even when an agency exists with the prescribed authority to take action, its credibility (and therefore its capacity) may be undermined by near-future uncertainty. England, specifically and as distinct from Great Britain, exemplified this in 2009–10. The prospect of a change of national government at a general election six months later, and the policies of the party likely to take office, read like a death sentence for the Regional Development Agencies or RDAs. Universities and local authorities therefore tended to discount as partners the very agencies which should naturally lead and focus regional collaboration for development.

Britain has long had a highly centralized political system. Despite devolution of some powers to Scotland and Wales, and less cleanly to Northern Ireland in recent times the tendency for power and control to drain to Whitehall remains strong. Regional agencies have always struggled to take a strong policy hold on the development of the region. Policy and its execution, if it joins up across portfolios at all, tends to do so centrally and then feed out to separated regional portfolios reporting back up the line. In general local government is not well liked and trusted, and the larger English regions are weak entities.

Federal systems have less difficulty in this respect. Even so, regions of whatever jurisdictional persuasion are naturally and generally outplayed by the central government. Countries such as Spain that are moving towards greater devolution still struggle with what are seen as standardizing and stifling bureaucratic instincts from the capital. The same applies to the Hungarian region within PURE. 'One size fits all' convenience instinctually outweighs the positive valuing of diversity, rhetoric to the contrary notwithstanding. This was evident in the OECD studies of Valencia and the Canary Islands.

Sometimes it is worse. National governments may distrust their regions, for example for separatist ethnic and other reasons as in the case of the Kurdish region of eastern Turkey. No amount of borrowed rhetoric from the documents of the European Union will quickly overcome the fear of an independent Kurdistan, and the instinct for hugely detailed central control that is both traditional and re-energized by each new manifestation of separatism. In heavily administered, hierarchical systems, whether actively corrupt or simply instinctually and traditionally conservative servants of strong central government, there is the likelihood of anti-intellectualism, and a distrust of universities as possible hotbeds of radicalism, if not insurrection, to be controlled rather than partnered. Memories of the sixties in Europe and the United States, and the part of student movements and campuses in non-OECD revolutions since then, feed authoritarian instincts. In a centralized system this leaves little room for the kind of varied and locally appropriate partnerships and development strategies that we are discussing here.

Even a stable well accepted regional authority which can reasonably expect long-term central trust and support may encounter problems in building engagement with the higher education sector. Regions with small populations, and limited resources and income, like the more rural and remote regions in the PURE project, have only a single university-level institution, supplemented perhaps by technical college type institutions. In the case of Lesotho this means a whole impoverished country. Such a region may lack the particular higher education expertise required to build a knowledge economy that connects with the region's specific needs and develops its potential. Less costly 'soft-end' disciplines may be available, and relevant to other social and community needs, such as health, ageing, strengthening civil society and social cohesion, maybe even environmental protection and the development of cultural industries. However there is no research and teaching capacity to underpin developments requiring advanced research, R&D and teaching in the main 'STEM' disciplines of science, technology, engineering and mathematics. For example, high-tech mining to the west of the Darling Downs region of Southern Queensland implies costly demands, beyond the expertise of the regional university.

Such a situation may mean persuading non-local universities or technological institutes with relevant expertise to enter into partnership at a distance, but scale and inconvenience may promise too modest a return on investment. If it does prove possible it may call for sensitivity in relation to existing in-region institutions. Also it precludes the wider institutional involvement of the whole university in the health and prosperity of the region that a full sense of engagement implies.

A superficially tempting administrative solution favoured by some countries seeking economies of scale (and perhaps imposed top-down rather than cultivated by local arrangement) is to aggregate thinly populated and poor authorities into larger regional entities. This may, however, merely mask the problem: almost every region in the PURE project has a 'rural-remote' hinterland, marginalized from the development gains of the main cities, towns and population centres, with its own distinctive needs. Great ingenuity, patience, good will, as well as a strong sense of equity (and/or electoral pressures) are needed to resolve periphery problems in larger regions. Moreover, aggregating and otherwise messing with local and regional authority names and boundaries risks jeopardizing the identity and community involvement available to a more anchored and organic region, thus diminishing and squandering intangible but invaluable social capital.

The other side of the same coin is found in large and more complicated metropolitan regions with or without a remote hinterland. Melbourne in Australia provides a good example. Multiple universities and Technical and Further Education (TAFE) institutions occupy the same regional territory. Partly complementary, they can in principle occupy different scholarly and market niches, but in a neo-liberal era of state-sponsored competition they are also highly competitive. Operationally the city region is tackling this by means of a recently created Office of Knowledge Capital (OKC) owned jointly by City, metropolitan and State-level authorities and interests, together with all the higher education institutions. Along with this attempt by the region to manage competition through negotiated collaboration ('coopetition' as it has been named) goes a concept of region in several concentric circles – Melbourne City, metropolitan Melbourne, the commuting region, and the wider surrounding State of Victoria. Each is real. Teasing them out in this way assists planning. It also helps to distinguish at which levels each institution has most to offer.

Here Australian geography – the 'tyranny of distance' – has benevolent incidental consequences: markets for domestic students and labour markets are relatively regionalized, despite national and overseas, direct and distance-based, competition. In England by comparison, an entrepreneurial and powerful institution like Imperial College can create a direct infrastructure presence and become a partner to a region away from London, but become a competitor to in-region universities there which have the same expertise. For many regions, handling tensions arising from such competition may seem almost as difficult as lacking relevant academic expertise altogether.

A small region like Varmland in Sweden can develop a strong, sustained and multi-stranded partnership with its one university, Karlstad, larger in both population and economy. Even here it has taken a decade to create a reasonably productive working partnership. More dense, complex regions in more crowded locations have a different kind of problem in developing long-term trust-based partnerships across a wide spectrum of university expertise. Here, local in-region loyalty may be weak or non-existent. Plurality of higher education institutions and socio-economic density nurture 'promiscuity': universities have a wide choice of local, and less local but still conveniently nearby, public and private sector organizations with which they can do business.

Thus the regional identity and sustained partnership of Varmland and Karlstad are absent from the Thames Gateway region stretching from east London to the North Sea coast. Many regional and local authorities have come together in this well-focused and high profile development agency. The region thus has strong meaning and identity, and some sense of shared history and destiny despite administrative fragmentation; it is both connected and divided by the River Thames. Yet the identification with the specific region of most universities within the geographical area is weak and fragmentary. Conversely, many other London-region based institutions can happily fish in these nearby waters – selectively and in the sense of full engagement somewhat 'irresponsibly'.

More obviously, larger regions may be pleased to find their less prestigious local universities open, cooperative and keen to engage. These HEIs see engagement as close to the heart of their mission. They may even need regional partners to survive. Whereas they are willing partners, high status elite and research-intensive universities tend to ally to achieve common purposes nationally (the so-called Russell Group in the UK, the US Ivy League, the Sandstones or Group of Eight in Australia) while jostling to out-perform others in global rankings, where such universities rank much higher. They have more generously provided research resources, perhaps highly relevant to the region's innovation aspirations. But they may be unwilling to engage locally.

Being called a regional university in Australia can be taken as an insult; there as in the UK and no doubt elsewhere, sometimes acrimonious competition between types and generations of universities bemuses and irritates regional authorities. There are a few good examples of voluntary collaboration between universities on a regional basis: new *OKC* in Melbourne, the long-lasting English consortium *Universities North-East*; *Universus* in the Italian region of Puglia. Most university groupings, however, have geographically dispersed membership based on historical and other affinities. They collaborate to lobby nationally, but avoid their neighbours and compete destructively for resources with other kind of institutions, locally and nationally.

Many other behavioural traits embedded in the history, culture and traditions of different universities may demoralize regional authorities, making them unlikely to pursue sustained partnership and long-term engagement altogether. Let us take just a few examples. The tradition of universities may be to focus exclusively on the traditional academic education of the middle class young. Mature age and part-time, let alone work-based undergraduates are exceptional. The contribution to the human resource needs of the region is thus narrowly corralled, indirect, probably unrelated to employer needs and development demands. This applies even if those graduating do stay in the region rather than moving out to sell their qualifications to better paying bidders elsewhere. The post-colonial HE systems of India and parts of Africa have long displayed these features. As elsewhere they do not find change easy.[7]

In the OECD countries the broadly North American and British or Anglo-Saxon orientation from the Thatcher–Reagan years has been neo-liberal, driving universities to be more entrepreneurial and competitive. In one obvious sense this makes them more amenable to engagement so long as it offers rewards. On the other hand the nature of the competition and of the status and other rewards pulls away from the local region towards global stature and now world rather than even national rankings. None of this helps regions which are anyway (and accurately) seen as second class citizens beside national governments.

In many of the continental European systems, due in part to EU policies including the Bologna Agreement, 'the entrepreneurial university' (Clark, 1998) is now being embraced, albeit with less enthusiasm even than in the UK. Management traditions and practices – strong faculties and weak rectors – militate against active university leadership; there can be no rapid engage-ment with the needs of the region. In places as far apart as Zagreb, Italy and Spain, old academic governance make it extremely hard for even an engagement-oriented region to get sustainable commitment and action from a short-lived elected rector.

Generalization is hazardous. There are great differences from the socialist Nordic traditions, now overlain with neo-liberalism, to the post-communist fast-but-shallow transformation of systems in Central and Eastern Europe, and the communitarian patterns of societies further south. Between countries as between regions, diversity is a reality, whether or not well respected. The European Commission itself, a strong and well-funding advocate of both regional development and engaged relevant higher education, can behave in standardizing and bureaucratic ways that do not always facilitate 'indigenous' and collaborative development – local learning through failures as well as successes.

As I put it to conference paper in Thessaloniki in late 2009, regional authorities even if strong and well trusted, as in some stable federal systems, have a plethora of duties, responsibilities, and delegations. Working with universities may not be self-evidently high among their priorities – especially if these in the past earned, and sometimes still project, the mystique of the ivory tower; and if they are led by vain and arrogant rather than public-spirited and collaborative heads. Regional authorities are self-evidently second tier, inferior in power to the national. They are likely to have less talented and well resourced administrations, and to feel second class, even when they are excellent. They are at the mercy of local as well as national elections; and of other political pressures and lobbying, private and third sector as well as public. Education, if it falls within their jurisdiction at all, is a big budget item, more of a political and financial headache than a natural resource for developing the region. If higher education is funded nationally, the regional authority lacks leverage to influence university behaviour through its reward systems; then it can only plead and persuade.[8]

This discussion has barely scratched the difficulties that may confront a region wishing to work with the higher education institutions in its territory. Little wonder that many of the approaches for regional involvement in the 2004–06 OECD as well as the current PURE rounds of studies came from universities rather than directly from regions; or that in many (though not all) cases this was from younger, more innovative and therefore less prestigious, institutions, rather than from those on the Shanghai top 200 list.

And from the university side

Other chapters in this volume examine how third mission is being adopted and perhaps embedded especially in North America. There are many stories of successful innovation meeting the needs of society. I confine myself here briefly to the cultural rather than resource difficulties facing universities. Their long tradition as conservers and transmitters of knowledge, values and traditions as well as of skills, then also as creators of new knowledge with ever larger research ambitions and achievements, makes them invaluable in principle but possibly remote in reality. Institutional and individual success depends on prestige: a highly competitive and qualified student intake; big research budgets from prestigious sources; a high profile in the most prestigious research journals. Position in world as well as national rankings assumes overwhelming importance in the way that universities judge and are judged.

None of this bodes well for those who want prestigious universities deeply involved in their local region. Smart university leaders invest well in communication and publicity. They ensure visible demonstrations of outreach and access that protect rather than alter teaching curricula, the research agenda, and if possible in-house control of key decisions. Working with the immediate region in even the most fortunate and harmonious of circumstances may feel, to managers and scholars like diversion of effort from the core business which leads to success in a highly competitive and unsympathetic world.

Along with these new pressures, there is the intensification of work brought on by the massification of elite systems; the need to conform to other strident central government priorities; and new demands for audit and accountability that go hand in hand with greater autonomy. Behind them lie deeper issues, manifesting themselves as pursuit of the ideal of being 'universal', untrammelled in both teaching and research, pursuing purposes of a higher moral order than making the university or any other agency more prosperous or even efficient. The crisis and demise of the ('true') university is a long-running drama. Angst persists. The political drive for more narrowly economic outcomes, skills and impact within what some herald as the demise of neo-liberalism, makes it more difficult for an institutional head to act like a CEO and command that third mission in this form be adopted.

Finally, the kind of engagement that appeals to the characteristic 'soft left old liberal' scholar tends to be at the 'soft' socio-cultural, environmental and civic end of regional development, well away from what governments want, and what helps the bottom line. The challenge of engaging higher education may be daunting for regions. It is not easy for a prestigious university to give more than token support, while driving up intake score, research output and financial investment reserves. Third mission becomes increasingly logical, natural and plausible to the 'modern', 'innovative', 'new generation', regional university. It is uncommon to find the most prestigious taking a lead.

What lessons can we draw?

We may conclude that there will never be a perfect and stable map and match of regions with the totality of higher education. The region will remain a vulnerable and malleable concept at the mercy of ideologies, state administrations and elusive characteristics such as trust and self-confidence versus bureaucratic and managerial instincts to standardize, direct and control. Different kinds and conditions of regions will allow, gain from, or inhibit different forms of engagement.

There will always be tension between different university objectives and priorities, along with complexity and probably excessive stretch of mission. Accountability and autonomy will likewise remain in tension with the developmental formative evaluation that support organizational and institutional learning. The notion of a totally independent free-spirited university is a myth, as indeed it always was. Like other institutions it is and will remain a creature of both inherited and contemporary culture which is itself fast-changing. Desirably it will also contribute to continuously refashioning and enriching it.

Some of the changes needed to make third mission (a) real and (b) the first and guiding mission lie beyond the reach of both region and university. They rest with national government, national culture, public opinion and the influential media. Some however do lie within the reach of institutions if they are well managed, self-managed, purposeful institutions and enjoy strong intelligent leadership. Some require a culture shift so that the full spectrum of university scholarship and the full spectrum of dimensions of development are valued; otherwise 'engagement' will be for the privileged and fashionable few, leaving other departments impoverished and, with poor life expectancy.

In any event it is necessary as part of a full and viable third mission for the student body to include all ages, not just successful high school graduates, and for the university to have a societal as well as a strictly individual-scholar grasp of what it is doing. From a national policy perspective, it may now make better sense to plan tertiary *systems*, with shared responsibility on a regional basis for HEIs between them to deliver across all aspects of universities' missions, rather than concentrating on each institution in isolation. It would not be difficult to arrange reward systems such that all suffer unless the full 'mission spectrum' is delivered between the regional HEI 'system' as a whole.

This would require strong and clear central government leadership. It would enable regional administrations along with other private and third sector stakeholders to get from the local higher education resource pool what they and the region need. HEIs and lower level colleges could be guided into locality-based partnerships, where with complementarity each can do well in pursuit of diverse and appropriate missions. In this case the kind of central government commitment to third stream funding for third mission development adopted in the UK a decade ago, but still eluding for example Australia, could give a lead and top-down direction, within which sustainable and self-interested regional partnership can grow.[9] Without an explicit lead, and in most systems an enabling financial mechanism as well as a supportive policy framework, it is difficult for even the most engagement-minded region and university to work fully together.

References

Bjarnason S. and Coldstream P. (eds) (2003) *The idea of engagement: Universities in society*. London: ACU.

Charles, D. (2009) *Characteristics modes of university engagement with wider society. A literature review and survey of best practice.* Newcastle: University of Newcastle. Available at: http://www.tufts.edu/talloiresnetwork/downloads/Characterisingmodesofuniversityengagementwithwidersociety.pdf Accessed 28 September 2010.

Charles, D. and Benneworth, P. (2001) *The regional contribution of higher education.* London: HEFCE and UUK.

Clark, B. R. (1998) *Creating entrepreneurial universities: Organisational pathways of transformation.* Oxford: Elsevier Press.

Gibbons, M. (2001) *Engagement as a core value for the university.* London: ACU.

Gibbons, M., Limoges, C., Nowonty, H., Schwartzman, S., Scott, P. and Trow, M. (1994) *The new production of knowledge.* London: Sage.

Goddard, J.B. and Chatterton, P. (1999) *The Response of higher education institutions to regional needs.* Paris: OECD.

OECD (Organization for Economic Cooperation and Development) (1973) *Recurrent education; a strategy for lifelong learning.* Paris: OECD.

OECD (Organization for Economic Cooperation and Development) (2001) *Cities and regions in the learning economy.* Paris: OECD.

OECD (Organization for Economic Cooperation and Development) (2007) *Higher education and regions: Globally competitive, locally engaged.* Paris: OECD.

OECD (Organization for Economic Cooperation and Development) (2008) *Higher Education Management and Policy, Special Issue. Higher Education and Regional Development*, 20, 2. Paris: OECD.

OECD CERI (1982) *The University and the Community: The Problems of Changing Relationships.* Paris: OECD.

PASCAL International Observatory, www.obs-pascal.com.

Talloires Network, http://www.tufts.edu/talloiresnetwork/.

Watson, D. (2007) *Managing civic and community engagement.* Milton Keynes: Open UP.

Wilson, B. (2009) 'Social inclusion: Universities and regional development'

Presented to the First National Conference on Social Inclusion in Education, Sydney, October.

Wissema, J.G. (2009) *Towards the third generation university: Managing the Universities in Transition.* Cheltenham UK, Northampton MA: Edward Elgar.

Notes

[1] See www.obs-pascal.com

[2] OECD tends to refer to higher education institutions, abbreviated as HEIs. In practice the scope is limited to universities and other high-level institutions recognised as fully their peers. At the same time OECD had been a leader in promoting the broader concept of tertiary (as in tertiary systems), thus raising the issue of 'the other binary divide' between 'college' or further and higher education. Different countries see the unitary-binary option in different ways and at different times, sometimes passing one another in opposite directions like ships in the night. I use university for convenience here, adding that the PURE project does indeed address the role of non-university tertiary-higher education. This is important: these more local colleges tend to be closer and more responsive to the needs of the local region, and more accessible to SME and other local interest groups, than most universities.

[3] But the jury is out again. Richard Florida (2002) and others argue the importance of good universities to successful creative cities. OECD asks which is a more valuable to regional development – a single world class university or a high-performing university system. Birmingham, Sheffield and Manchester cities were or are all world class in what they make and sell, from cutlery to small arms to high culture. Today their civic universities seek world class stature independently rather than in civic company.

[4] Universities have been vocational training schools in almost every time and place, but often less frankly so.

[5] At the time of writing such lobbying was rampant in the UK HE policy community, as criteria for assessing and funding research were reviewed. A distinct but linked conservatism closes universities in France and some other European states; students as well as staff rebel against government reforms offering greater autonomy in return for a more market- and fee-based approach.

[6] As always, language can be problematic. By third sector is meant non-

governmental, voluntary, civil society, not-for-profit. It is better distinguished from the (for-profit) private sector with which it is sometimes provocatively combined, as well as from the public or government sector. The necessity for separation becomes evident as soon as one considers the ideological differences underlying criticism of the 'big State' and neo-liberal preference for using the voluntary sector for service delivery, as well as hostility to neo-liberalism, the 'filthy rich' and widening poverty gaps.

[7] Ideally, this chapter would discuss these issues as they manifest themselves or by their absence, in Latin America, Africa and the huge and diverse Asian region. The complexity and diversity of history and context make this impracticable.

[8] Available in the e-book conference proceedings, The difficult realities of engaging for universities, *Educating the adult educator; Quality provision and assessment in Europe*, via the ERIC Website, direct access for the pdf from http://eric.ed.gov/ERICWebPortal/contentdelivery/servlet/ERICServlet?accno=ED508475 Accessed 28 September 2010.

[9] For a development of this idea see my paper published in the IMHE Journal *HEMP* following the OECD Conference in Valencia on engagement and regional development in 2007 (Duke, 2008).

Chapter 3

Social processes in regional development

Bruce Wilson

Introduction

Over the past two decades, the increasing internationalization of economic and cultural activity has led, perhaps ironically, to growing interest in the region and locality as the focus of much debate about economic and social development. Researchers from quite different disciplinary orientations have become involved with this work: urban geographers, economists, sociologists, and educationalists. Policy-makers have grappled with questions about how to intervene at the local or regional level in order to achieve economic and social policy outcomes.

While economic issues have often been key drivers, there has been strong interest specifically in the social dimensions of regional development. A variety of concepts to explore the 'social' have emerged, often crossing disciplinary boundaries: social capital, social cohesion, social inclusion/ exclusion, social participation, as well as community building and community strengthening. While the 'social' aspects of regional development have been shown to be very significant, progress in both research and policy development has been hindered by a lack of clarity about these concepts, by confusion about the extent to which they overlap or even contradict each other, and by difficulty in applying them consistently across different regional or national settings. Even the term 'social capital' itself has remained unclear and disputed:

> *Despite the immense amount of research on it, the definition of social capital has remained elusive. Conceptual vagueness, the coexistence of multiple definitions, the chronic lack of suitable*

data have so far been an impediment to both theoretical and empirical research in which social capital may play a role. (Sabatini, 2007, pp. 79–80)

This matters because the concepts of regional development, regional innovation systems, learning regions refer to processes that are pre-eminently social. Whilst their focus might be on the development and diffusion of clusters, new technologies, production systems, logistical arrangements and skills formation, the social dimensions frame, enable, mediate and limit the effectiveness of policies and programmes designed to enhance economic and social outcomes, irrespective of regional or national settings.

This insight is reflected in all the contributions to this book. Learning, teaching and research are of their very nature social processes; when framed within a community engagement paradigm, the complexities of the 'social' can be amplified much more than when they are undertaken within traditional institutional boundaries.

Hence, this chapter aims to assist with clarifying these issues through developing a framework for analysing social processes in a regional context. This would support not only universities' efforts at community engagement, but would also be useful in developing regional policy and programmes. The chapter offers examples of current contributions in the field, including analyses presented in previous PASCAL publications. It suggests a more consistent conceptual vocabulary in describing the 'social' in regional development, and in explaining the significance of diverse aspects of social processes. This is integral to an understanding of the different kinds of dynamics that are at work in regional settings, and of the kinds of policy levers that can enhance the effectiveness of new initiatives.

A more systematic social analysis is important not only in the design and planning of development initiatives, but also in research and project implementation. The more rigorous conceptual framing helps to understand why an emphasis on economic development independent of social and cultural context will always have only partial benefits.

Social capital

While a range of concepts has always shaped discussions about place, social relationships and regional development, Robert Putnam's book on

'American Community', *Bowling Alone* (Putnam, 2000), brought public debate and policy interest about the nature and implications of the 'social' into sharp relief. Putnam's initial research in this field was conducted with colleagues in Italy, on questions about the effectiveness of local government. Putnam himself proposed that community wealth depended on social ties, rather than social ties being a consequence of economic wealth. This carried the obvious policy implication that building stronger social relationships within a community would lead to enhanced economic activity.

However, as several writers including Fabio Sabatini (2007) have documented, Putnam was not the first to use the concept of 'social capital'; Putnam himself drew on the work of Coleman (1988, 1990), while the earliest reference to the concept was that of Hanifan (1916) who was interested in the role of community participation in enhancing school performance. Bourdieu (1980, 1986) distinguished amongst economic, cultural and social capital, the last referring to the way in which social relations could enable actors to advance their own interests, and thus to contribute to class struggle.

In a political and policy environment in which economic outcomes are seen to be the primary priority, linking the 'social' to 'capital' has resonated in public debate, even where different meanings are implied. However, as mentioned above, other theorists and policy-makers have developed other conceptual language in making sense of the 'social' aspects of regional development policy and practice. The next section explores the use of the concept of social capital and the alternative constructions, firstly through drawing on work sponsored by the PASCAL Observatory, and then through a review of the broader literature. The PASCAL Observatory was established in 2003 as an international network (see www.obs-pascal.com) that brought together leading ideas on social capital, place management and learning regions. In its early years, a series of authoritative 'Hot Topic' articles were published on the key ideas in these fields. The review of this and related work will be selective necessarily, as the concepts permeate widely through both academic and policy literature, and the popular media.

PASCAL and social capital

The first PASCAL Hot Topic addressed issues relating to the measurement of social capital. While Cavaye's primary interest was in measurement, he outlined a brief review of the social capital literature (2004; see also Duke *et*

al., 2005). He acknowledged that social capital had different meanings and interpretations, and summarized its key common characteristics as being:
- participation in networks;
- reciprocity;
- trust;
- social norms;
- a sense of the 'commons'; and
- proactivity and cooperation (2004, p. 3).

He noted that social capital can have a 'dark side' and that it should not be regarded as inherently desirable; one consequence could be the maintenance of community support for unjust power structures. This leads Cavaye to consider social capital as a 'confounding' concept, both cause and consequence in relation to economic and social improvement. However, Cavaye himself notes that social capital 'appears to have more to do with power and participation than with financial resources' (2004, p. 8). Discussion of these kinds of issues provided an introduction to Cavaye's principal concern, which was to present an overview of issues related to measurement of social capital. The priority given to measurement reflected the search by policy analysts, managers and others to develop evidence-based decision making and planning.

Hot Topic 3, by Martin Mowbray (2004), questioned Cavaye's and others application of the concept of social capital on the grounds that it focused excessively on local circumstances and interventions, at the expense of acknowledging the extensive and complex range of other forces and policies which can have direct consequences for trust and networks at the local level. The implication of Mowbray's critique is that initiatives around social capital should be integrated with the broader framework of public policy, rather than focusing on narrowly-constructed programmes around community-building. He proposed that governments should be more interested in understanding the effects of their policies on social capital, and should, as a matter of course, seek to conduct 'social capital impact assessment' studies on their major policy initiatives.

Field (2006) begins with the apparently self-evident observation that networks, innovation and social capital are inter-connected, and a positive force. As he then examines the complexity of policy formation, this proposition begins to unravel. Firstly, there are always risks of unintended consequences of policies to promote the social capacities for innovation. In the second place,

. . . it is by no means clear that innovation, learning and social capital are readily compatible with social justice and equality . . . Equally, policies designed to promote social cohesion may reduce capacities for innovation and knowledge exchange. (p. 4).

Nevertheless, he was able to reach a clear conclusion on the relationship between networks, innovation and social capital:

Strong social networks tend to be associated positively with learning and innovation. In order to achieve these benefits, policy-makers should seek to promote innovation and learning in ways that are socially embedded, socially inclusive, and create ties that bridge and link together actors from different social settings and different geographical entities (including the international level). (p. 20).

More recently, *Social Capital, Placement and Lifelong Learning* (Osborne *et al.*, 2007) included a chapter by Fabio Sabatini, in which he presented a critique of research on the empirical links between social capital and economic development.

Sabatini's work is interesting particularly because he describes the use of the concept of social *capital* in economics, as an identifiable resource that can be invested to order to generate ventures that will lead to growth of capital. This perspective might account for the substantial level of interest in the measurement of social capital. Apart from Cavaye's work, Field and Osborne (2006), Catts (2007) and Kilpatrick and Abbott-Chapman (2007) also addressed the question of measurement of social capital.

Taken together, the PASCAL writers, most of whom have published authoritatively in the field, seem to suggest that as a concept, 'social capital' is problematic. While other writers, not least Coleman and Bourdieu, have clearly played on the allusion to economic capital, this positions the quality of social relationships as an instrumental resource for achieving economic, political and social objectives. This can be interpreted as treating social interactions as forms of commodities, and giving priority to economic concepts and language as the frame for understanding social dynamics and social power.

This is clearly problematic, given the intangible complexities of human interactions, and the different kinds of social and emotional forces which shape them. Can other conceptual language provide greater clarity? A different kind of language might be important in clarifying issues of policy and also of values.

Other perspectives

Interestingly, policy itself has been dominated by other kinds of terminology, even where the underlying public debate has been shaped by reference to social capital. In Victoria, Australia, for example, the emphasis has been on social inclusion, as opposed to exclusion, and most recently, on 'liveability' and social participation – in education and training, employment, and civic affairs. In a speech entitled 'Liveability, Participation and Inclusion – New Approaches in Victorian Community Development Policy', the then Minister for Community Development, Peter Batchelor, observed that: '*A Fairer Victoria* is about social inclusion. It's about reducing inequalities which unfairly undermine the hopes of families and communities.' (2008, pp. 2–3)

In the government programmes themselves, the language of community building and community strengthening has provided the conceptual foundation. This recalls the seductive capacity of 'community' in discussion of the social. It has been a prominent theme in sociological analysis for well over a century, and evokes a positive spirit of relationship, even where ties of place and of identity have become fractured. Nevertheless, as Delanty (2003) has noted in his overview of the concept of community, it continues to carry an important connotation of sense of belonging, irrespective of whether the community is borne of place, association or virtual encounters online.

In Canada, social 'cohesion' has provided a dominant focus. Not unlike social capital, there are various meanings 'and the choice of which to employ as a definitional starting point has immediate consequences for what is analysed, what is measured and what policy action is recommended' (Beauvais and Jenson, 2002). For example, social 'order' and control, rather than social solidarity and equality, can imply a very different set of policy initiatives.

There has been debate in Canada also over whether social cohesion is a consequence or a cause of economic performance and well-being; the best conclusion that can be drawn from most studies is that a correlation exists.

> *However, as a quasi-concept useful for policy purposes, social*
> *cohesion remains robust ... It serves usefully as a framing*
> *concept for thinking through the complexity of policy issues.*
> (Beauvais and Jenson, 2002, p. 20).

They note that social cohesion has become a useful frame also for policies in the United Kingdom and France, which set out to address social exclusion in a multidimensional way, addressing simultaneously isolation, passivity and powerlessness (Beauvais and Jenson, 2002, p. 31).

Network theory and analysis have provided another quite distinct approach to understanding social relationships. The Organization of Economic Cooperation and Development (OECD) has adopted an approach based on networks as the central focus of its LEED (Local Economic and Employment Development) project. A network approach provides a clear framework for identifying and understanding the significance of collaboration amongst various entities as part of a place-based approach to economic change, highlighting in particular the interdependencies which exist amongst public, commercial and non-government organizations (see OECD, 2004). However, a range of questions arises about the social processes and actors within networks, especially in relation to governance (see Considine and Lewis, 2007).

A focus on 'networks' was central to the CRITICAL (City-Regions as Intelligent Territories: Inclusion, Competitiveness and Learning), project, a European Commission project (2003–07) which set out to understand how learning contributed to innovation in different kinds of networks. Focused in four European cities and one in Australia, case studies were produced on economic, social, political and cultural networks. While these case studies varied widely, and revealed a range of outcomes, they demonstrated the difficulties of distinguishing the social processes which occur in a regional context. This can be seen especially in the overlap between formal and informal relationships, where the apparent drivers of a government-initiated network might be less influential than the members who work behind the scenes (see Wilson *et al.*, 2007).

Organizational studies have also contributed to some of the conceptual language which has been used to describe social processes within a local or regional setting. In the CRITICAL project, for example, Wenger's concept of 'communities of practice' was used to describe the typically informal pattern which emerges when a group with common interests forms to share experience and to collaborate in generating new insights and practices. The broader literature on learning regions and regional innovation systems also acknowledges the importance of the 'social'. For example, Doloreux and Parto (2005) refer to the origin of the concept of regional innovation systems in two main sources: literature on innovation systems, and on regional science. With respect to the first:

> *The social aspect of innovation refers to the collective learning process between several departments of a company . . . as well as to external collaborations with other firms, knowledge providers, finances, training, etc.* (Doloreux and Parto, 2005, p. 3; see also Cooke et al., 2000)

Regional science, on the other hand, focuses on

> *. . . explaining the socio-institutional environment where innovation emerges . . . localized and locally embedded, not placeless . . . In other words, a regional innovation system is characterized by co-operation in innovation activity between firms and knowledge creating and diffusing organisations, such as universities, training organizations, R&D institutes, technology transfer agencies and so forth.* (Doloreux and Parto, 2004, p. 5).

The preceding discussion indicates that while there are a range of concepts that have been used to describe and explain the social dimensions of regional development, each is partial, contributing some insights but struggling to offer any comprehensive framework which could guide either local action or more general policy development.

Analysing the 'social' in regional development

Where to next? In analysing the social processes in regional development, the starting point is the proposition that regional development is a pre-eminently social process. The purpose of developing an analytical framework is to understand better the different kinds of social processes that arise in a regional context, and to provide insights into possible interventions into these processes that could enhance the effectiveness of regional development policies and initiatives.

To speak of a region is itself problematic. While governments regularly define regional boundaries, either for the purposes of governance (where state governments, for example, determine local government boundaries) or for managing service delivery (boundaries within government departments, not-for-profit or corporate entities, for example), these often do not match perceived regional identities or economic or geographic regions. For the purposes of this paper, this ambiguity might not matter greatly, except where overlapping or disjointed boundaries can create unnecessary confusion, duplication or neglect. Nevertheless, the assumption is that a locality or region can be identified for the purposes of undertaking an analysis based on the framework below.

A major problem which emerges from the review of the perspectives outlined in the preceding sections is that the reference to the 'social' masks a number of different kinds of actors, relationships and processes. It is not hard to see that there could be fundamentally different implications arising from whether people are engaged in activities as individual residents and community members, or as employees of different kinds of organizations, professional or otherwise, whether government, private industry or community. As an example, 'community' engagement has a very different look and feel if it involves, for example, unemployed young people from a public housing estate, rather than social workers from neighbourhood health centres.

How to make sense of these complexities? The framework which follows is a starting point for analysing the different kinds of social processes which occur within regional settings. The language used is relatively abstract, so that the framework can be applied in a broad range of diverse settings. It distinguishes those interactions of everyday life amongst citizens from those which involve more deliberative organizational activities and interventions. It becomes apparent quickly that there could be very significant differences between the kinds of dynamics which occur informally amongst citizens, when compared with formal negotiations between large organizations, yet all of these are submerged by the generic reference to the 'social'.

The clear implication is that agencies or organizations that are planning community engagement or regional development initiatives could use such a framework to think through the kinds of processes and relationships that will be important in shaping the effectiveness of their interventions. For example, community building initiatives in Victoria have focused on informal citizen-citizen processes, setting up new structures to facilitate projects, whereas neighbourhood renewal projects have had a much stronger involvement with existing organizational structures – it depends on the outcomes which are sought.

One of the implications of this approach is that university staff or regional policy-makers can identify more precisely the kinds of local/regional processes with which they wish to connect, and can anticipate some of the complexities which they might encounter. Specific questions which will help to understand the processes better are included in the relevant part of the framework. These also alert project leaders to issues which might arise in the interaction itself, where class differences, or competing interests can intrude and undermine the quality of interaction, as has happened often with efforts by universities to engage with industry or community. The very language and customs of academic scholarship can get in the way of effective communication with key audiences for the results of their work (see Wilson, 2009).

Complexity of processes

Each of these different kinds of social processes overlaps with the others, partly as individuals participate in one type of process or another, and partly as local/regional issues bring different kinds of processes together. For example, informal and formal processes in local/regional governance frequently connect with each other. This could be represented diagrammatically, which would indicate that the ensuing pattern of interacting social processes might seem like a bowl of spaghetti! The assumption here, however, is that the analytic distinction of the different kinds of processes can be useful in explaining why some kinds of interventions are more productive than others. Making sense of this would require more careful elucidation of each of these kinds of processes as they are observed in a particular setting.

As Table 3.1 indicates, making sense of the actual social processes in a particular local or regional setting requires considerably more care, with implications for both policy formation and engagement, than is apparent from a simple reference to social capital. This has been demonstrated through four case studies of regional innovation systems in Melbourne, Australia. Undertaken as part of Melbourne's participation in the PASCAL Universities and Regional Engagement (PURE) project, they set out to explore the structure, dynamics and opportunities offered through the regional systems which had emerged amongst universities (and other research institutes), local

Table 3.1 Social processes in regional development

Citizen–citizen	Citizen–organization	Local organization–organization	External organization–local organization
Informal processes that are the foundation of local/regional social life: interactions between neighbours, transactions such as those that occur through shopping and other aspects of commercial life, chance encounters in community settings (walking the dogs, taking children to playgrounds).	Transactional processes, commercial or service-oriented: health, finance, transport, recreational, educational for example, paid employment in local firms or organizations.	Informal processes, especially amongst community organizations (and possibly local government): networking, sharing information and possibly resources (e.g. buildings, parks). Relationships might be personal but interaction is business-oriented.	Typically formal processes, related to funding, reporting, accountability, and some areas of shared policy formation and decision-making.
Semi-formal processes that arise from civic initiative: voluntary work, street parties, local environmental action groups, perhaps some hobby or sports clubs.	Civic local / regional governance processes: these encompass the formation and operations of 'community' organizations, campaigns around specific issues, and activities associated with lobbying and elections related to (local) regional governance.	Formal processes: Industry, commercial and political, where private, public and community organizations interact in undertaking organizational business. Diverse organizations, including industry and commerce, universities and other research centres, different tiers of government and non-government organizations. Not all transactional, as some collaborative partnerships.	In some cases, regional offices/representatives/campuses mediate processes between international/national/provincial management and local/regional organizations.

Table 3.1 Continued

Policy interventions: processes instigated by local/regional or by extra-regional organizations (state or federal) to influence the character and parameters of (local) regional informal social processes. An example would be initiatives sponsored by the Victorian Government concerning community 'building' and 'strengthening'.	Formal processes in (local) regional governance: the formal politics of local/regional governance, and the actions of local/regional governments in service delivery to individual citizens, enforcement of local regulation, and policy and operational decision-making.	Interventions occur in local/regional governance. Extra-regional organizations (mostly state or federal governments) seek at times to shape the character of (local) regional governance to achieve policy objectives related to economic and/or social development. E.g. reshaping of (local) regional boundaries, leading to the reformation of decision-making and service delivery.
	Interventions might focus on: work organization, functional arrangements and decision-making in private, public and community organizations. Organizational capability is explicit focus of change and the character and parameters of organizational activity, with a view to enhancing economic and social regional development. Formation of strategic regional entities.	

Table 3.1 Continued

Questions

- What is the pattern and frequency of interaction?
- Do these patterns vary according to gender, class, culture/language of birth/race?
- Does professional or educational background affect the patterns of interaction?
- Does the interaction tend to be formal or informal?

- What is the pattern, density and frequency of interaction?
- Do these patterns vary according to gender, class, culture/language of birth/race?
- Does professional or educational background affect the patterns of interaction?
- Does the interaction tend to be formal or informal?
- How is the existence or otherwise of trust/mutual confidence demonstrated?
- What assumptions are made about the significance, practical or symbolic, of place?
- Do the patterns of relationships reflect distinct examples of individual and organizational learning/ communities of practice?

- Is there an infrastructure to support different kinds of interactions?
- What is the density of relationships within this region?
- How is the existence or otherwise of trust/mutual confidence demonstrated?
- What assumptions are made about the significance, practical or symbolic, of place?
- Do the patterns of relationships reflect distinct examples of individual and organizational learning/communities of practice?
- Do the processes vary according to context and activity (advocacy as compared with programme/ project development, for example)?
- Under what circumstances do the social interactions produce learning that generates innovation?

- Is there an infrastructure to support different kinds of interactions?
- Do the patterns of relationships reflect distinct examples of individual and organizational learning/communities of practice?
- Do the processes vary according to context and activity (advocacy as compared with programme/ project development, for example)?
- Who sets the vision, provides resources, shapes key decisions?

63

industry, local government and other stakeholders focused on innovation and economic growth in the north, south-east, west and south-west of Melbourne. In each case, an intermediary 'broking' entity had developed to facilitate improved relationships.

An example: Social processes in regional innovation systems

Insofar as the key players in regional innovation systems are 'firms and knowledge creating and diffusing organizations, such as universities, training organizations, R&D institutes, technology transfer agencies' (as Doloreux and Parto, 2004, identified), the relationships amongst these actors can be quite difficult. For example, some of the constraints that have limited universities' capacity to engage include:

- The scale of universities. Their organizational complexity is frequently very much at odds with the scale and orientation of regional and community organizations;
- They are increasingly lean as resources remain tight and demands increase, particularly in relation to time;
- They have competing priorities, as universities are under pressure already to maximize their efforts in teaching and research;
- The structure of staff careers, in which the priority put on research performance undermines staff willingness to support engagement activity;
- The contrast between the social characteristics of HEI staff, and the social class and race composition, and gender dynamics, in the relevant region and its communities. The use of language is one quite particular manifestation of the tensions which can arise in this respect.

While the framework outlined above was not available for use in these case studies, the findings of the case studies demonstrate the complexity of the processes involved, and indicate how the framework could be used in planning either government or university intervention. Each of the case studies centred on an organization which had been established to bring some strategic leadership and coherence to regional initiatives, with particular emphasis on enhancing innovation and economic and social development. Each included at least one university as a key partner, and most were based on organizational membership or networks, although one had very strong citizen engagement.

On this basis, the 'citizen–citizen' level of processes was not particularly relevant. The other three categories all encompassed processes which were integral to the regional entities. A number of the participants in the regional entities were small businesses whose proprietors were also prominent local identities and many residents had paid employment in local businesses or services. While the strongest set of the social processes was amongst local-regional organizations, external organizations such as state and federal government departments and corporate headquarters also played a prominent role. The questions above point to a number of key features of the regional processes which shaped the participation by different kinds of organizations, including universities.

For example, drawing on some of the questions in Table 4.1, the following insights into the processes in these four regions can be identified:

- Each of the regional entities represented a significant infrastructure to support collaboration and shared learning.
- Both formal and informal kinds of interaction were important in facilitating learning and the development of appropriate initiatives. The informal interaction, in particular, influenced the development of trust and mutual confidence.
- The sense of place, and identifying with the region, was a crucial driver of collaboration in at least three regions.
- Advocacy was a prominent role in each of the four regions, although this was based typically on specific research or consultative projects.
- Local government authorities were prominent in decision-making and providing resources.
- Collaborative processes were seen regularly as the key source of learning about new initiatives.
- The universities were a critical resource for learning and innovation, although perhaps linked more strongly with business and process innovation rather than technological innovation – not without a good deal of angst, such as described previously.

Based on these insights, both universities and government need to explore carefully the kinds of infrastructure that will facilitate constructive participation in regional innovation systems. This cannot be taken for granted; indeed, the constraints identified above are often compounded by the characteristics of HEI staff. For example, they are recruited frequently from outside the region (perhaps from very different locales); their own careers have required investment in an increasingly narrow sphere of expertise that is not easily connected to regional issues; their own class, gender or race background limits their capacity to communicate effectively with regional representatives. As Gibbons has noted, overcoming these issues is not an easy matter (see Nowotny *et al.*, 2001).

This means that HEIs need to build an infrastructure to support the linking of their academic staff with regional partners, even those who exercise regional leadership: local politicians, public, private and community sector managers, and professional workers. The infrastructure might include internal units, where staff have the skills to both understand their characteristics of their regions, and to assist academic staff to make the links. The other aspect of infrastructure is external units, housed in industry or regional settings, which can be bridgeheads for engagement, linking both staff and students with regional or local services and projects.

Whatever the approach adopted, either by universities or government towards engagement, the key proposition of this chapter is that their effectiveness will be increased if they attend to a more thorough understanding of the social processes which underpin regional development. The framework developed in this chapter is intended to facilitate their analysis of these kinds of processes, and to enable them to plan more effectively for their engagement.

References

Beauvais, C. and Jenson, J. (2002) *Social Cohesion: Updating the State of the Research.* Canadian Policy Research Networks Discussion Paper No. F/22. Ottawa, May 2002.

Bourdieu, P. (1980) 'Le capital social', *Actes de la Recherche en Sciences Sociales* 31, 2–3.

Bourdieu, P. (1986) 'The forms of capital', in J.G. Richardson (ed.) *Handbook of theory and research for the sociology of education.* New York: Greenwood Press, 241–258.

Catts, R. (2007) 'Quantitative indicators of social capital – roles in policy development and implementation' in M. Osborne *et al.* (eds), *Social capital, lifelong learning and the management of place: An international perspective.* London: Routledge.

Cavaye, J. (2004) 'Social capital: A commentary on issues, understanding and measurement', PASCAL Hot Topic No. 1, May. http://www.obs-pascal.com/resources/cavaye.pdf.

Coleman, J. (1988) 'Social capital in the creation of human capital', *American Journal of Sociology*, 94, 95–120.

Coleman, J. (1990) *Foundations of social theory*. Cambridge, MA: Harvard University Press.

Considine, M. and Lewis, J. (2007) 'Innovation and innovators inside government: From institutions to networks' *Governance*, 20(4), 581–607.

Cooke, P., Boekholt, P., Tödtling, F. (2000) *The governance of innovation in Europe*. London: Pinter.

Delanty, G. (2003) *Community*. London, Routledge.

Doloreux, and Parto, S. (2005) 'Regional innovation systems: Current discourse and challenges for future research', Scientific Commons: http://en.scientificcommons.org/32933102 Accessed 28 September 2010.

DPCD (Department for Planning and Community Development) (2008) *A fairer Victoria: Strong people, strong communities*. Melbourne: DPCD.

Duke, C., Doyle, L. and Wilson, B. (eds.) (2006) *Making knowledge work: Sustaining learning communities and regions*. Leicester: NIACE.

Field, J. (2006) 'Social networks, innovation and learning: can policies for social capital promote both economic dynamism and social justice?' PASCAL Hot Topic No. 3, May http://www.obs-pascal.com/system/files/johnfieldfebruary2006.pdf.

Field, J. and Osborne, M. (2006) 'Researching social capital in Europe: towards a toolkit for measurement', in C. Duke *et al.* (eds.), *Making knowledge work: Sustaining learning communities and regions*. Leicester: NIACE.

Hanifan, L.J. (1916) 'The rural school community centre', *Annals of the American Academy of Political and Social Sciences*, 67, 130–138.

Kilpatrick, S. and Abbott-Chapman, J. (2007) 'Community efficacy and social capital: modelling how communities deliver outcomes for members' in M. Osborne *et al.* (eds.), *Social capital, lifelong learning and the management of place: An international perspective*. London: Routledge.

Mowbray, M. (2004) 'Beyond community capacity building: the effect of government on social capital', PASCAL Hot Topic No. 3, May http://www.obs-pascal.com/resources/mowbray_dec_2004.pdf.

Nowotny, H., Scott, P. and Gibbons, M. (2001) *Re-thinking science: Knowledge and the public in an age of uncertainty*. Cambridge: Polity Press.

Organization for Economic Co-operation and Development (2004) *New forms of governance for economic development*. Local Economic and Employment Development Program. Paris: OECD.

Osborne, M., Sankey, K. and Wilson, B. (2007) *Social capital, lifelong learning and the management of place: An international perspective*. London, Routledge.

Putnam, R.D. (2000) *Bowling Alone: The collapse and revival of American community*. New York: Touchstone Books.

Sabatini, F. (2007) 'The empirics of social capital and economic development: A critical perspective', in M.Osborne *et al.* (eds), *Social capital, lifelong learning and the management of place: An international perspective*. London: Routledge.

Wilson, B. (2009) 'Social inclusion: Universities and regional development', Keynote Paper presented to National Social Inclusion and Education Conference, Sydney, October 2009.

Wilson, B., Badenhorst, A., Charles, D. and Duke, C. (2007) 'Urban networks, learning and innovation', Paper presented to the Australian State of the Cities Conference, Adelaide, November 2007.

Chapter 4

How to benchmark
university-community interactions

David Charles, Paul Benneworth,
Cheryl Conway and Lynne Humphrey

Introduction

There is an increasing recognition that there is a need to rebalance the contributions that universities make to society. The so-called third mission for universities, also described as external engagement, has evolved considerably in the past quarter-century, although the roots of engagement go back to the origins of most universities. In 1982, an Organization for Economic Cooperation and Development (OECD) report produced by the Centre for Educational Research and Innovation explored all dimensions of community engagement, with business, government, the third sector and society (OECD, 1982). However, the third mission has increasingly become equated with commercialization, patents and licensing, a trend enforced by the easy measurement associated with these variables. This chapter explores the ways in which measurement and benchmarking tools can be used to assess the wider contributions that universities make including engagement with 'harder-to-reach' groups such as smaller, potentially non-innovative firms, voluntary organizations, smaller charities and disadvantaged communities.

In part the desire to measure community engagement is being driven by increased government interest in, and in some cases funding for, engagement and hence a desire to assess the impact of such activity and investment. Some of this funding has been in the form of core programmatic support for engagement as in the UK, whilst other countries have seen ad hoc government schemes and the opening up of support for regeneration to university participants. At the same time the increased level of activity leads both universities and their partners to seek improvement and to look for ways to benchmark themselves against other universities and other university systems. This search for improvement has been encouraged by a number of international fora and projects, including the OECD.

However this presents considerable challenges as to what you measure and compare. A characteristic of university-community engagement is the pro-liferation of different schemes and programmes and the diversity of impacts and benefits realized. Some university activities can be readily codified, measured and hence compared, but the diversity of activities covered by engagement with the community presents great difficulties of comparison as well as fundamental problems of measurement.

A number of studies in recent years have tried to develop indicators and benchmarking tools for university engagement. Many of the earliest attempts to provide indicators have emerged from business engagement where standardization of the outputs and simple financial measures give the opportunity to provide easily comparable measures. Over time though more effort has been placed in expanding on these simple metrics to cover a wider set of relationships beyond the business community and wider set of project types. This chapter examines a number of different approaches to measurement and benchmarking and explores some of the strengths and weaknesses, but then examines in greater detail one particular approach initially developed in the UK and modified for the PASCAL Universities and Regional Engagement (PURE) project.

Key issues in university-community engagement

Whilst it may be difficult for a large educational institution such as a university to be truly disengaged from society and its local community, the debate about university-community engagement in recent years has focused on the extent to which engagement is seen by universities as a core element of their mission, alongside teaching and research (Goddard *et al.*, 1994; ACU, 2001; Kellogg Commission, 1999). Individual staff and students may undertake community service, but does the university as a corporate body seek to support such activities and recognize, as the American Association of State Colleges and Universities puts it, that they have duties as 'stewards of place': 'answering the call to join with public and private partners in their communities to take advantage of opportunities and confront challenges' (AASCU, 2002, p. 7). In some countries there is a long history of this kind of engagement: in the US the roots of engagement lie in the Morrill Act of 1862 which established the land-grant colleges (McDowell, 2003) whilst in the UK the civic universities of the 19th century were mainly established by local interests to support local industry (Sanderson, 1972). The dominance of national funding in the post war years particularly in the growth of a new generation of universities led to a downplaying of local and regional engagement within the mission, a process which governments have sought to rebalance in more recent years. In part this emerges from a mutuality of purpose in that universities benefit from the growth and success of their local surroundings, and their research and teaching can benefit from the engagement with real world problems, but also a sense of obligation reinforced by policy-makers that universities as publicly funded institutions should address some of the challenges facing society.

Defining university-community engagement is however not straightforward, as the 'community' is a multifaceted concept based on place, or the functions of the university (Goedegebuure and van der Lee, 2006), or other interests and needs. Even the apparently simple definition of a geographical community or region for a university is fraught with difficulties as universities choose to define their regions according to different criteria, and differently for distinct activities (Charles, 2003). A further difficulty is the wide range of activities covered which includes strategies for economic and social regional development, service learning, collaboration with business, social and cultural activities, support for local health and welfare and physical urban regeneration (Charles and Benneworth, 2001; Goedegebuure and van der Lee, 2006). The nature of community engagement for an individual university will be shaped by the history and disciplinary profile of the university itself, but also the nature of the local community, its needs and enunciated demands, and the incentives and funding made available to support such activities from the national as well as local level. Thus comparison between universities is difficult as there is no reason for two universities to have similar profiles of engagement given the likely variations in institutional and local context.

The measurement of university-community engagement is also a fundamentally complex and difficult task, and is still at a formative stage (Hart *et al.*, 2009). Indicators are a means of measuring that which is codifiable and measureable, whereas much university-community engagement defies measurement and is highly heterogeneous. So the development of indicators is problematic, unlike in other aspects of university activities where there are relatively clear, repeatable and codifiable outputs. In teaching, for example, there are standard units of work (lectures, seminars) and of outputs (students, graduates, degrees or modules examined). Research also yields some standardized performance measures in the form of research grants, levels of income, publication outputs etc. Whilst there are problems with assessing quality, only partly addressed by citation counts etc., at least all universities are seeking similar kinds of inputs and outputs. For community engagement the outputs may be highly disparate, and the kind of engagement as a process also very varied.

A particular difficulty with community-oriented activities is the difference in perspective between the university and the community. From whose perspective should we measure engagement projects? A project that delivered research income and publications might be positively viewed by a university, but if it was expected to deliver improvements to services in a community and didn't, then the community might take a very different view.

Governments in recent years have been interested in measuring community engagement following on from the considerable effort placed on measuring business engagement. In the latter case there are a few codified and well established indicators such as patents, licences, spin off firms etc., which can be measured and, more importantly, counted and compared across universities and even across national boundaries.

In business engagement the codification of relationships partly emerges for legal reasons. In order to establish clear ownership of intellectual property, universities need to patent ideas, which can then be licensed to firms. Knowledge may be handed over freely but in such a case the firm would not be able to take out intellectual property protection and could not therefore protect its own investment. So legal agreements are necessary for successful knowledge transfer (in some areas) and hence the codification provides easy-to-measure metrics, especially if, like patents, they are placed in the public domain. As patents are public documents and are searchable on databases then details of university patent holdings are public knowledge and databases can be assembled by researchers without needing universities to provide the information. Universities also have a financial duty to monitor the numbers of patents as they are both expenses and potential assets, and as such are monitored closely, whereas softer forms of interaction are not required to be monitored and therefore usually monitored on an ad-hoc basis if at all. Engagement with business is often also supported by public programmes and hence is subject to audit and formal monitoring by the funding organization, but even here there are problems with capturing knowledge exchange.

Another dimension of the measurement task is the contrast between quantitative and qualitative measures. There are several problems with quantitative indicators which derives from the need for such indicators to be repeatable, measurable and codifiable. The focus on measurement (and auditability) requires such indicators to reflect what has already happened, so as such they reflect past actions and policies rather than current strategies. The emphasis on deliverables or outputs reflects what has been achieved rather than the intentions. This is exacerbated sometimes by the significant time-lags in ultimate success, so actions taken now may not yield outcomes for several years, and measured outcomes today may be the result of very different policies than those in place now.

Quantitative indicators may be highly influenced by the structure of universities and inputs such as the quality of students. Large well resourced universities may have higher impacts on some indicators even if adjusted by scale as the available budget for engagement activity rises above threshold levels which allow greater impacts. It is also easier to measure absolute outputs rather than value added, which again tends to emphasize the larger and better resourced institutions.

Quantitative indicators often don't even measure what is intended but are only crude surrogates for what needs to be measured, and there is a risk of seeking to deliver the required indicators rather than the desired outcomes.

Finally, significant economic impacts may require risk-taking, and hence there is a likelihood of short-term failure and poor performance even if the approach is correct.

Qualitative assessments also have shortcomings though. Whilst many studies focus on identifying 'good practices', these may depend heavily on the context, so the relative success of one approach may be difficult to judge if abstracted from the institutional situation. Most qualitative evaluation is also akin to description, and generalization is difficult.

Both quantitative and qualitative assessments suffer from a problem of scale. At what scale should measurement take place, and what measurements can be applied across a wide range of departments and activities? Many activities are undertaken by parts of the university only, or are small elements within the work of a department, and hence tend to be unmeasured or unreported to the centre of the university. The efforts of individuals may be significant but go unnoticed within their departments

Previous approaches

There have been a number of different approaches to the issue of measurement and benchmarking of university-community engagement in recent years. Analysis of previous projects and tools gives a simple classification of approaches:

- Survey approaches. Where indicators can be codified and reliably collected from one year to the next, there has been scope for regular surveys, primarily in the area of business links. This includes the annual survey of the Association of University Technology Managers (AUTM, 2009) in North America, and the Higher Education Business and Community Interaction Survey undertaken by the Higher Education Funding Council for England (HEFCE, 2008) in the UK. The latter includes some metrics relating to community engagement as well as business linkages. Mollas-Gallart *et al.* (2002) have also proposed a very similar set of indicators.

- Project analysis and templates. Much interest in community engagement is focused at the project level and some groups have developed formal templates for collecting data on projects for comparison and benchmarking. Two examples from the UK include the Russell Group engagement tool (CCC, 2004) and Salford University's UPBEAT (Powell *et al.*, no date) project. The UPBEAT project has collected data and stories about successful engagement projects from a wide range of universities internationally using templates for presentation of information about widely diverse cases.

- Institutional reviews by questionnaire. At an institutional rather than project level a number of bodies have developed a process for assessing university strategies for engagement as well as actions and outcomes using some form of template or questionnaire. So the OECD Institutional Management in Higher Education programme has a process for assessing regional engagement of universities in case study regions where the universities have to provide information on their strategies and actions against a self assessment questionnaire format, and are then subject to peer review by a panel (OECD, 2007). The Australian Universities Community Engagement Alliance (AUCEA) has developed a benchmarking approach based on a series of instruments including an institutional questionnaire, partners perception surveys and good practice cases (Garlick and Langworthy, 2008).

- Institutional indicators. A more formal approach to bench-marking at an institutional level is to use a set of indicators or key performance indicators at university level. Some institutions have developed this approach and monitor their performance against these indicators (e.g. RMIT University, University of Western Sydney)
- Benchmarking. The final category is a benchmarking approach where a range of indicators are used in an approach which is comparative and can be seen as part of a wider benchmarking process (Charles and Benneworth, 2002; CIC, 2005).

In these different approaches we can contrast audit, benchmarking and evaluation. Audit usually involves the description and simple measurement of interventions to see what has been done, or whether what was promised was delivered, and is usually represented by surveys relying on quantitative measures and template descriptions of projects. Evaluation is concerned with assessing whether the best outcome was realized and which approaches work best and may include standard indicators and surveys as well as institutional reviews. Benchmarking by contrast tends to be focused on a process of self-improvement and the collection of information that allows an organization to compare itself with others in ways that show opportunities for change. Such benchmarking usually requires a combination of quantitative indicators as well as comparison of practices and thus often builds upon other forms of analysis.

Looking in more detail at some of these different approaches we can assess the strengths and weaknesses.

In terms of surveys of quantitative indicators, the UK uses an annual survey, the Higher Education – Business and Community Interaction Survey, originally developed by two of the authors (Charles and Conway, 2001), but based heavily on standard indicators used by the AUTM in North America and earlier ad-hoc surveys in the UK. This makes full use of those standardized indicators such as patent licences which have been well developed over time and are reasonably comparable internationally, but also includes a wider set of new quantitative indicators and some qualitative questions also. Initial work on the very first survey found that many universities struggled to complete novel questions due to the limitations of their databases, and we may presume varying degrees of accuracy in response depending on the maturity of the indicator. Some benchmarking questions from the HEFCE Charles and Benneworth (2002) tool were included in the survey, but we cannot make assumptions about the ways in which they were answered, so they may not have been answered by reflection among a mixed group of staff as would be suggested in a benchmarking exercise. The nature of surveys is such that we normally regard all answers as equally reliable, but here we know the reliability of response varies between questions, and that some of the questions are only rough proxies of the core issues. It remains however an effective way of collecting some standardized information across a national university sector.

A completely different approach is the project level and frameworks for the preparation of case studies of individual projects. The UPBEAT project led by the University of Salford takes this approach and provides a template for the evaluation and comparison of project-level activity. The project has developed tools for the preparation of project case studies but also their assessment against a grid which displays four qualities – academic business acumen, social networking intelligence, individual performance and foresight enabling skill – against a six-point scale. The focus here is to identify success stories and assist the transfer of experience to encourage good practice, but it avoids the collection of standard performance data.

Institutional reviews also tend to focus on templates and questionnaires, and in some cases come close to benchmarking, although mainly focusing on audits, lists and descriptions, with examples of good practice often identified without real comparison across a range of institutions. There is a tendency to rely on peer review to identify good practice, and use of a consistent peer-review team makes cross-regional comparisons possible (Garlick and Langworthy, 2008) but it is often practically difficult to use the same reviewers across a number of cases so consistency may be hard to achieve. A key disadvantage is the effect of the home system and culture on reviewers (Garlick and Langworthy, 2008), which may blinker perspectives. Good institutional reviews will use some standardized indicators, and many universities are developing their own indicators to monitor progress over time, but there is a great tendency to reinvent the wheel and to develop case-specific lists of indicators.

This all leads to a desire for some standardized approaches to comparison across institutions in different contexts, but which are sensitive to the weaknesses of simplistic metrics and where the focus of the activity is a culture of improvement and communication rather than the production of league tables, and this is where benchmarking can play an important role.

The example of the HEFCE/PURE approach

The approach used in the PURE study originated as a tool developed for the Higher Education Funding Council for England in 2001, with the support of Universities UK (Charles and Benneworth, 2002), to identify and communicate the regional contributions made by universities in England. The project focused on the existing activities of universities in their regions, and examples of good practice and the results were published in a series of reports each covering one of the English regions, with a national overview report ('The Regional Mission' reports are available from Universities UK, including Charles and Benneworth, 2001). Alongside this descriptive activity a benchmarking tool was developed to help universities develop a process and apply a set of criteria to help prioritize their engagement activities.

The objective of the tool was to give individual universities a means of assessing their regional impact. The key challenge is to highlight not just linear relations between a university and its region, but also a wide range of strategic interactions. Strategic priorities for regional engagement should be regional development processes which link between, for example, economic development and educational attainment, or community regeneration and the formation of new firms.

The tool assesses whether or not, across a broad range of processes, a university contributes significantly to regional development. It does not assess how well managed the university is, nor its success in educational or research terms. Not every university will want to contribute in all possible ways identified. All universities will have a combination of strengths and areas of lower contribution. The latter may be strategic choices rather than weaknesses. What is important is that universities seeking to contribute to particular regional development processes should aim to achieve good practice.

The university benchmarking tool therefore has four functions:
- to assess improvements in the strategy, performance and outcomes of university-regional engagement by providing a set of indicators that can be reviewed at different points of time to see how well the university addresses regional development processes and how this might change over time;
- to help the university set its own strategic priorities by examining how well it performs across a range of different areas so senior management can decide whether to devote resources to

strengthening existing strengths or building up areas with a poor performance;
- to support joint strategies within a regional partnership, by allowing comparison between universities within a region and the identification of mutual or complementary strengths;
- to enable comparisons to be made between universities and regions through the mapping of indicators either at an individual university level or for groups of universities.

The benchmarking tool has several elements:
- analysis of existing quantitative indicators, and the development of new quantitative measures of core, regionally-oriented activities;
- benchmarking questions on aspects of institutional management and culture related to promoting regional engagement; and
- questions on the main themes of regional economic and social development. For each of these, good practice in the support of regional processes is the benchmark to be attained.

The tool was primarily for use at an institutional level, but certain aspects may be applied to sub-units such as campuses or faculties. It is designed to be implemented within cross-functional and cross-departmental groups in a university, and to involve staff at all levels and students.

A five-point scale represents the spectrum from poor to good practice, which can be used to produce scores for groups of indicators. Institutions can use these results, with the quantitative data, to identify areas in which they are performing well. This can be extended to internal analysis of which departments or units are achieving good practice.

More importantly, the process of benchmarking can stimulate discussion and internal assessment of where to focus effort, for the benefit of both the region and the university. Such discussions could consider:
- What are the mechanisms within the university to establish a consensus on strategic priorities for regional development?
- What mechanisms can be established within the university to link existing regionally-focused activities and add value to them?
- What mechanisms exist within the university to balance its different geographical roles and create synergy between them?
- What mechanisms exist within the region to consider issues such

as health, culture, the economy, and community regeneration, in a joined-up way?
- What mechanisms can be established to bring together those involved in the regional development process such as regional governments and agencies, community groups and central government, so they can prioritize which regional needs should be addressed?

A distinct aspect of the tool is its focus around regional development processes, so rather than a set of indicators relating to a university's activities, the questions are grouped according to regional development priorities and are mainly seen from the perspective of the region. Rather than asking whether what the university does is relevant to the region the tool asks whether what the university does addresses the needs of a region. As such, seven main groups of processes were identified that underpin regional competitiveness:
- Enhancing regional infrastructure. Supporting the regional infrastructure, regulatory frameworks and underlying quality of environment and lifestyles. This includes the university helping the region to identify where improvements can be made, or providing direct input to the quality of the local environment.
- Human capital development processes. Supporting the development of human capital through education and training both within the university and in other organizations. The emphasis here is on how the university adds to the stock of human capital by facilitating the development of people in the region, and retains both local and non-local graduates. (The education of people from outside the region who then leave it does not add to the stock of human capital in the region, and therefore is not relevant for this process. However it may be important at the national level, and it does add to regional GDP.)
- Business development processes. The creation and attraction of new firms, as well as support for developing new products, processes and markets for existing firms.
- Interactive learning and social capital development processes. Encouraging co-operation between firms and other institutions to generate technological, commercial and social benefits. Regional collaboration and learning between organizations are important in regional success. Universities can promote the

application of knowledge through regional partnerships, and encourage networking and the building of trust.

- Community development processes. Ensuring that the benefits of enhanced business competitiveness are widely shared within the community, and that the health and welfare of the population are maximized.
- Cultural development. The creation, enhancement and reproduction of regional cultures, underpinning the other processes above, and interpreting culture both as activities that enrich the quality of life and as patterns of social conventions, norms and values that constitute regional identities.
- Promoting sustainability. Long-term regional development must be underpinned by processes seeking to improve sustainability, even though some of these objectives may appear to conflict with business development objectives.

These seven processes form the framework for the questions in the benchmarking tool and ensure that the activities of the university can be related back to perceived needs of the region rather than the internal interests of the university.

Modifications and developments

For the PASCAL Universities and Regional Engagement (PURE) project there was a need to have a benchmarking tool which allowed for some comparison between universities both within and between regions, as well as coverage of a wide range of forms of engagement and activities. The international nature of the project was a particular challenge as different national HE systems tend to emphasize different forms of engagement and the benchmarking needed to be sensitive to these differences. It was decided that the HEFCE benchmarking tool provided the right balance of relative simplicity of comparison, breadth of coverage and focus on improvement processes, but it needed to be modified from a focus on the UK, and needed some further development in certain areas.

In order to meet the requirements of the project therefore the tool was edited and enhanced. The coverage of topics was increased slightly with additional questions, including a new section on internal university processes. This particularly strengthened the community aspects of engagement relative to the existing emphasis on business engagement. Some of the wording was

Example benchmark from the tool

Benchmark 5.2 Support for community-based regeneration

Type
Practice

Rationale
Considerable support is required to address the problems of disadvantaged communities in many cities and rural areas. Much of this is provided through government programmes that require partnerships to deliver assistance. Universities can provide support in a number of ways, through expertise based on research into the nature of community problems and regeneration policies, through direct services, through educational programmes, and as neighbours and landlords in many inner city areas. The benchmark examines whether the university seeks to provide integrated support for needy communities, and uses resources in a way that meets needs and maximizes partnerships while also supporting the university's mission.

Sources of data
Internal assessment

Good practice
Good practice goes beyond support for individual departments wishing to engage in community regeneration, and prioritizes specific target communities for integrated support from the institution as a whole. Support may be provided within a compact involving a wide variety of departments and schemes. In the case of neighbouring communities this may extend to using the university estates strategy as a pump primer for physical regeneration. Senior staff within the university may seek to take leadership roles in regeneration partnerships or companies, and ensure that expertise from the university is made available to the community and other local partners.

Levels

1	2	3	4	5
No engagement with community regeneration schemes, apart from individual efforts.		Some representation of the university on local partnerships at senior management level, but with limited implementation capability. Main focus is on research role and possible property development due.		Active and creative engagement with community programmes, with the university taking a leadership position and applying a wide variety of resources. Community regeneration seen as a mainstream activity with role for access policy, link to student community action, and staff involvement as part of staff development.

also modified to remove references to specific UK institutions or practices, and to increase the international applicability.

The example benchmark shows the format of the questions used in the tool. Each one is identified as being either a practice or performance benchmark, and is provided with a brief rationale for its selection, expected source of data and good practice statement. The university team is then expected to select their position on the scale of 1–5, depending on how well the statements in the table describe their university. Three statements are provided so allowing the participants to also select a position between these three. The statements were selected so as to give an extremely good practice as Level 5 on the scale, no activity or only very indifferent activity as 1, and an intermediate position as 3. This way the participants are given reasonably objective criteria for the grading of the university, rather than just poor to good, and a limited number of statements from which to select.

Conclusions

The nature of university-community engagement as a complex relationship covering a wide range of activities and contributions to the community requires a benchmarking approach that addresses that complexity through a multifaceted instrument and an inclusive form of assessment. A great many tools and approaches for assessment have been developed but it is argued here that a benchmarking methodology can overcome some of the difficulties and draw on some aspects of other approaches.

The choice of approach, whether audit, evaluation or benchmarking depends however on the objectives of the study and the role played by the assessor. An external assessment to make comparisons for funding purposes will usually draw on standardized indicators and some form of survey approach where the data can be audited, but this will usually fail to capture the richness of engagement or identify ways to improve performance except along narrow tracks. The particular benefits of the benchmarking approach is as part of a culture of self improvement within the university and within a strategic discussion with regional partners where decisions can be made as to which areas of engagement are necessary for the community, which need to be improved or ignored, and how two or more universities might negotiate mutually complementary programmes.

This kind of approach is very much at odds with league tables and raw indicators where size of institution may skew results and limited quantitative indicators, usually involving business tend to dominate the rankings. Instead there is a focus on the process by which the university examines its approach and prioritization rather than a slavish attention to metrics.

References

AASCU (American Association of State Colleges and Universities) (2002) *Stepping forward as stewards of place.*Washington DC: AACSU.

ACU (Association of Commonwealth Universities) (2001) *Engagement as a core value for universities: A consultation document.* London: ACU.

AUTM (Association of University Technology Managers) (2009) *AUTM U.S. licensing activity survey: FY2008.* Deerfield, IL: AUTM.

Charles, D. R. (2003) 'Universities and territorial development: reshaping the regional role of English universities', *Local Economy*, 18, 7–20.

Charles, D. R. and Benneworth, P. (2001) *The regional mission: The regional contribution of higher education: National Report.* London: Universities UK.

Charles, D. R. and Benneworth, P. (2002) *Evaluating the regional contribution of an HEI. A benchmarking approach.* Bristol: Higher Education Funding Council for England www.hefce.ac.uk/pubs/hefce/2002/02_23.htm Accessed 28 September 2010.

Charles, D. R. and Conway, C. (2001) *Higher education business interaction survey.* Bristol: Higher Education Funding Council for England http://www.hefce.ac.uk/pubs/hefce/2001/01_68.htm Accessed 28 September 2010.

CIC (Committee on Institutional Cooperation) (2005) *Engaged scholarship: A resource guide.* Champaign, IL: Committee on Institutional Co-operation http://www.cic.net/Home/Reports.aspx Accessed 28 September 2010.

CRC (Corporate Citizenship Company) (2004) *Higher education community engagement model: Final report and analysis. A report for the Russell Group of universities.* London: CCC.

Garlick, S. and Langworthy, A. (2008) 'Benchmarking university–community engagement: Developing a national approach in Australia', *Higher Education Management and Policy*, 20(2) 1–12.

Garlick, S. and Langworthy, A. (undated) 'Assessing university-community engagement', Discussion paper prepared for the AUCEA Benchmarking Project.

Goddard, J., Charles, D., Pike, A., Potts, G. and Bradley, D. (1994) *Universities and communities*. London: Committee of Vice-Chancellors and Principals.

Goedegebuure, L. and van der Lee, J. (2006). *In search of evidence. Measuring community engagement: A pilot study.* Brisbane: Eidos.

Hart, A., Northmore, S. and Gerhardt, C. (2009) *Briefing Paper: Auditing, Benchmarking and Evaluating Public Engagement, Research Synthesis No 1.* Bristol: National Coordinating Centre for Public Engagement.

HEFCE (Higher Education Funding Council for England) (2008) *Higher education – Business and community interaction survey 2006–07.* Bristol: Higher Education Funding Council for England http://www.hefce.ac.uk/pubs/hefce/2008/08_22/ Accessed 28 September 2010.

Kellogg Commission (1999) Third report on the future of state and land-grant universities, *Returning to our roots: The engaged institution.* Washington DC: National Association of State Universities and Land-Grant Colleges http://www.eric.ed.gov/ > ERIC#ED426676 Accessed 28 September 2010.

McDowell, G. R. (2003) 'Engaged universities: lessons from the land-grant universities and extension', *Annals of the American Academy of Political and Social Science*, 585, 31–50.

Mollas-Gallart, J., Salter, A., Patel, P., Scott, A., Duran, X. and SPRU University of Sussex (2002) *Measuring third stream activities. Final report to the Russell Group of Universities.* Brighton: SPRU. www.lse.ac.uk/collections/CCPN/pdf/russell_report_thirdStream.pdf Accessed 28 September 2010.

OECD (Organization for Economic Co-operation and Development) (2007) *Higher education and regions: Globally competitive, locally engaged.* Paris: OECD.

OECD Centre for Educational Research and Innovation (1982) *The university and the community: the problems of changing relationships.* Paris: OECD.

Powell, J.A., Khan, S. and Wright, E. (No date) 'Case Study: UPBEAT at the University of Salford', http://www.eucen.eu/BeFlex/CaseStudies/UK_SalfordUPBEAT.pdf Accessed 28 September 2010 (also see the project website: http://www.upbeat.eu.com/).

Sanderson, M. (1972) *The universities and British industry, 1850–1970.* London: Routledge and Kegan Paul.

Chapter 5

Measuring the impact of university-community research partnerships: A literature review of theories, concepts, tools and practices

Nirmala Lall

Research, engagement and society

University-community research partnerships engage in the co-creation of knowledge and have the potential to inform and co-produce policy. These research partnerships tackle complex challenges such as housing, homelessness, food and water security, health and education. Such partnerships contribute to social action and social change at a time when communities are in economic, environmental and social crises. The inter-related nature and complexities of issues and challenges faced by communities, regions and nations require systematic partnership, collaboration and networking between and across all sectors and disciplines (GACER, 2009.)

Although not commonplace, there are a small number of researchers and practitioners within communities, universities and other sectors engaging in university-community research partnerships. Community–research collaborations, combined with organizational structures that support these partnerships, are able to reach local, regional, national and international spheres (Hall, 2009). Efforts are currently fragmented, requiring a systematic support for university-community research partnerships to respond to regional sustainable development. There are many barriers that challenge the knowledge co-creation and mobilization system of university-community research partnerships.

Institutionalizing research partnerships between higher education, communities and civil society is one way to address the fragmentation of common efforts by social actors and stakeholders aiming to achieve societal outcomes such as poverty reduction, social innovation, health promotion and environmental sustainability. Community-university partnerships reform the role of higher education in research engagement. This process requires a key shift from higher education's monopoly on knowledge creation and dissemination using traditional research methods to the use of community-based research (CBR) and participatory action research strategies which have roots in civil society organizations and rural communities. The fact that there has been an active Office of Community-Based Research (OCBR) at the University of Victoria for the past three years is one indicator that a shift is occurring.

Community-university partnerships in research

Engaged scholarship provides mechanisms for the multidisciplinary co-creation and mobilization of knowledge to deal with complex and interrelated social issues. Community-university research partnerships are one of several ways in which universities and communities collaborate for mutual benefit addressing challenges within the community and society (Carnegie Foundation, 2008; AUCC, 2008). Four broad categories of community-university partnerships in research have been identified (Hall, 2009). Type one involves individual faculties engaging in partnership with community without systematic institutional support. Type two describes centres or institutes with particular foci that support partnerships with communities having similar interests. Type three identifies systematic organizational structures functioning within a university to intentionally engage university and community partners in research for mutual benefit. Type four involves multiple higher education institutions and community partnerships engaging in ongoing research and strengthening engaged teaching and research at regional, national or international levels.

The Office of Community-Based Research (OCBR) is a type three community-university research partnership. The OCBR and the Community-University Partnership Programme (CUPP) at the University of Brighton in England are two examples among a growing number of systematic organizational structures that operate within higher education institutions. These structures actively encourage and mobilize government departments, research councils, government supported agencies, civil society organizations and philanthropic foundations to invest in and support partnership models. The OCBR and CUPP work with community-university research partners who are engaged in multi-disciplinary and multi-sectoral approaches to deal with complex issues and challenges specific to their local and regional communities. Since it is suggested that a systematic approach is required to create effective partnerships (Hollander and Hartley, 1999) it is valuable to investigate the impact of systematic organizational structures in creating effective partnerships.

A proposed case study to measure impact

The author is currently designing a study to measure the impact of the Office of Community-Based Research (OCBR) at the University of Victoria. Created in 2007, the OCBR is an active organizational structure with local, regional, national, and international partnerships. OCBR's mandate is to facilitate collaborative community-university research and partnerships that enhance the quality of life and the economic, environmental and social well-being of communities (OCBR, 2009). Using an assessment lens, this mandate elicits the following questions: What kind of impact community–university research partnerships are making toward creating vibrant, sustainable and inclusive communities? How does the OCBR add value to what community-based researchers have already been doing? What difference does the OCBR make to the institution and to the community stakeholders? These questions have initiated the study of measuring the impact of the OCBR.

Drawing from the definition of community-based research by Strand *et al.* (2003), the OCBR frames community-based research in its university context as:
  * a way of integrating research and teaching, an opportunity for experimental learning in real-world settings, as a contribution to recruitment through the creation of a dynamic and engaged atmosphere, a means of making our region;
  * a better place to live and as a contribution to national and global understanding of ways in which the creation and co-creation of knowledge are used for social innovation. (OCBR, 2009, p. 4).

The work of the OCBR includes equipping, facilitating and supporting engaged and traditional scholars within the university as well as scholars and practitioners outside the context of higher education, referred to as 'the community'. In this context, organizational knowledge creation can be 'understood in terms of a process that organizationally amplifies the knowledge created by individuals, and crystallizes it as a part of the knowledge network of organization' (Nonaka, 1994, p. 17). The OCBR's 2009 Service Plan recognizes that a combination of evaluation tools is needed to address the impact of the work being conducted in and through the Office. Developing the tools to measure the impact of OCBR's knowledge mobilization is a timely challenge.

The work and impact of the OCBR will be documented in a case study. Stoecker (1991) argues that case studies 'help define abstract concepts [and] provide concrete illustrations of those concepts' (p. 108). Impact is often considered an abstract concept until it is consciously and intentionally concretized through a process involving indications of impact and assessment tools to demonstrate and identify impact. A working definition of impact assessment that emerged through consultation and case studies is offered by Chris Roche (1999) in his book, *Impact Assessment for Development Agencies* as: 'the systematic analysis of the lasting or significant changes – positive or negative, intended or not – in people's lives brought about by a given action or series of actions' (p. 20). Impact assessment is by no means a new phenomena, it is often done intuitively in our daily lives. The difference between what we do to assess impact in our daily lives and formal impact assessment is the process of developing a structure, a systematic or complex process, involving indicators, outcomes and timelines, which can be used to map unchartered territory using a pathway of change (Connell and Kubisch, 1998; Roche, 1999; Hart *et al.*, 2008). Identifying a pathway of change is one way to study a particular initiative or an intervention. Weiss (1995) defines a theory of change as describing how and why an initiative works in the context of theory-guided programme evaluation.

Community-university research partners at the University of Brighton's Community-university Partnership Programme (CUPP) apply a theory of change to identify a pathway of change, which include indicators to measure success leading to particular outcomes (Hart *et al.*, 2007). There is value in incorporating a theory of change approach to evaluate partnership processes and the impact of these processes (Anderson, 2005) because it aids in understanding whether community-university partnerships achieve their desired outcomes, how they achieve those outcomes and how university participation adds value to the process (Hart *et al.*, 2008). Mapping a pathway of change is one of the approaches being considered in designing an impact assessment framework for the work of the OCBR.

Critical to this discussion is the understanding that the significance of impact being assessed depends on whose views are represented, which involves the process of how various agendas of stakeholders are being met and how the pathway of change is being mapped and revised to reflect meaningful indicators and outcomes for the community, university and their respective stakeholders. Challenges include dealing with indistinct concepts such as outcomes, effects and impact, as they tend to overlap. Many factors contribute to how impact is assessed and whether impact is determined as valuable (good return for investment, contributes to the public good) positive, negative, detrimental or beneficial.

Impact assessment: Research councils

In addition to institutional structures such as the OCBR and CUPP, funders are also interested in assessing the economic and social impact of collaborative research initiatives. A knowledge co-creation and exchange approach is being applied between particular national research councils and higher education institutions to develop creative and effective ways for assessing the impact of the research conducted, the knowledge co-created, and the work accomplished through the support of funders.

Funders need to question who benefits from research, and democratize the dissemination and use of knowledge; funders and funding councils are better able to inform, rethink and revise their processes of assessment and evaluation. I have chosen to address the changing roles and requirements of funders for assessment and evaluation using the following examples.

The Social Sciences and Humanities Research Council of Canada (SSHRC), one of three federally funding councils in Canada, initiated the funding of community-university research partnerships through their Community University Research Alliance (CURA) programme in 1999. In their grant application guidelines, the SSHRC-CURA expects that projects will produce significant outcomes and impacts. They have been engaged in the ongoing process of revising assessment and evaluation frameworks as they apply to community-university research partnership projects. Such projects and initiatives are highly competitive for limited funds, while generally requiring longer periods of time, increasing requests to extend funding. Dialogue and on-the-ground engagement between funding councils and those involved in projects, including institutional structures that support community-university research partnerships and their networks, are reshaping the assessment and evaluation landscape of funders.

In 2005, Canadian Institutes for Health Research (CIHR) began a collaborative process to measure the impact of health research (McAuley and Borbey, 2009). They involved academics, government, research agencies, health organizations and associations in the process of developing an impact framework and indicators. CIHR is the largest government funder of health research in Canada with a focus on the creation and translation of new knowledge to improve the health and health services of Canadians. CIHR's five broad categories of impact for use in their impact framework are heavily based on the Buxton/Hanney model, a conceptual categorization of how to best determine benefits of funded research projects. Indicators, higher and lower orders of effect at different levels have been identified in the following impact categories: Advancing knowledge, building capacity, informing decision-making, health and health system impacts and broad economic impacts. CIHR's impact assessment unit will consult with CIHR and their partners to plan impact assessment project for the next three to five years (McAuley and Borbey, 2009). These projects will include types of research that have not yet been studied.

The Higher Education Funding Council for England (HEFCE/HEFC) has funded the South East Coastal Communities (SECC) Project £3 million pounds over three years. An additional £3 million of generated matched funds renders a combined total of £6 million. The South East Coast of England is a region with some of the highest income levels in the country coexisting with some of the most severe deprivation across multiple sectors such as income, employment, health, disability, education and training, crime, and barriers to housing and services. Fragmentation across initiatives, disjointed ways of working between government departments and the duplication of services reflect a few of the concerns. Government, communities, community organizations and universities generally agreed that there was a failure to understand the issues and meet the needs of these communities (Coastal Communities, 2007).

The SECC Business Case is a document outlining a strategic well-resourced approach to community knowledge exchange created by nine south east coastal higher education institutions to work in partnership with each other, local organizations and communities. This case details project initiatives for this region to address the current fragmented approach to inter-related and complex health and social issues, funding collaboration, and regional and sub-region foci, which include different strands of the community knowledge exchange agenda such as social enterprise, regeneration, and specific communities of practice.

The Higher Education Funding Council's Business and Community Strategic Committee, which reports directly to the HEFCE Board, supports the South East Coastal Communities project as one that will inform how funding 'can leverage partnership, expertise and resources from local and regional stakeholders' (Coastal Communities, 2007, p.1). Outputs and outcomes will be used by HEFCE to demonstrate the knowledge in and funding for community knowledge exchange in the context of a community engagement investment model. This project focuses on generating evidence to benefit community knowledge exchange, to determine how those benefits may be funded and measured, to begin to concretize effective models or metrics for assessing the impact of community-based initiatives and to develop a collaborative model of funding that will serve to both initiate and sustain university-community knowledge exchange across the south east coastal region of England.

More work is required in the area of data collection, analysis and com-munication about the roles, requirements and expectations of funders for assessment and evaluation of community-university research partnerships. Print and website content provide information about the requirements necessary to apply for grants but assessment of community-university research partnership projects and initiatives, by funding councils, are limited. An initial critical step has been accomplished through a recent research report on the funding and development of community-university research partnerships in Canada. This publication maps the sources and types of funding created to support community-university research partnerships (Hall, 2009). It was commissioned by the Strategic Programs and Joint Initiatives Branch of the Social Sciences and Research Council of Canada and is an example of collaboration between a national research council (SSHRC), representatives from a community-university network across Canada (Community-Based Research Canada) and the Office of Community-Based Research, a systematic community-university research partnership structure within the University of Victoria. An important next step would be to identify the roles, requirements and expectations of funders for assessment and evaluation within the sources and types of funding created to support community-university research partnership.

Collaboration between research councils, higher education institutions, and networks involving community and university representatives benefits funders in developing effective and relevant programmes and assessments. Such collaboration also benefits universities and communities in being able to use their unique knowledge and experience in a process of co-creation and mobilization, creating social and policy changes within complex social, environmental and economic sectors.

Measurement: Tools and practices

The economic value of community engagement is not the only thing we need to know. We need to know whether we can make serious statements about the way in which certain community engagement outputs generate outcomes that we value for their social and cultural as well as economic benefits. (Pearce, Pearson and Cameron, 2007, p. 35)

Evaluation literature in the field of community-university partnerships, indicates that self and/or external evaluation and deliberative assessment processes such as assessment of short and long-term impact, baseline auditing, monitoring, and benchmarking are applied when attempting to measure the value and/or the impact of community-university research. These measurement processes can also be applied to institutional support structures, as evidenced particularly by Brighton University's Community-university Partnership Programme (CUPP); an institutional support structure similar in type to the Office of Community-Based Research (OCBR). Innovative structures such as the OCBR and CUPP engage in complex and inter-related activities, relationships and networks within the university, local and regional communities, and across national and international spheres.

Assessing short and long-term impact is a complex and multi-tiered challenge requiring a combination of measurement tools, which must be deconstructed into manageable portions that ultimately converge to construct a web of measurement activities involving university and community researchers and practitioners. The following are different types of measure-ment activities described within certain arenas of practice, also summarized in Table 6.1. These measurement activities are being conducted in various combinations creating hybrid approaches to address and assess the impact of different aspects of community engagement including community-university research partnerships.

Table 5.1 Four types of measurement activities, adapted by N. Lall. Based on a combination of Hart *et al.*, (2008) and Roche (1999).

	Audit	Benchmark	Evaluate	Addressing and assessing impact
Timing	Cyclical series of reviews.	Ongoing process.	Periodically.	Short-term and long-term impact assessed throughout and after the intervention using a combination of measurement activities.
Analytical Level	Collect routine data.	Exchange of information.	Examines processes.	Identify change. Mapping a pathway of change. Short-term and long-term outcomes and consequences. Challenge: lines between outcomes, effects and impact are not distinct; these concepts overlap.
Specificity	Review of what practitioners actually do.	Review of best practice in the sector.	Process and value oriented.	Consider external influences and events. Challenge to determine connection between influences and outcome.
Examples	Community-University Partnership Programme (CUPP, UK).	Australia Universities Community Engagement Associates AUCEA (piloting).	AUCEA, CUPP, SECC. South East Costal	Communities Project (SECC), Impact Survey 2008 (CUPP), CIHR (Canadian Institutes of Health Research).

Hybrid approach within a benchmarking framework

Benchmarking identifies best practices and problem areas. It is an ongoing process of exchanging information and can be used to make comparisons (Hart *et al.*, 2008). The Australian Universities Community Engagement Alliance (AUCEA) is comprised of multiple universities, which are involved in developing and piloting benchmarking activities. Their benchmarking project aims to develop a community engagement assessment framework to be piloted by selected AUCEA member universities. The Benchmarking Project has progressed through several stages including an initial workshop in 2005 at the AUCEA conference, the development of a Collaboration and Structural Reform grant application to support the pilot that is currently in progress, preparation of position and discussion papers, a benchmarking framework, indicator filters, benchmarking workshop reports, and publications discussing the challenges of benchmarking (Garlick and Langworthy, 2004, 2006 and 2008; Garlick and Pryor, 2004; Langworthy, 2007). The AUCEA's ambitious undertaking uses a hybrid approach with benchmarking at the core. Measurement activities include self-evaluation, assessment by the community and the university in partnership, a metric assessment based on agreed upon quantitative measures and the need for measures and targets that address both the process of partnership and the progression toward intended outcomes. Short and long term assessments recognize both the need to report to stakeholder groups on a regular basis and the need for a long term view of the way university knowledge contributes to meaningful outcomes for society and the environment, locally, regionally and nationally. Challenges include keeping measurement activities simple, relevant, cost-effective and applicable across sectors; linking outcomes, indicators and objectives together and keeping measures well-defined using reliable data that can be tracked over time.

Hybrid approach: Audit, evaluate and assess impact

An audit measures what is being done through a series of reviews. It is a collection of routine data documenting what practitioners are actually doing but it is not possible to generalize from the findings (Hart *et al.*, 2008). Evaluation determines value through a series of individual assessments over time. Complex data is collected, research methodology is rigorously defined and it is often possible to generalize findings (Hart *et al.*, 2008). An impact assessment is: 'the systematic analysis of the lasting or significant changes – positive or negative, intended or not – in people's lives brought about by a given action or series of actions' (Roche, 1999, p. 20).

The University of Brighton's Community-University Partnership Programme (CUPP) has been applying a variety of measurement activities to their work. Evaluation reports conducted by Rodriguez (2005) evidenced the value and impacts of CUPP's Helpdesk. Among the impacts identified, were the Helpdesk's 'contribution to helping local, community, voluntary and statutory sector organizations build capacity and aid the development of more sustainable services, as well as showing the benefits for individual academic development of the University.' (Hart *et al.*, 2007, p. 39). In addition, three stages of CUPP evaluations conducted by an external evaluator, (Roker, 2005, 2006 and 2007) included a baseline audit, identification of learning and good practice and an impact survey. Roker conducted a relatively small-scale overview and evaluation, involving a total of 50 people, focusing on key success criteria of CUPP's projects, activities and experiences.

Citing her use of seven success factors which emerged from the literature, as a structure for the evaluation results, Roker questioned the extent to which CUPP was able to demonstrate the seven key factors and investigated other factors to help understand what works in CUPP's activities. The seven success factors are 'a shared vision of university-community collaborations in general, in individual projects and activities; mutual benefit and learning; good personal relationships and 'openness'; individual and organizational flexibility; leadership and commitment of senior staff; commitment and enthusiasm from universities and communities and organizational infrastructure and support' (Hart *et al.*, 2007, p. 184). Key findings included: the interconnected importance of CUPP in forging, developing and negotiating links; participants' belief that their partnerships would not have existed without CUPP; the value of an active steering committee; the importance of having accessible individuals as points of contact such as the Helpdesk manager and Project Manager; provision or money for meetings, transportation and refreshments; project funding; access to administrative and technical support; and having an organized infrastructure to create opportunities for networking and learning (Hart *et al.*, 2007, p. 195). Challenges noted were overwork due to lack of capacity and time, differing priorities and procedures of university and community partners and staff, sustaining projects over the long term, the use of academic language in all forms of communication, the perception and reality of community expertise being undervalued and issues around ownership. Currently, CUPP is revising and implementing the REAP measurement framework (Pearce *et al.*, 2007) for use in their projects and initiatives. The REAP tool uses Reciprocity, Externalities, Access and Partnership as categories to examine the way outputs generate outcomes in the context of social, cultural and economic benefits.

The literature reflects two kinds of questions being asked from the institutional context of assessing and evaluating community-university research partnerships. Questions such as, 'How do we know that our work makes a difference?' (Gelmon, 2000), seek to address short and long term impact within the university and community. Questions such as, 'Do these measures indicate what really matters and is the process enabling universities to improve and progress?' (Langworthy, 2007), take a critical look at the value of what is measured and how it contributes to higher education reform. These questions resonate with the work of the AUCEA, CUPP and the OCBR, as they initiate and pilot a combination of measurement activities to address and assess the impact of their work and the effect on their higher education institution(s). The literature suggests the use of a combination of measurement tools to measure the impact of the Office of Community-Based Research. However, the particular combination to be developed will be somewhat unique since no single approach can be fully applied outside its intended context (Garlick and Langworthy, 2008; Gelmon *et al.*, 2005; Hart *et al.*, 2008, Holland and Ramaley, 2008, Pearce *et al.*, 2007). In order to measure the impact of community-university research partnerships and the structures that support them, universities are modifying existing evaluation resources to develop informative and suitable combinations. Considering the broader context of society, strategic and effective use of measurement tools and an understanding of what to measure (not only what can be easily measured or counted) can play a significant role in the improvement and progression of universities to contribute to the public's social, cultural, environmental and economic good.

Conclusion

The turn of the century brought with it a proliferation of publications by scholars in Australia, Canada, the United Kingdom and the United States; all seeking to frame the purpose, indicators, language and context of how to assess university-community engagement. Recently, attention has been turned to the challenge of developing meaningful measures to assess the impact of community-university research partnerships.

The purpose and function of higher education institutions are extending beyond knowledge production and transfer to the co-creation, exchange and mobilization of knowledge through systematic approaches to community-university research partnerships; with the intent to mutually benefit the university, and its local and regional communities (Pearce *et al.*, 2007). The literature reflects a need for systematic and intentional institutional approaches to community-university research partnerships and such structures are increasing in number across the globe. These institutional structures support and facilitate community-university research partnerships using democratic approaches to research such as community-based research. They are mobilizing and creating knowledge in new ways, contributing to change in practices, policies and impact in higher education, in the research councils that fund them, and within their local communities. It is valuable and necessary to measure and understand the impact of community-university research partnerships and the structures that support them. In this way, universities can continue to move from knowledge production to knowledge co-creation and mobilization across the university and community; extending practice, policy, and contributing to the public good at local, regional, national and international levels.

References

Anderson, A. A. (2005) *The community builder's approach to theory of change: A practical guide to theory development*. New York: The Aspen Institute. Retrieved 16 February 2009 from http://www.aspeninstitute.org/.

AUCC (Association of Universities and Colleges in Canada) (2008) *Momentus: 2008 report on university research and knowledge mobilization*. Ottawa: AUCC.

Carnegie Foundation (2008) Meet the Carnegie Classification for Community Engagement. Retrieved 20 November, 2008 from http://louisville.edu/communityengagement/Carnegie%20Overview%206-6—08.ppt.

Coastal Communities (Universities of Brighton, Chichester, Sussex, Portsmouth, Southampton Solent, Southampton, Canterbury Christ Church, Greenwich, Kent and Solent Energy) (2007) 'South east coastal communities project business case'. Retrieved 21 September 21, 2008 from http://www.coastalcommunities.org.uk/.

Connell, J. and Kubisch, A. (1998) 'Applying a Theory of Change approach to the evaluation of initiatives: progress, prospects, and problems', in K. Fullbright-Anderson, A.C. Kubisch and J.P. Connell (eds.), *New approaches to evaluating community initiatives: Volume 2:Comprehensive community initiatives: theory, measurement and analysis.* Washington DC: The Aspen Institute.

GACER (Global Alliance on Community Engaged Research) (2009) 'GACER policy brief to the World Conference on Higher Education'. Victoria, BC: GACER.

Garlick, S. and Pryor, G. (2004) *Benchmarking the university: Learning about improvement.* Commonwealth of Australia: Report for the Commonwealth Department of Education Science and Training.

Garlick, S. and Langworthy, A. (2004) *Building a culture of improvement through evaluation in university/regional engagement.* Sydney, Australia: University of Western Sydney.

Garlick, S. and Langworthy, A. (2006) *'Assessing university engagement: Discussion paper prepared for the AUCEA Benchmarking Project.* Commonwealth of Australia: AUCEA.

Garlick, S., and Langworthy A. (2008) 'Benchmarking university-community engagement: Developing a national approach in Australia', *Higher Education and Regional Development, Special issue: The engagement of higher educational institutions in regional development, an overview of the opportunities and challenges,* 20(2), 153–164.

Gelmon, S. (2000) 'How do we know that our work makes a difference?' *Metropolitan Universities,* 11 (2), 28–39.

Gelmon, S. B., Seifer, S. D., Kauper-Brown, J. and Mikkelsen, M., (2005) *Building capacity for community engagement: Institutional self-assessment.* Seattle, WA: Community-Campus Partnerships for Health. Retrieved 21 August 2008 from www.ccph.info/.

Hall, B. L (2009) The funding and development of community-university research partnerships in Canada. Ottawa: SSHRC.

Hart, A. and Wolff, D. (2006) 'Developing communities of practice through community-university partnerships', *Planning, Practice and Research,* 21(1), 121–38.

Hart, A., Maddison, E. and Wolff, D. (eds.) (2007) *Community-university partnerships in practice.* Leicwster: NIACE.

Hart, A., Northmore, S. and Gerhardt, C. (2008) *Auditing, benchmarking and evaluating university public engagement.* University of Brighton: The National Co-ordinating Centre for Public Engagement.

Holland, B. and Ramaley, J. (2008) 'Creating a supportive environment for community-university engagement: Conceptual frameworks', in HERDSA 2008 Conference proceedings. http://www.herdsa.org.au/wp-content/ uploads/conference/2008/media/Holland%20&%20Ramaley.pdf Accessed 28 September 2010.

Hollander, E. and Hartley, M. (1999) 'Civic renewel in higher education: The state of the movement and the need for a national network', in Ehrlich, T. (ed.), *Higher education and civic responsibility*, Phoenix AZ: Oryx Press.

Langworthy, A. (2007) 'The challenge of benchmarking community engagement: The AUCEA Pilot Project', Paper presented at the Australian Universities Quality Forum 'Evolution and renewal in quality assurance', Hobart, Tasmania

McAuley, L., Borbey, P., Cox, Dr. D., Cozzens, S., and van Ark, G. (2010) 'Implementing impact assessment at the Canadian Institutes of Health Research' in *Evaluation of Impacts of Medical Research.* Swedish Research Council 2010. Retrieved October 12, 2010 from http://www.vr.se/download/ 18.5adac704126af4b4be2800026596/Evaluation+of+impacts+of+medical+r esear

Nonaka, I. (1994) 'A dynamic theory of organizational knowledge creation', *Organization Science*, 5(1), 14–39.

OCBR (Office of Community-Based Research at the University of Victoria) (2009) 'Draft service plan', October 2009. Victoria BC: OCBR.

Pearce, J., Pearson, M. and Cameron, S. (2007) *The ivory tower and beyond: Bradford University at the heart of its communities.* University of Bradford.

Roche, C. (1999) *Impact Assessment for Development Agencies.* Oxford: Oxfam GB with Novib.

Rodriguez, P. (2005) 'CUPP's Senior Researchers Group and the one to one research support service, monitoring and evaluation report', September 2004–August 2005. Brighton: University of Brighton.

Roker, D. (2005) 'Evaluation of the Community-University Partnership Programme (CUPP), Stage 1 report: A review of progress to date.' Brighton, United Kingdom: University of Brighton.

Roker, D. (2006) 'Evaluation of the Community University Partnership Programme (CUPP), Stage 2 report: A review of progress to date.' Brighton, United Kingdom: University of Brighton.

Roker, D. (2007) 'The impact of CUPP projects and activities: Facts and figures. The results of a final survey.' Brighton, United Kingdom: University of Brighton.

SSHRC-CURA guidelines: http://www.sshrc-crsh.gc.ca/site/apply-demande/program_descriptions-descriptions_de_programmes/cura-aruc-eng.aspx Accessed 28 September 2010.

Stoecker, R. (1991) 'Evaluating and rethinking the case study', *Sociological Review*, 39, 88–112.

Strand, K. J., Cutforth, N., Stoecker, R., Marullo, S. and Donahue, P. (2003) 'Principles of best practice for community-based research', *Michigan Journal of Community service learning*, 9(3), 5–15.

Weiss, C. (1995) 'Nothing as practical as good theory: Exploring theory-based evaluation for comprehensive community initiatives for children and families', in J. Connell *et al.* (eds.), *New approaches to evaluating community initiatives: concepts, methods, and contexts*. Washington DC: Aspen Institute.

Chapter 6

Institutionalizing university engagement

Patricia Inman

Margaret Swedish asks the question, 'How do we live at the end of the world?' (Swedish, 2008, p. 1). This timely and provocative book documents the toll our extractive culture has taken. Swedish states that we must make drastic changes in the way we live if we are to have a place in which to live. Life as we know it must end and we are asked to consider sustainable alternatives making the most of our precious remaining resources.

What resources do we have to turn the train around? This paper suggests engaged educational institutions developing curriculum and research around regionally-defined issues is an approach we have long ignored. An argument for utilizing the power of engaged institutions in place-focused policy is presented as well as a tool to facilitate collaboration between institutions and local stakeholders. An example of the use of this methodology is also discussed.

Why regional policy?

The questions offered in this opening section provide a framework for the focus of the paper. Regional policy and engaged educational institutions can use their power of research and applied learning to change the course of destructive policies that ignore local landscapes. Regionalism provides an organizing principle to address economic and social issues while maintaining the priority of environmental integrity. The basic premise of regional policy is that economies have a physical sense (Kemmis, 1990). The strength of an economy is based on utilizing and preserving the resources around which the urban hubs are structured. Commerce and economic development are centred around natural centres rather than political.

> *Regionalism is an integrative approach that follows this geographical focus, looking beyond political and jurisdictional boundaries. This allows for the study of social, economic, and environmental issues through the creation and sustaining of organizations that do not fit into the established framework of local, state, and federal governments.* (Inman and Swanson, 2007, p. 181).

Large cities provide the business hub but rural space extends and connects smaller communities. Jane Jacobs explains that natural resources are an inheritance from the earth's past expansion that initiated the first clusters of economic development (2000, p. 54). Economies follow natural centres rather than political. The seminal unit of organization filters down to the community which addresses the concern in the opening of this paper – the need to connect to the human community with what Illich refers to as 'convivial tools' (Illich, 1973). By honouring the environment we honour those with whom we share our local space. We exist globally; but it is a web of local connections that provides the tightly woven fabric to support a transformed world.

Analysis of regional issues

Once regions are defined (Swanson, 2000) we can address issues and concerns. All too often past institutional engagement consisted of 'experts' carrying out their own research agendas or agendas defined by government or corporate bodies. Policies were standardized for an abstract 'place' by individuals and groups who chose to impose their agenda and priorities on unrecognized stakeholders. A deficit-based approach demanded that institutions be 'fixed' rather than transformed.

Building regional capacity requires us to consider what we *have* rather than what we do not. Acknowledging regional resources and the recognizing natural diversity is key. How else can we honour our rich ecology? And who knows their strengths and resulting issues better than the regional stakeholders themselves? So how do we foster collaborative definition of regional issues, articulate strengths, and allow the regions to choose the institutional supports they see as most appropriate? Research indicates that highly flexible frameworks of diverse stakeholders incorporating systems thinking and holistic education are what best serve university-community partnerships (Hollander and Hartley, 1999). What is lacking in the literature is the documentation of a specific process that constructs community while incorporating the considerations of diverse stakeholders.

Fourth Generation Evaluation provides a methodology to 'frame the forum' as communities of learners move forward in working with universities to problem solve (Guba and Lincoln, 1989). This new approach moves beyond previous generations of evaluation that focused only on measurement and judgment by including negotiation and education of all stakeholders. However, working with the differing views of stakeholders often distracts from a discussion of the real issues. The Fourth Generation process allows regions to pay attention to issues warranting discussion and set aside issues that are already held in common, providing a scholarly path to community involvement, as well as formative programme evaluation.

The essence of this protocol is a cyclical interview process that uses open-ended responses to questions providing university representatives with quotations, the main source of raw data for defining regional issues to be addressed. Stakeholder groups are questioned about potential issues for collaboration. Stakeholder groups are defined as: 1) agents, those who use or implement an evaluand, 2) beneficiaries, those who profit in some way from the use of the evaluand; and 3) victims, persons negatively affected by the use of the evaluand. Once broad issues are defined by each stakeholder group, a second round of interviews produces a more sophisticated articulation.

Data analysis differs from traditional qualitative methodology in that a form of the narrative is written after each contact rather than looking for emerging themes in completed narratives. This approach differs from the traditional analysis of qualitative data that looks for emerging 'themes'. The purpose of the Fourth Generation protocol is to educate all interviewees. Each stakeholder is made aware of other viewpoints before providing input. This design not only allows for all stakeholders to be aware of diverse viewpoints but also minimizes the grandstanding that can occur in more public meetings. Such relational meetings provide ongoing construction of the regional reality. While the university representatives conduct the interviews, they serve as mediator and educator rather than taking on the role of the expert. It is the role of the university to assure that all voices are heard and document the reality that is constructed.

The second distinction of this methodology is the use of qualitative data as the frame of issue analysis. Traditionally, quantitative data provide the frame for issue analysis with qualitative data providing the 'thick description'. This often results in inappropriate or misleading data being selected and analyzed.

Finally, the product is a highly readable case study. If done correctly, the narrative is engaging and representative of all defined stakeholders. As important is that stakeholders have been educated in the process and, hopefully, have a greater insight regarding issues and concerns that affect their lives. Providing this common ground facilitates collaboration.

Recently, this methodology has been used to address such diverse issues as finding solutions to a state nursing shortage, defining workplace learning issues for a federal agency, providing effective literacy programmes for local industrial clusters, and evaluating a specialty crop grant to a farmers' market. In each case, the incorporation of data from all stakeholders brought issues to the table that would have otherwise remained invisible.

Methodology

Fourth Generation Evaluation is a process that allows one to define the scope of an issue, as well as come to a sophisticated articulation of issues as viewed by various stakeholders. Assumptions upon which this process is based include the fact that reality is constructed in a value-laden context; the researcher is not an objective, authoritative, politically neutral observer; and truth changes constantly with increases in sophistication of perceptions.

The Fourth Generation methodology is described below.
- An initial respondent is selected for any convenient or salient reason (decision makers, beneficiaries, advocacy groups).
- The respondent is asked to describe the focus of an issue (the evaluand) as he or she constructs it.
- These comments might include observations about stakeholder claims, concerns or issues, and observations about what is liked and disliked.
- The respondent is asked to nominate another respondent who is much different in her or his construction. ('There must be someone in this context who feels very different from the way that you do. Would you be willing to give me that person's name?)

- The central themes, concepts, ideas, values, concerns, and issues proposed by the first respondent are converted by the researcher into an initial formulation. Data analysis follows closely on the heels of the data collection, and is completed for the first respondent before the second is approached.
- If an issue is of great importance it may be necessary to go back to the respondent to be sure the researcher 'has it right'.
- The second respondent is interviewed with the same freedom of expression, but as soon as s/he has contributed as much as s/he is willing, the themes of the first respondent are introduced and the second respondent is asked to comment on them. This interview results in not only new information, but also a commentary of the first respondent's inputs and constructions.
- As the process proceeds, the basis on which successive respondents are selected varies. Initially the effort is to identify new respondents who can add something to the emerging construction(s) that enlarge the scope. The object of this portion of the evaluation is to maximize the *range* of information collected to assure that as many stakeholding groups and persons can be identified and have an opportunity to contribute (color coding of responses can help here).
- If some stakeholders are initially more sophisticated than others, steps must be taken to correct the inequality. This might entail providing education, role-playing, and practice – whatever steps must be taken to restore the balance of power between stakeholders.
- As the constructions begin to take shape certain elements appear more salient because of more frequent mention by respondents or because of the vehemence with which the stake-holding groups discuss an issue.
- The process of selection of salient issues gradually changes the respondent sampling from securing diversity to achieving articulation about the emerging salient themes.
- When the circle of respondents has been completed, it may be useful to do a second iteration. The circle may also be 'spiraled' by making it a second time with a set of respondents similar to the first.
- *Documents* may be searched for relevant information to the emerging constructions, *analects* (selections from relevant literature) may be introduced, and the researchers own construction may be introduced for critique.

- To avoid becoming dependent on 'expert' judgment, external materials are introduced in a way that does not reveal their source.

Advantages and disadvantages of the process

This process allows one to know how stakeholders make sense of an issue within their life context. Sense of place becomes critical in such discussion. This process can be used for research, evaluation, or policy analyses and allows one to look at the scope of an issue, as well as provide a sophisticated articulation. The process allows us to gather an even deeper sense of an issue.

Fourth Generation is a simple process allowing for client ownership in future iterations. The transparency allows for greater stakeholder involvement. The role of the evaluator is that of mediator or educator providing a conduit for information being generated throughout. The case study provides a readable format for evaluation which makes it more likely that the data will be used. This strong link between evaluator and stakeholders during all stages of the project increases the probability that the results will be used.

The disadvantages of the methodology include the fact that both the client and evaluator must be comfortable with open structure. The emphasis on readability of product often requires creative reporting to document the process. Finally, the multiple interviews can be time intensive which can make contract negotiations difficult.

Application of the process in university engagement

Most recently, this process was used with a local farmers' market to evaluate a grant they had obtained for specialty crop promotion. Farmers' markets are public spaces offering locally grown food for sale during certain times of the week. Woodstock is a town of 25,000 residents located 51 miles northwest of Chicago, Illinois. Serving as a hub of small farms, it was incorporated as a village in 1852, and was designated as the seat of county government shortly thereafter. The Woodstock Opera House was built in 1890, reflecting an ongoing support of the arts. The combination of a conservative farming population and avant-garde art community provides a complex social picture. In 2007, the city was named as one of the Nation's Dozen Distinctive Destinations by the National Trust for Historic Preservation. Woodstock Square currently serves as the location of the Woodstock Farmers' Market.

The Woodstock Farmers' Market (WFM) originally included approximately five vendors. This number remained fairly consistent over the 22 years of its existence as did the extremely limited income generated from sales. While the grant was to be used for promotion only, using the Fourth Generation methodology allowed the Market to look at issues and concerns that had impeded growth by interviewing various stakeholder groups. It was decided to use the grant funding to support improved signage, newspaper ads, and radio spots with the signage being the least expensive option and radio time the highest.

The WFM originated and continues as a producer-only market. This means that vendors can sell only what they have grown or produced. This limits offerings but provides the essence of local flavour. The market had opened in 1982 selling a limited number of vegetables and plants. While located on the picturesque Woodstock Square, its space consisted of a small area donated by a local merchant. There was a constant worry that the property would be sold and the Market would be forced to relocate. For a period of time the vendors assembled in the parking lot of the train station but this reduced traffic. To minimize insurance liability, the market operated under the auspices of the Woodstock Chamber of Commerce but this further minimized its autonomy. It was open 8:00 a.m.–1:30 p.m. on Thursdays and Saturdays from the first week in May to the last week of October.

Stakeholders were defined as vendors, merchants on the square, the City of Woodstock Governance, community groups and customers. Interviews were to take place in May, July, and at the end of the market in October so that all phases of the seasonal offerings would be represented. As mentioned earlier in the paper, the first round of interviews is intended to broadly define the issues with later interviews to provide a more sophisticated set of improvements. The intent was then to see where the market could find institutional collaboration to support enterprise.

Evaluation results

The initial intent of the market promotion had been to increase the number of vendors and variety of products offered. The intent was to increase individual vendor income. The vendors also wished to determine which forms of promotion worked best. Another concern had been determining why customers visited the market, the location of the customer base, and the appropriateness of the days and times. Conducting business on Thursdays and Saturdays was a bit close for harvests of smaller specialty crops. Vendors found the Thursday and Saturday markets had very different feels. The Saturday provided a more leisurely pace and an experience to be savoured. Thursday consisted of a more local crowd taking and purchasing food in a more business-like manner. Finally, there were questions regarding restrictions from the McHenry County Health Department regarding sampling.

Merchants were concerned about the diminished parking on the Square on Market days and the effect of Market offerings on business. This was especially true for bakeries and restaurants as there were vendors selling baked goods.

The City of Woodstock was concerned with the need to expand city services due to increased pedestrian and vehicular traffic. They were also concerned with the ability of the Health Department to maintain control if vendors initiated food sampling. Since there had been talk of extending the market around the square on the street, safety of customers also emerged as a concern.

Customers desired increased options for local and organic produce, especially berries, mushroom, eggs, free-range meats and dog treats. Many customers expressed interest in joining as a vendor but felt they needed more information before committing. They indicated they came not only to support local farmers but also perceived the market as an 'event' and requested activities such as music and cooking demonstrations. Several customers were active in community groups and indicated they would like the use the market space for educational purposes.

Each stakeholder interview was followed by a consideration of what documentation was needed to validate of invalidate the narrative. For example, when customers and business owners expressed a concern regarding a lack of parking opportunities, city documents indicated adequate public parking available. This information was then included in the narrative presented to the interviewee. Improved signage to these areas was eventually used to increase access.

Connecting to institutions

One of the most immediate concerns was to expand market offerings. Market board members looked to past research to address this issue. A conference of regional universities was conducted in Chicago on increasing offerings for specialty markets through the development of value-added products. A board member obtained an invitation via the University of Illinois Extension Service. Universities represented were regional and had identified local food production as a research interest. They included Cornell University, University of Illinois, Indiana University, University of Wisconsin, and Purdue University. Research presented at the conference demonstrated that the most effective promotion venues included word-of-mouth and signage. Radio spots, while the most expensive, were the least effective method of promotion. Funding for market promotion was greatly informed by this research.

One of the most innovative strategies regarding value-added product was taken by a veterinarian who has become one of the most successful vendors. He had been servicing local dairies and found them to be floundering financially. The smaller farms were struggling to keep up with milk production of the larger agribusinesses in the Illinois/Wisconsin area.

Value-added products provided another option. Cheese seemed a viable option as neighbouring Wisconsin, having been settled by German and Swiss immigrants, provided numerous educational opportunities through the University of Wisconsin. A dairy co-op was formed and decided to approach a marketing class at the University of Illinois to help develop a plan for production and promotion. This was done as a class project at no cost to the dairy farmers. Students determined the co-op should produce a unique cheese (Butter Kase) and suggested Farmers' Markets would provide a window to other commercial opportunities. This has been an immensely successful venture. Prairie Pure Cheese now produces not only Butter Kase but also Swiss and aged Cheddar. While the Woodstock market has its most faithful following, they also sell at the Chicago Green Market and Whole Foods. They are featured in a least one local supermarket as well. Master Preserver classes offered by the University of Illinois Extension are being funded by an Illinois Specialty Crop Grant to teach vendors how to produce value-added product throughout the year.

Addressing the issue of educating future vendors and potential customers, McHenry County College, a two-year institution of higher education, was approached regarding the offering of Farmers' Market 101. A February date was set that would allow time for individuals to prepare for a spring sale. It was developed as a panel presentation of vendors who addressed issues defined in the initial evaluation. These included such questions as: What products are most requested? What about insurance liability? How does a vendor deal with the department of Health? and What is the income potential from market sales? Attendees filled a small auditorium and applications to sell at the market doubled. The class has been offered for three years and venders now number about 35, depending on the season and day.

Customers had requested further education on the various labels for local food (organic, natural, pesticide-free, etc.) and so the University of Illinois Master Gardeners were approached to assist with educating the consumer. They offer gardening advice at space provided by the WFM. This group of volunteers provides education not only on types of local foods but also answers agriculturally related questions. This is the first season this service will be available but the hope is that the booth will not only provide community education, but also draw additional customers.

Finally, customers suggested that local K-12 schools be involved with the market. An invitation was extended to all school groups with the enticement of free vendor space. So far the schools have raised over $1,000 selling plants, market bags, and planters. Interestingly, student groups not traditionally represented in extracurricular activities have been the ones participating. These include the Art Club, which also provided free demonstrations; the Life Skills students who donated their income to the victims of hurricane Katrina; and the Hispanic Club, which sold plants indigenous to various states in Mexico. An interesting anecdote to the Hispanic Club's participation was the eagerness of the students to interact with the community. Students signed up for shifts of two hours but most stayed for the duration of the five-hour market.

Additional action taken

Additional changes were made to the WFM in response to stakeholder interviews. In response to customer requests for entertainment, music is provided at each market. Musicians are paid a minimal amount but receive substantial donations from customers. In response to merchants on the square, signs directing patrons to additional parking have been provided. Also, several cross-marketing initiatives have resulted with local produce being served by various restaurants. Market vendors advertise the establishment using their produce and restaurants provide advertisement for that specific vendor as well as the market in general.

The WFM has split from the Chamber to achieve greater autonomy. They are now directed by a Board with two advisory members. These advisory members include one representative from the City of Woodstock and one who now facilitates collaborations with educational institutions. These additional board positions are non-voting and provide increased feedback.

One of the issues most frequently mentioned by the vendors was the difficulty in sampling due to McHenry County Health Department requirements and fees that were prohibitive ($40.00/vendor each market). The WFM board met with a representative from the Department of Health to discuss a creative option. It was agreed that if all vendors wishing to sample their offerings were to take training in food safety from one of the community classes, the Market could pay an umbrella fee ($350) for the season. A successful state grant paid for the tuition of interested vendors who then took the course from the local community college.

One other health-related concern raised was the difficulty in finding an approved kitchen to make value-added product such as jams or salsas. The market is in the process of working on collaborations with community kitchens, including those of local schools and churches. Small rental fees would provide additional income for these institutions while providing low-cost facilities to increase vendor income.

Current status of the Woodstock Farmers' Market

The Woodstock Farmers' Market was voted the best farmers' market in Illinois, 41st in the nation by *Local Harvest*, a non-profit organization promoting local food systems (www.localharvest.org). Increased customer attendance provided additional funding from the city of Woodstock for the past two years in the form of grant support from the hotel/motel tax base. Customers often spend the night in Woodstock either before or after visiting the market. While several factors underlie the growth of the WFM, vendors believe the information provided by the Fourth Generation methodology has helped guide market strategy.

As mentioned earlier, one benefit of the Fourth Generation methodology is its simplicity and ability to serve as a source of continuous improvement. The result of the interviews, a case study, is easily composed and, more importantly, easily read by all stakeholders. While a representative of Northern Illinois University conducted the first set of interviews and produced the resulting case study, the market has been able to conduct the interviews for the past two years. The issues raised have allowed them to integrate a rapid response survey developed by Oregon State University. This has allowed increasingly specific market promotion. Market days and hours have changed to Tuesday and Saturday to better accommodate harvest patterns. Time has been changed to 8:00 a.m.–1:00 p.m. cutting off a half-hour during the lunch hour to minimize parking impact when local restaurants are busiest.

The Market winds around the entire Square. Crafts have separate space within the interior park. The space occupied by the Market is offered by the City of Woodstock. Offerings have increased to include honey, cheese, dog treats, free-range meats, eggs, herbs, landscape plants, jams, knife sharpening, berries and additional fruits. Two vineyards add an even more festive touch. Additional spaces are occupied by community groups offering community education. These spaces are donated at the discretion of the Board. Increased income to the Market from vendor fees has allowed donations to various local charities as well as the donation of plants for community gardens.

Increased vendor fees have also supported hiring a Market Manager. With 35 vendors, this has become a necessity especially in light of the collaborative arrangement with the city and the sensitive issue of parking impact.

Finally, Market growth has had a significant economic impact. The majority of vendors self-report that they can now make a living from the sale of their local produce. Most have additional venues such as the provision of a weekly vegetable box through Community Supported Agriculture (CSA). Others offer dinners on their property. Landscape services are also offered by several vendors. Interviews with customers indicate they visit businesses when attending the Market. Not surprisingly, businesses indicate an increase in business during market hours.

The inclusive evaluation methodology discussed in this chapter allowed the Woodstock Farmers' Market to collaborate with local high schools, a community college and several regional universities. Furthermore, they connected to government agencies at the city, county, state, and national level. Business owners became supporters rather than antagonists of the Woodstock Farmers' Market and both reaped the economic and civic benefits of collaboration. While other factors such as an increased promotion of local and organic foods in the media support such initiatives as the

Woodstock Farmers' Market, the ability of stakeholders to build relationships through an ongoing conversation and educational process has been identified by stakeholders as the prime engine for collaboration and future growth.

Conclusion

This chapter described the need for a regional focus as we protect our environment and its resources. It also suggested a methodology to define issues and educate stakeholders as the issues are addressed. The cyclical interview process discussed provides a 'convivial' tool to define regional issues and frame institutional collaboration. Collaboration with educational institutions, especially institutions of higher education, is a potent tool yet to be maximized. Universities have worked with communities (rather than regions) in the past but it was most often in the role of 'expert' rather than 'partner'. The Fourth Generation construction of issues is linked to a particular context. The context provides the environment within which individuals try to make sense. The education of interviewees throughout the process allows stakeholders to come to share a construction of reality. This shared reality sets the table for collaboration in addressing regional issues.

While the Woodstock Farmers' Market was able to eventually connect with various institutional resources, it should be the role of higher educational institutions to make their services transparent to increase collaborative opportunities. These resources include knowledge, technique, scholarship, and science. The Kellogg Commission (1999) found that our institutions of higher education are perceived as inaccessible. Even students find it difficult to navigate the complex culture. The obscurity becomes even greater for marginalized populations that find it so difficult to access education at this level. Some types of institutional portfolios serve as inventories of services (e.g., the Institutional Portfolio Project funded by Pew Charitable Trust) allowing institutions to meet civic needs. One can find a description of this project at www.imir.iupui.edu/ceinv. The 'Urban Universities Portfolio Project: Assuring Quality for Multiple Publics' brings together six leading public universities to develop an electronic institutional portfolio. This project has three emphases: to enhance internal and external stakeholders' understanding of the mission of the urban public universities; to develop a new approach to cultivating ongoing internal improvement; and to experiment with new ways of demonstrating and evaluating effectiveness and accountability in the context of their mission (Inman, 2004, p. 143).

The Harris Centre of Memorial University of Newfoundland has developed research support for regional initiatives in a broad range of academic disciplines (www.mun.ca/harriscentre). The quarterly meetings between the university and regional stakeholders in both Newfoundland and Labrador provide a basis for collaborative research activity that starts a two-way exchange of information between researchers and the local communities. The centre sponsored the Knowledge in Motion conference in October 2008 where regional collaborations they had facilitated were showcased. Projects included research on public policy, mapping the social economy of the region and communication strategies to increase civic participation within the region. All projects were based on a celebration of a region's unique qualities. These included what regions brought to the table in both physical resources and human strength. The beauty of the centre's work is their ability to integrate education and research while supporting regions as they exist. They did not view their university as an engine of economic development but rather as a support to regions in preserving their resources and retaining their uniqueness.

The challenge

These practices support institutional culture change. Rather than organizing around disciplines we must organize in response to service. 'The lessons about connection and interrelationship learned from such disparate fields as physics and women's studies would encourage a more flexible, integrated approach to teaching, research, and service' (Martin, Manning and Ramaley, 2001, p. 101). The greatest challenge to society today is the creation of genuine learning communities that encourage lifelong learning and celebration of relationships. This is differentiated from an individual lifelong learning agenda. The lifelong learning covered in this paper is collaborative and defined by diverse stakeholders. These learning communities transform our institutions into vehicles of individual opportunity rather than barriers to change. Universities previously defined by separation of powers enter into relationships based on collaborative problem solving. The most significant issue is the elevation of *local* knowledge. Wendell Berry states:

> There can be no such thing as a global 'village'. No matter how much one may love the world as a whole, one can live fully in it by living responsibly in some small part of it. Where we live and with whom we live define the terms of our relationship to the

*world and humanity. We thus come again to the paradox that
one can become whole only by the responsible acceptance of
one's partiality* (Berry, 1977, p. 123).

The inclusive methodology described in this chapter provides a bridge
between academic research and the solving of practical local questions –
research done *with* community, not *to* it. The basic tenets of conversation and
education serve as the basis for ongoing collaboration facilitating the process
of regional transformation.

References

Berry, W. (1977) *The unsettling of America: Culture and agriculture*. San
Francisco: Sierra Book Clubs.

Guba, E. G. and Lincoln, Y. S. (1989) *Fourth generation evaluation*.
Newbury Park, CA: Sage Publications.

Hollander, E. and Hartley, M. (1999) 'Civic renewal in higher education: The
state of the movement and the need for a national network', in T. Ehrlich
(ed.), *Higher education and civic responsibility*. Santa Barbara, CA: Oryx
Press.

Illich, I. (1973) *Tools for conviviality*. New York: Harper and Row.

Inman, P. (2004) 'The engaged institution', *The Journal of Adult and
Continuing Education,* 10(2), 135–148.

Inman, P. and Swanson, L. (2007) 'Cities as engines of growth' in M.
Osborne, K. Sankey and B. Wilson (eds.) *Social capital, lifelong learning
and the management of place: An international perspective*. London: Taylor
and Francis, 181–189.

Jacobs, J. (2000) *The Nature of Economies*. New York: Random House.

Kellogg Commission (1999) Third report on the future of state and land-
grant universities, *Returning to our roots: The engaged institution.*
Washington DC: National Association of State Universities and Land-Grant
Colleges. http://www.eric.ed.gov/ > ERIC#ED426676 (Accessed 28
September 2010).

Kemmis, D. (1990) *Community and the Politics of Place*. Norman, OK:
University of Oklahoma Press.

Martin, R; Manning, K.; and Ramaley, J. ((2001) 'The self-study as a chariot for strategic change' in J. Ratcliff, E. Lubinescu, M. Gaffney (eds.) *New Directions for Higher Education: How Accreditation Influences Assessment.* San Francisco: Jossey-Bass, 95–115.

Swanson, L. (2000) *User's Guide to READ: Using Regional Economies Assessment Database System.* Missoula, MT: O'Connor Center for the Rocky Mountain West.

Swedish, M. (2008) *Living beyond the end of the world: A spirituality of hope.* New York: Orbis Books.

University of Minnesota (1999) *CURA update.* Minneapolis: Center for Urban and Regional Affairs.

University of Minnesota (2002) *An engaged university: Renewing the land-grant mission.* Minneapolis: University of Minnesota.

PART 2

NORTH AMERICAN PERSPECTIVES AND EXPERIENCE

Chapter 7

The third mission and the history of reform in American higher education

Robert E. Gleeson

Introduction

Important policy questions regarding the proper scale and scope of higher education are under review in almost every nation today. Policy choices inevitably revolve around different, and strongly held, points of view regarding how best to answer the question, 'What is the mission of higher education?' (US Department of Education, 2006; OECD, 2008a and b, 2009).

The most visible issues about mission involve scale. Just how big should each nation's higher education system be? How much funding should be provided compared to other priorities? What is the best mixture of public and private? How many students should be enrolled, and in what types of colleges and universities? What percentage of young people should benefit from a post-secondary degree? How can higher education expand to serve underrepresented minorities? Debates about these questions tend to be very visible because they take place in the public square.

Debates about the proper scope of higher education tend to be less visible. These debates occur more often within the walls of colleges and universities, or among policy experts in the field. A frequent topic of debate is whether colleges and universities should, or should not, be encouraged to expand their activities to include programming that is collectively referred to as the 'third mission.'

This paper is an initial attempt to enrich the discussion of these issues by providing some historical perspective based on the history of higher education in the US. Although the US context does not capture the full variety of other national settings, policy-makers outside the US may benefit from a better understanding of the US experience.

Adding value through historical perspective

An excellent place to start for anyone who seeks to weave historical perspective into a contemporary policy debate is Neustadt and May's classic book *Thinking in Time* (Neustadt and May, 1986). This is not an easy task. Historians by their nature revel in the complexity of human affairs. Decision-makers and those who advise them seek the opposite. Their standards of performance stress rational simplification of issues. Alternatives must be compared so preferred options can be identified.

Neustadt and May acknowledge these differences and propose common ground based on a pragmatic belief that making even marginal improvements to important decisions can yield large benefits. They start by observing that the different points of view held by various factions in most policy debates are rooted partly in different understandings of the past. Whether they acknowledge it or not, those who see themselves as change agents and those who define themselves as defenders of the status quo alike define themselves in reference to their own stories about how the present came to be, and whether the future should be different. Policy debates are about the struggle between the forces of change and the forces of continuity.

Historians can add value to policy analysis by clarifying the important assumptions people make about the past and subjecting those ideas to critical analysis. Although there certainly is no 'correct' history against which different assumptions can be measured for accuracy, there can indeed be many assumptions about the past that are simply inaccurate, or that at least need to be understood more fully. Clearing away 'impediments embedded in impressions of the past' (Neustadt and May (1986) p. 235) is an important way for historians to help contemporary policy-makers. And like many other useful tools of policy analysis, historical analysis helps decision-makers 'take care not to pursue the wrong story' (Neustadt and May (1986) p. 236).

Several challenges, however, deserve brief recognition. First, there is a great deal that we simply do not know about the past. Historical scholarship on any particular topic is limited to only those aspects that were thought to be worth examining by scholars in the past. Historians in the last fifty years have greatly expanded the topics of historical inquiry. But many topics remain unexplored. Most are not retrievable since the historical evidence of most people, most organizations, and most topics that were not previously thought worthy of retention is lost. The case of higher education is better than most. Academic institutions fare better than others in respecting their past. But still, the record is weighted very heavily by the experiences of a relative handful of elite institutions.

A second challenge is the methodological difficulty of capturing the actual behaviour of people through the historical records that remain. Language is dynamic and words mean different things to different people, and in different eras. This is hampered even further by an even more fundamental third challenge. Behaviours themselves can mean different things to different people depending on the social contexts in which they occurred.

These challenges will never be overcome entirely. No set of events can generate a universally accepted history. Yet that does not mean that all possible historical interpretations of the same events are created equal. Historians can contribute to contemporary policy debates by critically assessing different points of view to ascertain those that are based on evidence.

The contemporary debate about the mission of higher education

It is fair to say that in most nations today, there is broad consensus about the two core missions of higher education. The first is the mission to educate. In the words of Will Durant, 'education is the transmission of civilization.' The most important measure of this mission is a steady flow of graduating students who have earned degrees in prescribed fields of civilized study.

The second is the mission to create. This usually translates into a mission to create new knowledge through different types of research. But it also includes the mission to create new works of art and culture. The tangible products of this mission include faculty publications, patents, exhibits, performances, etc.

Consensus about the centrality of these two missions is strong. Indeed, the complex calculus of status within the vast network of colleges and universities throughout the world today is assessed mostly in reference to these two missions.

Lofty status is reserved for those institutions that achieve high levels of performance in each mission, and that fuse the two missions together whenever possible. Education at the doctoral level is expected to achieve this goal. And the more an institution can align its research and creative activities with its educational programmes at other levels (masters-level, professional, and undergraduate), the higher its status rank will be. Lower status is given to institutions that de-emphasize research and focus more on instruction. Yet even those that place the highest emphasis on instruction would not abandon faculty research and/or creative work entirely. To do so would risk the institution's legitimacy, and perhaps even its formal accreditation.

The third mission is the mission to engage the community beyond the campus gates. It is here that consensus about mission dissolves into debate. What responsibility does higher education have to reach out beyond teaching its students and conducting faculty research in order to directly affect the broader world?

Today's dominant academic culture still views the mission of engagement with great skepticism and mistrust, despite the advocacy of many academic leaders (Kellogg Commission, 1999; Simon, 2009; Walshok, 1995). Practices that fall within this category are characterized as distractions from the first two, more legitimate, missions. Although the exact definition of engaged practices is notoriously elusive, the most widely used description is the one used by the prestigious Carnegie Foundation for the Advancement of Teaching.

> *Community Engagement describes the collaboration between institutions of higher education and their larger communities (local, regional/state, national, global) for the mutually beneficial exchange of knowledge and resources in a context of partnership and reciprocity.* (Carnegie Foundation, 2007)

The Carnegie Foundation further subdivides engaged activities into two broad categories. The first is 'curricular engagement' and the second is 'outreach and partnerships.' Other commonly used terms to describe engagement activities include 'outreach,' 'technology transfer,' 'knowledge transfer,' and, perhaps of most concern to critics, 'service.'

Some critics argue that the entire mission of engagement is simply misplaced in higher education. They don't dispute that these practices can benefit communities. Rather, they assert that colleges and universities are not very efficient at making them work. The activities should be performed by some other set of institutions.

Others argue more forcefully that giving full legitimacy to the third mission is dangerous for higher education. Although the community benefits that can come from engagement are attractive because they are tangible and sometimes very visible, they are none the less small when compared to the less visible, longer-term benefits that society obtains from traditional practices in instruction and research. The allure of engagement threatens to undermine awareness of the more fundamental contributions of higher education. The result is too many one-way flows of time, talent, and treasure out of the university and into the community in an era when the resources needed to accomplish the first two missions are already too scarce.

Mixing these two critiques together creates a widely-held third line of argument that is particularly devastating. The third mission is often characterized as a sort of consolation prize for those colleges and universities that do not create enough public value through the traditional first two missions. Institutions that do not earn high marks on traditional measures of status can pursue engagement as a supplementary activity. The legitimacy of the third mission, therefore, is in inverse proportion to accepted measures of university status.

Third mission advocates fight back with several arguments of their own. One common theme applauds exactly the kinds of visible, short-term public benefits that some critics fear. Creating those visible benefits, they assert, won't undermine the public's belief in the long-term value of higher education. That confidence has already been lost. With the possible exception of the health sciences, they argue, the public already views the great bulk of university teaching and research as detached from the problems of society. Popular culture is filled with lampoons of university life and its lack of pragmatic utility.

Cutting state appropriations to higher education has become a popular sport in state politics throughout the US. This sport thrives because of the loss of public trust, despite the fact that the voting public has never before contained so many college graduates. Faced with this political climate, advocates assert, colleges and universities must create visible examples of their value by pursuing clearly perceived public goods like revitalizing distressed neighbourhoods and rural towns, improving human services and homeland security, alleviating poverty, improving P-12 education, cleaning up the environment and pursuing social justice. Third mission practices do not endanger public support. They are essential in order to restore the pool of social capital that once supported higher education. (Kaplan, 2004)

Another important theme relates to more tangible types of capital. Some assert that newly emerging economic and social dynamics within the last few decades are creating unprecedented demands on higher education to perform functions in society that were not necessary before. Douglass, King and Feller summarize this point of view well. 'To a degree only recently realized, universities have become the anointed agents of social and economic transformation in the 21st century' *(Douglass, King, and Feller (2009), p. 3)*. The old missions of instruction and research are no longer adequate to meet new demands placed on higher education in a world dominated by global networks of knowledge regions, knowledge-intensive business sectors, radically transformative technological innovations, self-actualizing creative class workers, and hyper-mobile financial capital.

This summary does not include all points of view in the debate over engagement. But it does reveal the depth of the divide. The challenge for this paper is to see whether some historical perspective from the history of higher education in the US can add value to the resolution of this issue today.

Historical assumptions in the third mission debate

The current debate allows one to identify some widely-held assumptions about the past that frame the contemporary debate about the future of the third mission.

To begin with, advocates and critics alike accept the notion that granting legitimacy to the third mission for all levels of higher education would be something new. Engagement activities, they agree, have never before served as a dominant force of change or upward status in the US system of higher education. Critics may praise this aspect of history. Advocates may lament it. But all agree that engagement has been a sideline topic. The larger story about how the US system grew to global prominence over the last century is driven by topics related to the history of education and research activities among a relative handful of prestigious, research-intensive universities.

Today's policy-makers generally accept the idea that colleges and universities transformed themselves into high status institutions through a series of internal reform movements beginning in the late 19th century and continuing through the present. Those internal reform movements disengaged higher education from external ties (especially religious) and allowed academia to cultivate a culture of learned autonomy. That culture was essential for setting in motion a cycle of continual reform in which increasingly specialized and detached fields of research could produce new knowledge that would continually alter and expand curriculum. (Jencks and Riesman, 1977; Geiger, 1986 and 1993)

Much of the character of this point of view was articulated best by Clark Kerr (1963) when he envisioned the ultimate achievement of higher education's role in American life. Writing in 1963, he described the emergence of the 'multiversity.' Kerr's multiversity would be a complex institution comprised of fully autonomous faculties, independent from each other, independent from the communities they inhabited, and, he quipped, united only by their common complaint about inadequate parking. Kerr argued that these supremely autonomous faculties, and the students they created, were nonetheless worthy of generous public support out of enlightened self-interest because they could be counted on to produce and consume most of the new knowledge that would lead the world forward into a new global age.

Against the backdrop of this story, the history of engagement is positioned as a humble sub-plot. Indeed, both sides of today's debate reinforce the peripheral nature of the third mission by connecting its origins with the founding of the land-grant universities after passage of the Morrill Act by the Federal government in 1862.

Proponents use the origins story to associate engagement with the virtues of democratic civic culture. The land-grant tradition highlights higher education's service to people and communities who are not part of the elite, and who are not leading the broader forces of social or economic change. Common people continually face difficult adjustments to social and economic changes beyond their control. The land-grant tradition uses public money to bring the benefits of education and practical, applied science to underdeveloped states so that common people can adjust to change. The land-grants would educate the children of farmers and mechanics while also serving the needs of the current generation of ordinary people through outreach, applied research, and extension services.

Some proponents use the humble origins story to build a bridge from the past to the present by stressing the continuity of civic virtue inherent in third mission activities. Others go further by asserting that many of those traditional civic virtues also overlap with the changing sources of local and regional economic development in today's global knowledge economy.

Critics use the same origins story to associate engagement with relative mediocrity. Connecting the third mission exclusively to the land-grant tradition of continuing education and public service confirms to the critic that engagement lies outside the mainstream of how colleges and universities have risen in prominence. The history tells that engagement emerged as a strategy to help lower-status schools provide services to lower-status adults and lower-status communities located at the nation's periphery. None of these matters relate to the broader story of how higher education rose to high esteem in American culture by establishing patronage among social, political, economic, and cultural elites.

Critical assessment of key historical assumptions

The first assumption to examine is the notion that the origins of the third mission were confined to the early years of experiment in educational programming and community service within land-grant institutions. Making use of the Carnegie Foundation's definition, one can ask whether the historical record contains evidence of 'collaboration between institutions of higher education and their larger communities' to exchange information and resources in the context of reciprocal partnerships beyond the setting of land-grant institutions?

If this first assumption is found to be inaccurate, additional questions arise. If engagement-related activities were more widespread in the history of US higher education, how did those activities relate to concepts of status, and how did those activities relate to the larger forces of reform in education and research that propelled the US system of colleges and universities to global prominence?

A full exploration of these questions is beyond the scope of this chapter. What follows is a first attempt to examine the issue of origins, followed by some initial ideas about how a better understanding of the past can add value to contemporary policy-makers.

What were the origins of engagement?

Historical scholarship does indeed raise fundamental challenges to the accepted story of humble origins in regard to the third mission of higher education in the US. The literature challenges the notion that community engagement played only a limited role in the development of US system of higher education. It also challenges the accepted story that engagement was limited to the use of public funding to build working partnerships with non-elite partners, and that engaged, reciprocal relationships dealt exclusively with educational programming for adults and extension-type services.

The historian Peter Dobkin Hall (1982) provides a good starting point for the history of higher education engagement in the US. Hall argues that beginning shortly after the founding of the republic, churches and the church-affiliated colleges that dominated the early years of higher education in the US entered into a pattern of mutually advantageous relationships with wealthy New England merchants as part of a broader movement that created the social and legal framework of the modern, privately governed, state-chartered corporation. Merchants could use the private corporate form to shield financial wealth from the power of government. Churches could use the same corporate form to enforce the separation of church and state. Colleges began to use the form to separate themselves from the religious denominations that founded them, and to offer social status to newly wealthy merchants and emerging industrialists by granting them positions on college governing boards. Hall argues that these mutually advantageous actions helped lay the foundations for a distinctively American culture by creating a non-democratic source of legitimate private authority that could counterbalance growing popular power in the increasingly democratic republic. Once the pattern of mutually advantageous ties between wealthy elites and private colleges was established, the consequences spread gradually into more and more aspects of elite American culture.

Dorothy Ross (1991) expands on this theme throughout her seminal history of American social science. She places the origins of social science in the US squarely within the broader context of how US elites sought intellectual justification for their fervent belief in the core concept of American exceptionalism. As Ross summarized, 'America, unlike Europe, would forestall the mass poverty and class conflict that modernity appeared to be creating in Britain.'

As a national ideology, American exceptionalism was an

intellectual construct, the work of cultural and political elites, and hence it had to be propagated, learned, and accepted by the diverse strata of American society. Neither its dissemination nor its affirmation could be taken for granted. (Ross (1991) p. xiv)

Many of the leaders of America's most influential private colleges built strong mutual ties with elites in the fast-changing communities outside their campus gates beginning in the years after the Civil War and extending through the early 20th century. Historians have been rediscovering how communities and universities interacted with each other during this time. (Recchiuti, 2006; Longo, 2007; Westhoff, 2007; Morelock, 2008).

College and university leaders sought to assure the vitality of their institutions by transforming them into recognized contributors to achieving the local, regional, and even national goals that were embraced by their elite partners. As the post-Civil War generation of college leaders used the new corporate form to disengage their colleges from religious denominations, they eagerly re-engaged them with the newly emerging, local, regional, and national elites whose authority rested on more secular sources.

No one contributed more to this movement in the years after the Civil War than Harvard's new, reform-minded president, Charles W. Eliot. In an article he published in *Atlantic Monthly* in 1869 titled 'The New Education,' Eliot connected the future of higher education with the aspirations of his day. 'The American people are fighting a wilderness, physical and moral, on the one hand, and on the other are struggling to work out the awful problem of self-government. For this fight they must be trained and armed,' he argued. Colleges needed to help the nation produce 'commissioned officers in the army of industry' (Hall, 1982).

The new generation of university leaders like Eliot was joined by a new generation of likeminded faculty. Unlike their older colleagues, many of the newly hired faculty had received research training in European universities. They shared Eliot's ambition for civic engagement and their careers flowed in and out of academia in ways that kept them connected to the wider world. They had worked in business, they maintained close friendships with labour leaders and other reformers, and they travelled widely. They had first-hand ties to the extremes of wealth and poverty that characterized life in the Gilded Age. These ties helped them recruit students and helped them gain access to people from all walks of life to inform their research and writing.

The two-way flow of ideas that they established was not always appreciated by university administrators and their powerful patrons. Ideological passions were strong in American politics, and tolerance for debate was limited. Many academic careers were interrupted, sidetracked, and ended when professorial engagements strayed beyond the ambiguous lines of acceptable discourse and were branded as too 'radical,' or worst of all, 'socialist.'

But most who encountered problems were able to put together careers like that of the influential economist Henry Carter Adams (Ross (1991) pp. 115–116). He was pushed off the faculty at Cornell after he upset the university's major benefactor, Russell Sage, by supporting railroad workers during the great southwestern railroad strike of 1886. Yet despite that misstep he was able to secure a permanent position for himself at the University of Michigan shortly afterward by negotiating with Michigan's president James Burrell Angell and issuing a carefully worded statement that distinguished his views from socialism.

Those who navigated the complexities of engagement in their research were the most productive scholars of their time. As Ross summarizes, 'The paradigms they formulated – neoclassical economics, liberal economic interpretations of history, a sociology and ideology of social control, and pragmatism – laid the groundwork for twentieth-century social science' (Ross (1991) p. 143).

The rise of the social sciences enabled faculty and administrators to foster internal curricular reform. Major new published works created specialties around which new courses could be developed. More and more colleges abandoned the traditional curricula, based on study of the classics, and replaced it with the broader 'elective system' urged by Eliot and other leaders. More specialized elective courses fed the need for more engaged social science research, which in turn produced more material for even more courses. Once set in motion, this cycle gained considerable momentum as external sources of power in American society began to tap into university-based research to help inform the broad-based reform movement that became known as the Progressive Era.

The powerful ties that grew between private colleges and their elite patrons in the middle of the 19th century established a pattern of reciprocal behavior between university faculty and administrators and members of local, regional, and national elites that can justifiably be described with the modern terminology of 'engagement' and 'third mission activities.' These ties created the milieu that gave birth to the social sciences in American culture, and the rapid rise of higher education as an influential source of reform in American society in the late 19th and early 20th centuries.

The desire to align the teaching and research agendas of higher education in those years with the needs of elite groups in American culture, however, was not confined to a small handful of elite private colleges. When public universities began to multiply and expand, leveraged by resources available through the Morrill Act, they sought legitimacy by hiring faculty and recent graduates from the private institutions. Their faculty brought with them the same desire to build strong ties to elites, and emerging elites, in each state. They used those ties to align teaching and research in the new land-grant colleges with the needs of their external partners, both elite and common.

Academic entrepreneurs in newly established, and much less prestigious, scientific and technical schools followed the same engaged path. The result was a widely based academic culture that placed high value on cultivating strong ties with external partners. The experience of Carnegie Tech provides an instructive example. Founded by Andrew Carnegie as the Carnegie Technical Schools in 1900, and later renamed the Carnegie Institute of Technology, its founder was a harsh critic of old-time classical college education. In Carnegie's own words,

> *While the college student has been learning a little about the barbarous and petty squabbles of a far-distant past, or trying to master languages which are dead, such knowledge as seems adapted for life upon another planet than this as far as business affairs are concerned, the future captain of industry is hotly engaged in the school of experience, obtaining the very knowledge required for his future triumphs . . . College education as it exists is fatal to success in that domain.* (Cited in Veysey (1964), pp. 13–14)

Carnegie Tech's early engineering faculty worked hard to develop mutually beneficial ties with the world outside the sylvan campus that Carnegie was building for working-class young people on parkland donated by the City of Pittsburgh. By 1909, more than twenty firms were paying an annual fee to support its Division of Cooperative Research, including the Equitable Life Assurance Society, the Ford Motor Company, US Steel Corporation, H. J. Heinz Company, and the seven largest department stores in Pittsburgh.

Engaged relationships permeated curriculum development as well. The constant interplay between engineering faculty and local business leaders is captured well in the annual summary of curricular reform efforts written by Walter F. Rittman in 1924. Rittman served as faculty chair of an engineering division within Carnegie Tech. At that time he also served as national president of the Society of Industrial Engineers.

> *The co-operative work with the industries of Pittsburgh has now reached the point where we may consider it established and on a permanent basis. During the year we have had forty-five speakers, prominent in their respective industries, who have given instruction in problems of production and distribution. The personnel of these speakers is the same from year to year, which means that the programme is a co-ordinated one. The speakers in turn feel themselves to be a part of the Carnegie Institute of Technology. Each week is devoted to a different industry. For example, we have a National Tube Company week. On Monday, Mr Cornelius speaks to the students on the production of their plants. On Tuesday, the students visit the plants of the National Tube Company. Later in the week, Mr Schaeffer, of the same company, instructs the boys in the procedure used to advertise and sell National Tube Company products. By the following Monday each student turns into the department a comprehensive report dealing with the National Tube Company business . . . In a similar way the co-operative work deals with the twenty-seven industries of the district.* (Walter Rittman, 'Annual Report of the Department of Commercial Engineering, May 1924', pp 1–2. Carnegie Mellon University Archives, Applied Science Box)

The broader growth of professional education beyond engineering is, perhaps, the most enduring example of the central role that third mission-related activities played (and continue to play) in the evolution of the US higher education system. The literatures on the history of various types of professional education are large. And social science literature is filled with examples of how different occupational groups in American life entered into long-term, mutually beneficial relationships with university educators to develop research foundations for their occupations that could be translated into acceptable college curricula for degree programmes.

The result of this process gave birth to new professions that could enjoy upwardly mobile social status. It also created dramatic increases in enrollments and revenues for the colleges and universities that were part of the partnerships. Middle class and working class families both embraced higher education as the point of entry for achieving higher social status through vocational utility. Enrollments boomed in professional degree programmes, both undergraduate and graduate.

Business became the most common course of study in many colleges by 1900. But professional programmes produced growing numbers of physicians, dentists, social workers, teachers, veterinarians, engineers, nurses, and almost any other occupation that could claim a scientific basis of specialized knowledge for practice. By the peak of the Progressive era just before the US became involved in the First World War, higher education not only supplied the 'commissioned officers in the army of industry,' it also supplied the legions of professionals that Progressive Era reformers hoped would constrain the worst excesses of the American form of industrial capitalism. Higher education institutions emerged as vital and widely engaged partners in US society's broader ambition to reap the benefits of industrialization without experiencing the harsh class conflicts that plagued Europe. Pervasive engagement between higher education institutions and the multitude of groups that made up America's growing local, regional and national elites was thought to be an important strategy for ensuring the future of American exceptionalism.

How can historical perspective affect the contemporary policy debate?

As discussed previously, supporters and critics disagree about what role, and what status, should be given to engaged activities, and those who pursue them, in the future of US higher education. They agree, however, about the past. Both sides in the contemporary debate connect the origins of the third mission with the 19th century land-grant movement in public higher education. This popular origins story disconnects engagement-related activities from the larger story of how higher education rose to social and cultural prominence.

The widespread consensus about the past heavily influences the contemporary debate about the future. Placing land-grant institutions at the centre of the history of community engagement determines the roles played by each side. Third mission advocates are positioned as reformers who must justify the need for change. Opponents are defending the status quo against the perceived forces of mediocrity.

The initial review of historical scholarship in this paper, however, raises serious questions about the accuracy of these presumed positions. The records of the past seem to contain many examples of third mission-type activities that were not part of the land-grant movement. Indeed, there is strong evidence to suggest that engagement with outside partners played a much more central role, and a much more systematic role, in creating the conditions that allowed the modern university to emerge in the US. Indeed, when we look at the period of time in which the US system of higher education first emerged, i.e. the Gilded Age and the Progressive Era, it seems almost impossible to identify a history of the third mission that is separate from the cycle of reform-minded activities that drove change in the first two missions.

One could even suggest that the history of reform in US higher education has an unexplored pattern in which engagement plays an essential role. A fresh look at the historical record suggests a recurring pattern in which many of the most innovative academic scholars embraced third mission activities in order to create new education and research initiatives. These new initiatives deepened the reciprocal ties between internal and external partners and created new benefits for all. This point of view even suggests that there never has been a separate history of the third mission in US higher education. Rather, engagement activities may be interpreted as a recurring strategy for stimulating reforms in education and research and aligning those reforms with the broader needs of society at different points in time.

Although this brief paper has not explored whether there is evidence of this pattern across all the eras of reform in US higher education, especially the most recent, it has uncovered evidence that suggests that a pattern of engaged activities did play an important role in the founding era of twentieth century social science. Since the strongest voices against the third mission in higher education today tend to come from the traditional social sciences, further investigation seems warranted.

Revising our interpretation of the past based on a fresh look at primary historical evidence would have many consequences for our debate about the future. Most policy-makers today recognize the growing importance of higher education in producing new knowledge and talented labour for the global economy. But this brief essay suggests that we still do not have answers to many basic questions about the social relations that led colleges and universities in the US to emerge as central players in the production and dissemination of knowledge and human talent over the last century.

The lack of clarity about these issues robs us of a better informed historical perspective against which we can assess the aspects of both change and continuity that underlie different proposals for how higher education can play this historic role better in the fast-changing social, economic, and political world of today.

References

Carnegie Foundation for the Advancement of Teaching (2007) *Elective classification: Community engagement 2008 documentation framework.* New York: Carnegie Foundation.

Douglass, J. King, C. J., and Feller, I. (eds.) (2009) *Globalization's muse: Universities and Higher Education systems in a changing world.* Berkeley, CA: Berkeley Public Policy Press.

Geiger, R. (1986) *To advance knowledge: The growth of american research universities, 1900–1940.* New York: Oxford University Press.

Geiger, R. (1993) *Research and relevant knowledge: American research universities since World War Two.* New York: Oxford University Press.

Hall, P. (1982) *The organization of American culture, 1700–1900: private institutions, elites, and the origins of American nationality.* New York: New York University Press.

Jencks, C. and Riesman, D. (1977) *The academic revolution.* Chicago: University of Chicago Press.

Kaplan, Anne C. (2004) 'Outreach in the twenty-first century: survival strategies for a unique environment', *Continuing Higher Education Review,* 68 (2004), 117–128.

Kellogg Commission (1999) Third report on the future of state and land-grant universities, *Returning to our roots: The engaged institution.* Washington DC: National Association of State Universities and Land-Grant Colleges http://www.eric.ed.gov/ > ERIC#ED426676 Accessed 28 September 2010.

Kerr, C. (1963) *The uses of the university*. Cambridge, MA: Harvard University Press.

Longo, N. (2007) *Why community matters: Connecting education with civic life*. Albany, NY: SUNY Press.

Morelock, K. (2008) *Taking the town: Collegiate and community culture in the bluegrass, 1880–1917*. Lexington, KY: The University Press of Kentucky.

Neustadt, R. and May, E. (1986) *Thinking in time: The uses of history for decision makers*. New York: Free Press.

OECD (Organization for Economic Co-operation and Development) (2008a) *Higher Education to 2030 (Vol. 1): Demography*. Paris: OECD.

OECD (Organization for Economic Co-operation and Development) (2008b) *Four scenarios for Higher Education*. Paris: OECD.

OECD (Organization for Economic Co-operation and Development) (2009) *Higher Education to 2030 (Vol. 2): Globalization*. Paris: OECD.

Recchiuti, J. (2006) *Civic engagement: Social science and progressive-era reform in New York City*. Philadelphia: University of Pennsylvania Press.

Ross, D. (1991) *The origins of American social science*. Cambridge: Cambridge University Press.

Simon, L. A. K. (2009) *Embracing the world grant ideal: Affirming the Morrill Act for a twenty-first century global society*. Michigan State University.

Thelin, J. (2004) *A history of American Higher Education*. Baltimore: Johns Hopkins University Press.

US Department of Education (2006) *A test of leadership: Charting the future of U.S. Higher Education*. Washington DC.

Veysey, L. (1965) *The emergence of the American university*. Chicago: University of Chicago Press.

Walshok, M. (1995) *Knowledge without boundaries: What America's research universities can do for the economy, the workplace, and the community*. San Francisco: Jossey-Bass.

Westhoff, L. (2007) *A fatal drifting apart: Democratic social knowledge and Chicago reform*. Columbus: The Ohio State University Press.

Chapter 8

Public universities and regional development

Kathryn Mohrman

In early 2008, the University Design Consortium, a joint project of Sichuan University (SCU) in China and Arizona State University (ASU) in the United States, conducted case studies of fifteen universities in seven countries engaged in regional development. From policy entrepreneurship in water pollution problems to technology-delivered education for rural residents, the case studies demonstrate the scope and variety of community-university partnerships. This chapter draws recommendations and conclusions from these case studies, published under the title *Public Universities and Regional Development* (Mohrman *et al.*, 2009), providing suggestions for other institutions seeking to strengthen their contributions to the communities around them. SCU and ASU began the project with a pragmatic rather than a theoretical mindset; the project was seen as a service and the resulting book a policy and practice report rather than a research study.

As large research universities located in underdeveloped parts of their respective countries, SCU and ASU share a commitment to serving the people in their respective regions. Sichuan is one of the largest provinces in China; SCU has been involved in developing the human and economic capacity of the province for many years. After the devastating Wenchuan earthquake of May 2008, the university took on even greater responsibility to serve the needs of the people of Sichuan.

Similarly, ASU is the largest institution of higher education in Arizona and one of the largest in the United States. Like its Chinese partner, ASU is committed to economic development and social progress of the region. Among its priorities, encompassed in the New American University concept, are community embeddedness and use-inspired research. One important outgrowth of this commitment was the creation of the new downtown campus as part of a larger effort to revitalize the hollow core of the city of Phoenix.

Both universities believe that dramatic changes in higher education are essential if institutions are to play a key role in societal development in the 21st century. As Wiewel and Perry (2009, p. 8) explain, new institutional challenges to the state, market and politics in an era of globalization are influencing a new global set of patterns in higher education. The changing political and economic relationships and the cross-border movement of information in the knowledge economy set the stage for new institutional practices in both the developing and developed economies of the world.

Case studies

The case studies involve fifteen public universities from China, Mexico, United Kingdom, Portugal, Sweden, Australia, and the United States. Some cases represent institution-wide priorities while others are smaller, more focused activities. The guiding questions were:

- How do university leaders articulate their regional development vision and strategies?
- What strategic actions can university leaders effectively use to manage the interactive relationships between university goals and regional development?
- How can public universities effectively promote, direct and reinforce regional development internally as well as at the local and/or national level through specific regional partnerships?
- What outcomes are important when evaluating public universities' performance in regional development?
- What issues and challenges arise from regional development activities?

The brief descriptions below indicate the variety of community and regional issues addressed by the fifteen participants.

University at Albany, State University of New York (SUNY), USA

University at Albany presents lessons learned from two collaborative projects supporting youth and families, on the one hand, and elder-friendly communities on the other.

Arizona State University, USA
Arizona State University's Downtown Campus contributes to the revitalization of Phoenix's downtown and creates an economic stimulus while providing more educational opportunities and new ways of engaging the community.

Center for Research in Higher Education Policies (CIPES), Portugal
Massification, geographic diversification, and greater institutional autonomy in Portuguese higher education were all policies intended to increase the institutions' responsiveness to regional vocational education demands of students and employers, but there remains a mismatch between regional supply and demand of higher education.

Chongqing University, China
Chongqing University uses 'adapting to social and economic development' as a model to link university researchers' collaborations with local businesses to meet regional challenges and maximize public benefit.

Cornell University, USA
Cornell University's Urban Scholars Program provides summer internships with leaders in the non-profit sector in New York City, resulting in many talented students taking public service positions after graduation.

University of Guadalajara, Mexico
The Manantlan Institute of Ecology and Biodiversity (MIEB), created by the University of Guadalajara in the heart of the Ayuquila–Armería river basin, contributes technical expertise and community leadership to implement an integrated watershed management approach. Researchers have become policy entrepreneurs in the process.

Louisiana State University, USA
The loss of land, homes and livelihoods from Hurricanes Katrina and Rita in 2005 presented an opportunity for LSU students to become directly involved in the recovery process through service learning, internships, research projects, and community-based courses.

Luleå University of Technology, Sweden
University–business collaborations at Luleå University of Technology contribute to regional and company-based development; the case study looks at the roles and perceptions of the different players in these partnerships.

Monash University, Australia

As Monash University develops into a global university with international campuses, it faces a challenge in balancing its regional responsibilities with its global ambitions. The case addresses what outcomes are important when evaluating universities' performance in regional development and the particular challenges of multi-national, multi-campus research initiatives.

Nanjing University, China

Over ten years, more than 400 scholars and government leaders have come together in the Senior Forum on Jiangsu Province Development, the highest-level platform of policy consultancy for the province. Key issues for discussion have included sustainable development, rule of law, and the development of a modern service industry in the province.

Newcastle University, United Kingdom

Funding changes and institutional restructuring after 2000 drove Newcastle to rediscover its original role in regional development. A key element of the successful implementation of Newcastle's projects has been the participation of the university's policy research group, the Centre for Urban and Regional Development Studies (CURDS).

Ohio State University, USA

Ohio State created Campus Partners and worked with the City of Columbus and residents of the University District to improve neighborhoods around the campus, an example of university leadership through engagement of key stakeholders in both private and public sectors.

Sichuan University, China

As the leading university in the western part of China, Sichuan University has focused on poverty reduction in one of the poorest regions of the country. Its efforts in Sichuan Province and in Tibet include five areas of activity: technology, talent development, medical support, financial aid for students, and think tank contributions.

Texas Tech University, USA

This case study examines the need for further education in rural communities. Texas Tech has pursued strategies of distributed learning, mutuality and reciprocity of agreements between partners, technology as an enabler of partnerships, and financial infrastructure for sustainable delivery of hybrid academic programmes.

University of Utah, USA

The University of Utah case study provides examples of regional development emphasizing a full continuum of engagement. The successes of such partnerships are attributed to a focus on leadership, resident empowerment, and community capacity building; issues of reciprocity and sustainability are vital.

In selecting the case studies, different types of public universities were identified – based on size, location, rural/urban focus, and project goals – that are involved with communities outside the campus. The editors identified four overarching themes:

- Universities engaged in *economic development* include, but are not limited to, partnerships with business, industry, and/or government to improve the growth, potential or sustainability of the region. Project outcomes include downtown development, retail or business enhancement in the region, community revitalization, or employment in the region of the university's graduates.
- Within the category of *communication and technology development*, examples include rural technology expansion, technology transfer, business corridor development, commercial growth, and interdisciplinary innovation.
- *Social development* programmes in a region include strategic faculty-student engagement, social entrepreneurship, local educational development, community-building programmes, student citizenship and civic engagement (catalyzing student and community commitment).
- *Sustainable environmental development* is defined as a university project engaged in contemporary scientific and social efforts to expand sustainable environmental practices.

The editors identified a number of examples in each of these categories, as well as cases that combined more than one category in intriguing ways. There was a bias in favour of projects that have not received wide publicity in other publications on community engagement.

The case study authors provide self reflection and analysis around the questions outlined above, although not all case studies address all the issues. Authors had wide latitude to respond to these issues in ways that allowed the story of each institution best to be told. The case study authors were not required to follow a strict outline or order of topics, although many of the cases have similar structures. When authors 'told the story' in simply descriptive terms, the editors pushed hard for analysis and broader generalizations in order to build a larger sense of common issues and problems.

While it was relatively easy to find good examples of American institutions engaged with their regions, it was more difficult to find comparable programmes in other countries. Sichuan University took on the responsibility of locating Chinese case studies. The examples from Sweden, Australia, Portugal, Mexico, and the United Kingdom came largely through personal connections.

Terminology

The study conducted by the Organization for Economic Co-operation and Development, *Higher Education and Regions: Globally Competitive, Locally Engaged* (OECD, 2007), considers regional engagement of higher education in several dimensions:

- knowledge-creation in the region through research and its exploitation via technology transfer;
- human capital formation and knowledge transfer;
- cultural and community development contributing to the milieu, social cohesion and sustainable development on which innovation depends. (p. 22)

The case studies in this chapter touch in varying degrees on all these dimensions.

Terminology in this field is often vague and sometimes slippery. As Harloe and Perry (2004, p. 212) point out, over the last century or more, there has been a significant degree of separation and segregation between the university, the state and the market. The more recent focus on the relationship between institutions of higher education and the communities surrounding them is for many universities a new role or expanded mission.

The title of the ASU/SCU volume emphasizes 'regional development' although some of the case study universities use 'community engagement' or 'university-community partnerships' to define their commitment to the localities in which they reside. These overlapping terms have slight differences, however, in the level, scope and depth of involvement by key stakeholders in the relationship. Institutions can offer a series of unrelated projects in the community, they can develop serious relationships with agencies and organizations in the region, or they can be deeply involved in the social and economic development of the communities in which they are located. Often a university will begin with small projects, then develop partnerships, and gradually embed community issues into research and teaching across the campus.

Community outreach is connecting with the local or regional community in a meaningful and beneficial way. The word 'outreach' suggests that the centre of action is the university itself; people move out beyond its walls to interact with previously unengaged persons and organizations. Projects are connected to the institution's overall mission to improve the health of the community and to increase the university's role as a community institution as defined by the university. Ongoing conversations with multiple segments of the community help to guide strategic decision making. The tie to the university mission is apparent, although projects are often one-way actions.

In the foreword to *Creating a New Kind of University*, Percy *et al*. (2006) speak to the limitations of this approach: 'Higher educational institutions should go beyond a *rhetoric* of collaboration and conscientiously *work with* communities, rejecting a [unilateral], unidirectional, top-down approach, which too often describes the actual practice of university-community interaction' (p. x). The editors of the volume suggest that members of both community and university should treat each other as ends in themselves, rather than as means to an end. For many institutions, however, outreach is the first step in a continuum of engagement, a way for institutions to initiate their community activities. In moving beyond outreach, Percy *et al*. (2006) encourage universities to think about the relationship itself as the goal, placing the greatest value on the community partners and their welfare, not developing a specified programme or completing a research project.

University-community partnerships go further, in which each stakeholder, having enlightened self-interest, takes part in the development, effort and rewards of the partnered project. The relationship is mutually beneficial as well as mutually developed and directed. Many of the case studies, and most authors on the subject, emphasize the importance of serious two-way partnerships. In these cases, there is support and interest from the leadership and a clear connection to the institution's mission. Most important is equality in stakeholder decision-making and participation in the endeavour from beginning to end.

Expectations flow in both directions. In the results of a survey conducted by the Council of Independent Colleges, Liederman and her colleagues (quoted in Brukardt *et al.*, 2006) outline what communities expect of universities:

- *A commitment to outcomes.* This often means sustained involvement beyond an academic semester to a school year to reach project completion in whatever time it takes. One way in which universities can help to provide continuity for partnerships is by creating structures . . . that can support long-term relationships.
- *Shared authority and financing.* Engaged institutions may lead, follow, or step together, depending on the shared goals of the partnership.
- *A willingness to support the partnership in the community.* This may require stepping up to advocate for the partnership in other civic forums, not just within the partnership. It also involves a mutual sharing of success and learning to celebrate together for hard-won victories.
- *Welcoming community partners on to campus in roles normally reserved for faculty or staff.* The idea of a trusting and mutually beneficial relationship between campus and community requires the academy to recognize the assets that the community can bring to the table (p. 14).

Regional development for most case study authors is an outward and visible sign of the public service role of higher education, including economic competitiveness but not limited to that. In the most extensive examples, community-university connections focus on the social relevance of research and teaching and on the building of civil society. At this level, university leadership has a clear, consistent message of continuous responsibility to the region in the work of the institution. New knowledge and other outcomes of the university directly answer to the needs of the region; community issues are integrated into academic courses and faculty research. There is also a broad view of what is considered 'community' within examples of regional development, often reaching beyond city boundaries to engage in state and national issues as well as local concerns.

Harloe and Perry (2004) describe the key characteristics of a university engaged in what European academics often call the 'Mode 2 university' in the global knowledge society:

- close to government and the market;
- directly responsive to national and regional needs in teaching, research and specific enterprise activities;

- engaged in a number of different networks;
- a key player in evolving systems of regional and local governance;
- research is conducted in an interdisciplinary fashion;
- research is sensitive to economic and social relevance;
- changes in mission and practice are accompanied by internal turmoil, reorganization and restructuring. (p. 217)

Cooperative work in improving a region often involves direct collaboration between university officials and high-level officials such as mayors, governors, industry CEOs and key civic leaders. Together they develop and implement a large scale, long-term agenda that sets the tone for the entire community. More than a single project or even a series of discrete efforts, regional development is best described by the long-term nature of the agenda for the enhancement of the region.

Table 8.1 presents this continuum in matrix form, looking at levels of commitment from low relevance to full integration across a range of characteristics, including mission, leadership, institutional policies, organizational structure, and faculty and student activity.

As noted above, many universities in the nineteenth and twentieth centuries became divorced from their locations. Goddard and Puukka (2008, p. 17) describe the development of research universities in continental Europe as institutions transcending their actual location. The ideal of scientific inquiry is to strive for universalism, to search for truth irrespective of time and place. In this view the university is a detached site for critical enquiry, exchange of ideas and advancement of knowledge for its own sake, characteristics of vital importance to the credibility and legitimacy of the institution. At the same time, research universities were to contribute, if only indirectly, to the development of the state (p. 17).

Humboldt's model of the German university and the American concept of the land-grant university, both developed in the nineteenth century, were linked to economic, agricultural and industrial growth. Somewhat later, Asian universities were created, often by Westerners, to educate the people in a community or colony. As a result a number of the universities in this study have community service or regional engagement in their mission statements.

Too often, however, the specifics of such engagement are scattered and unrelated, as suggested by Table 8.1. A successful outreach project is created by a dedicated individual but dies when that person is no longer involved. The Cornell Urban Scholars Program is an example of the vulnerability of small, isolated projects. The university has been happy to embrace the programme as long as external funding was available, but was less enthusiastic when the granting organization expected the university to incorporate the project into the base budget.

Other activities have limited scope. Nanjing University's policy forums have the specific goal of advice to provincial leaders, demonstrating engagement but not incorporation into the fundamental structure of the university (perhaps *Medium Relevance* but not *Full Integration* in the terms used in Table 8.1). Still other projects are limited by circumstance. Louisiana State's response to hurricane disaster relief waned as time passed and urgency disappeared, although the units involved in the projects continue to be connected to the community but with a focus on other issues.

In this study, only a few projects appear to be comprehensive. Both Utah and Ohio State talk about a long-term, broadly based strategy for community engagement. Sichuan University also takes a wide scope, focusing on poverty alleviation in Tibet and Sichuan Province, although the case study does not describe an institution-wide strategy of the same sort as Utah and Ohio State.

What is a region?

The term can mean an official governmentally determined territory (county, township, province), an economically integrated area, or a self-defined sense of shared cultural connection not clearly bounded by geography. The fifteen cases in this study represent these and yet more definitions of region. Several use the official territory approach; Lulea University of Technology's 'ProcessIT Innovations' serves the two northernmost counties of Sweden, for example, while the University of Utah's comprehensive community partnerships serve the Salt Lake City metropolis.

The larger regional approach is encompassed by Newcastle University, which helped to foster a cohesive sense of the North East of England as an industrial area in need of a new sense of purpose and economic strength. Monash University in Australia serves a region defined in part by its absorption of smaller educational institutions within the state of Victoria.

Louisiana State University launched projects in the coastal sections of Louisiana and Mississippi that were ravaged by Hurricanes Katrina and Rita.

A more self-defined approach can encompass both large and small areas. For example, Texas Tech University has outlined its service area as rural communities in the western two-thirds of the state of Texas (a very large geographic area). In contrast, Cornell University's Urban Scholars Program focuses on the social and human services sector of New York City, defined as much by common professional goals as by geography. Ohio State University's urban revitalization was targeted largely at the poor, transient neighborhoods adjacent to the campus; the blighted areas were discouraging students from applying to Ohio State and living on or close to the campus. Thus the characteristics of the area, more than geography, determined the focus of the Ohio State project.

This study, then, lets the university-community partnership define the 'region' most appropriate to its goals. Sometimes the region determines the project (as with the United Way service area surrounding Albany, NY), while in other cases the need for action defines the region to become engaged. In most cases, however, region includes a sense of the people who must work together face-to-face to achieve common goals. In a small physical area, human interaction is relatively easy to organize. In geographically large areas such as western Texas, universities use community partners, multiple technologies, and distributed learning methods to bring people together, even if only virtually. Universities are also the honest broker in many cases, hosting study groups, coordinating committees, teams of student volunteers, and service-learning courses as part of the regional effort.

Common elements

While each case study demonstrates the unique characteristics of the featured institution, the fifteen case studies permit some broad generalizations about public universities and regional development. Four are highlighted here: leadership, partners, finances, and context.

Leadership
Many of the case study authors emphasize the importance of leadership, especially when the goal is university-wide involvement with the community or region. For example, Ohio State University's president created Com-

Table 8.1 Levels of commitment to community engagement

	Level 1 Low relevance	Level 2 Medium relevance	Level 3 High relevance	Level 4 Full integration
Mission	No mention or undefined rhetorical reference	Engagement is part of what we do as educated citizens	Engagement is an aspect of our academic agenda	Engagement is a central and defining characteristic
Leadership (Presidents, Vice Presidents, Deans, Chairs)	Engagement not mentioned as a priority; general rhetorical references to community or society	Expressions that describe institution as asset to community through economic impact	Interest in and support for specific, short-term community projects; engagement discussed as a part of learning and research	Broad leadership commitment to a sustained engagement agenda with ongoing funding support and community input
Promotion, tenure, hiring	Idea of engagement is confused with traditional view of service	Community engagement mentioned; volunteerism or consulting may be included in portfolio	Formal guidelines for defining, documenting and rewarding engaged teaching / research	Community-based research and teaching are valid criteria for hiring and reward
Organization structure and funding	No units focus on engagement or volunteerism	Units may exist to foster volunteerism/community service	Various separate centres and institutes are organized to support engagement; soft funding	Infrastructure exists (with base funding) to support partnerships and widespread faculty/student participation

Student involvement and curriculum	Part of extracurricular student life activities	Organized institutional support for volunteer activity and community leadership development	Opportunity for internships, practice, some service-learning courses	Service-learning and community-based learning integrated across curriculum; linked to learning goals
Faculty involvement	Traditional service defined as campus duties; committees; little support for interdisciplinary work	Pro-bono consulting; community volunteerism acknowledged	Tenured/senior faculty may pursue community-based research; some teach service-learning courses	Community-based research and learning intentionally integrated across disciplines; interdisciplinary work is supported
Community Involvement	Random, occasional, symbolic or limited individual or group involvement	Community representation on advisory boards for departments or schools	Community influences campus through active partnerships, participation in service-learning programmes or specific grants	Community involved in defining, conducting and evaluating community-based research and teaching; sustained partnerships
External communications and fundraising	Community engagement not an emphasis	Stories of students or alumni as good citizens; partnerships are grant dependent	Emphasis on economic impact of institution; public role of centres, institutes, extension	Engagement is integral to fundraising goals; joint grants/gifts with community; base funding

Based on an analysis by Barbara Holland in Kenny *et.al.* (2002)

munity Partners, a not-for-profit organization that handled much of the work of regenerating the area around the campus. Using the categories in Table 8.1, Ohio State may be placed somewhere between the *High Relevance* and *Full Integration* categories (the case study does not discuss faculty and student involvement, although it may well exist). At the University at Albany, the president's office plays a key coordinating role across nine colleges and schools; once again, leadership is demonstrated at the *Full Integration* level. Newcastle University 'rediscovered' its community in the 1990s in part because of a pro vice chancellor who established a network of regional universities in support of local industries. Newcastle involves all elements of the university, from faculty research to complex involvement with community and governmental entities. The case study of Sichuan University in China also emphasizes the power and importance of leadership.

The Council on Competitiveness (2008), in its effort to promote regional development for innovation, makes four recommendations for institutions of higher education. One is 'Make regional development part of the president's personal mission' (pp. 7–8). The Council believes that, even though universities are decentralized organizations, presidents of higher education institutions play a crucial role in setting university priorities. The active commitment of the president is a necessary but not sufficient condition for effective collaboration.

At the University of Utah, community engagement is embedded in the academic programme of the institution, not something done only by administrators or peripheral offices. Priority issues to the community are framed as research questions for faculty and graduate students; narratives by community residents are used as reading material for an interdisciplinary seminar co-taught by university faculty and community residents. Such teaching counts in the regular faculty workload, and community engagement is considered in the promotion and tenure process. This is the only case study where the faculty reward system is explicitly mentioned, thus placing Utah most clearly in the *Full Integration* category.

Braskamp and Wergin (1998, quoted in Wergin 2006, pp. 25–26) outline some of the challenges facing leaders who want to embed community–university partnerships into the academic fabric of the institution:
- Faculty members are not accustomed to the messiness of direct engagement in societal problems.
- Faculty members often lack experiential knowledge of the issues being addressed.

- Faculty engagement in social partnerships creates major personal and professional challenges.
- Collaboration does not occur without the partners spending time together to foster mutual trust.
- Collaboration is not always beneficial.

The case studies present other leadership lessons as well. The authors of Cornell University's Urban Scholars Program express their frustration and anxiety about future funding for the project. In this case the original idea for the programme came from a New York City foundation seeking to train the next generation of public service professionals. Now, years later, the foundation hopes that Cornell will support this successful venture from university funds, but the authors express their disappointment that the university seems not to embrace the Urban Scholars Program sufficiently to integrate this small programme into the larger efforts of the institution. Without commitment from institutional leaders, even very successful activities may not continue.

But leadership is not limited to presidents and provosts. The University of Guadalajara case highlights professors and research scientists becoming policy entrepreneurs, exercising leadership with the local people affected by pollution. Going beyond their mandate – and even their authority at times – Guadalajara faculty help to create new forms of civic involvement to deal with major industries in the affected river basin. In Table 8.1, Guadalajara can be placed somewhere between *Medium* and *High Relevance* with its emphasis on the public role of the university in using its knowledge base to address the economic and environmental needs of Mexican society.

Leadership can come from anyone and everyone in the institution sensitive to changes in the expectations of higher education by the larger society. The challenges and difficulties are well known, but Harloe and Perry (2004) also emphasize the opportunities available to universities willing to embrace the implications of global changes.

> *The shift from universities being largely linked to the reproduction of elites to a broader, more democratic social role means closer working not just with local business, but with local communities too, and this is creating new opportunities for academic work. Similarly, the interdisciplinary pursuit of research in the context of application and in partnership with industry and government also has the potential to lead to*

exciting new areas of research at the ever blurring interface between disciplines and organizations (p. 218).

Reconceptualizing the academic work of the university requires initiative by the intellectual leaders of the university – the faculty – not just the individuals with the most prestigious titles at the institution.

Virtually every case study describes the importance of individuals, not all with high level positions, acting on their dedication to building partnerships between universities and their communities. Small-scale projects, focused on specific problems and involving only a few people, provide much needed support for the communities involved. From an institutional perspective, however, their individual nature and lack of infrastructure leave them in jeopardy. Table 8.1 suggests that institutional commitment must be more than a collection of discrete projects; *Full Integration* requires involvement of the university at every level.

Partners

All successful projects in regional development are partnerships. This is not something that universities can simply do on their own; they must collaborate with stakeholders from government agencies to businesses, not-for-profit organizations and local residents. Too often universities are viewed as institutions acting only in their own self-interest, whether collecting research data or fixing up a disadvantaged neighborhood, rather than working cooperatively with others to develop a shared vision for the future. The most successful partnerships, according to Boucher *et al.* (2003, p. 888), are networks of local institutions, not just individual organizations operating on their own.

A number of the case studies use words like mutuality and reciprocity to describe successful partnerships. For example, Texas Tech University offers degrees in rural areas of the state through distributed delivery using multiple technologies. Each community defines its specific educational and development needs; Texas Tech then works with community partners to create formal written agreements that outline expectations on all sides, including financial terms. These partnerships must be beneficial to all the stakeholders in the agreement. In this regard, Texas Tech is definitely in the *Full Integration* column.

Nanjing University focuses on a different form of partnership, in this case between academic experts and the leaders of the Jiangsu provincial government. Here the cooperation is based on mutual benefit: through the Senior Forum on Jiangsu Development, government leaders receive recommendations on important policy issues from the best minds in the university and beyond, while academics are engaged in real-world issues with the genuine prospect of affecting public decisions. The case study describes the equal status of all parties at the Forum, with no hierarchy distinctions based on title and seniority (and this in a country that tends to be very hierarchical).

Several of the case study authors go so far as to say that universities should not engage in community activities unless there is shared power and reciprocal benefit. It is sometimes hard for students and faculty to move from a service model, in which academic experts tell community groups what would be best for them, to a true partnership in which local citizens have equal voice in the decision-making process. Nanjing's Forum certainly fits this definition, although the scope of the project is limited to high level bureaucrats, faculty and university administrators, much narrower than some of the case studies in this volume.

Mutuality does not necessarily mean identical benefits, however, just a balance of benefits. Extending educational opportunities more widely can mean increased revenue as well the satisfaction of service to the community. Internships and service learning courses contribute to students' education as well as to the wellbeing of the clients being served. And response to disasters, as in the case of Louisiana State University after Hurricanes Katrina and Rita, or Sichuan University after the May 2008 earthquake, reflects humanitarian outpourings as well as academic objectives. At Louisiana State, the response to the devastation occurred in individual courses and departments (thus *Low Relevance* to the university as a whole) while Sichuan's response was more institutional. As Table 8.1 shows, true integration means that university and community work together in sustained ways as equals.

The Council on Competitiveness (2008, p. 10) also reminds universities that partnerships can go beyond community leaders or neighborhood organizations. In urging universities to build long-term relationships within the region, it also recommends that universities partner with other higher education institutions. Different educational institutions in a region typically have different – and often complementary – strengths. Identifying those areas where joint action makes sense and formalizing the relationship opens up new opportunities that institutions could never address on their own and may not even have recognized.

Finances

Partners include funders. All the case studies talk about financing, and in every instance some of the money comes from outside the university, at least as start-up funding. When government agencies contract with academic units to deliver social services, as in the Department of Social Work at Albany, the connection is logical. When Ohio State develops new commercial property near its campus, it uses city and federal authorities to fund construction and infrastructure, with an eye to market-based returns to pay back the bonds and loans. When Luleå University of Technology conducts research related to local industries, the corporations in question often fund both research projects as well as industrial doctoral students to work on the research. When Arizona State University builds a new downtown campus, partially supported by the city of Phoenix, it is contributing to a larger civic goal of revitalizing the centre of the city. When a private foundation supports Cornell's Urban Scholars Program, the expectation is that students will choose public service careers because of the experiences that philanthropic support provides. No university among these case studies supports regional development activities solely from the base budget of the institution.

Some of the case study universities use outside funding for one-time activities such as disaster relief or a particular project, so the issue of long-term financing is not at issue. Most funding agencies, however, do not expect to support regional development activities with 100 per cent support over many years; they often see their funding as seed money or grants for pilot projects which the stakeholders must support in the long run. Among the case studies are several larger comprehensive programmes (Guadalajara, Monash, Newcastle, Sichuan, plus several American institutions) that are multi-year partnerships requiring long-term staffing and operational support. Some universities fund such programmes with a mosaic of grants and contracts, often providing institutional base funding for key staff members to keep the programme running. Looking back at the levels of commitment in Table 8.1, it seems clear that financing of university-community partnerships is a shared responsibility, but one in which truly engaged universities must make serious financial commitments.

In a time of economic contraction in particular, such fiscal commitments are difficult to maintain unless community partnerships are embedded in the core values and fundamental activities of the university. For example, if students in the honours programme are required to complete internships, then that form of engagement will continue regardless of the state of the economy. When community issues are the focus of professors' research projects, then the collaboration will move forward. When the mission of the university includes regional development as a serious priority, then community engagement will not be threatened. But projects that are seen as peripheral, 'third stream' or otherwise not vital will be vulnerable to fiscal crises.

Context

Context is critical, especially when making comparisons across national boundaries. For example, most American public universities have a heritage of public service going back more than a century and a half to the land-grant concept expressed in the Morrill Act of 1862. This national legislation provided public lands to support new universities developed for the agricultural and mechanical arts. The Monash University case highlights the special meaning of the term 'region' in Australia connoting non-metropolitan in a pejorative sense (Beer *et al.*, 2003, p. xi.). Texas Tech's history is one of thinking big, defining a service area larger than most of the states in the United States.

The case study that best demonstrates the importance of context, however, is that of Portugal's expansion of its higher education system in the 1970s and 1980s. First, the nation shifted to a new policy goal of massification after many years of an elitist system. More significant for the theme of this chapter, however, was the desire to expand the university and polytechnic systems geographically to all regions of the country in order to contribute to economic and social development that was more evenly distributed throughout the nation.

The new regional universities were closely linked to the economies of the different regions, from textiles to wine, but the national, European, and world economies were changing at the same time. Textile production was moving to Asia; ceramics manufacturing became less competitive; and increasing desertification in inland regions reduced agricultural productivity. In addition, student demand shifted from traditional industries to professions such as medicine, law, civil engineering, and architecture. Portugal, like many nations, has experienced increasing urbanization with people moving to the major cities of Lisbon and Porto, and students desiring to study in those urban centres. As a result, these exogenous variables created a context in which the strategy of higher education for regional development was not as successful as everyone had hoped.

There is a more fundamental contextual factor which Shi and Chow (in Mohrman *et al.,* 2008, pp. 312–316) identify as 'metapolicy' in the concluding chapter of the ASU/SCU volume. They describe metapolicy as dealing with the functioning of policy-making systems (structure, process, inputs and stipulated outputs) and master policies (overall goals, basic assumptions and conceptual frameworks). Thus, for example, administrative centralization of higher education policy in China and Portugal is a metapolicy that places decision-making power in the hands of government agencies.

In contrast, United States metapolicy puts government control of higher education in the hands of the states rather than the national government, but even there the role of government is limited. Perhaps because the first American colleges and universities were private, history and metapolicy allow individual universities to determine their own mission and vision. US institutions, public and private, have the discretionary power to combine teaching, research and service in ways appropriate to the mission, including their contributions to regional development.

Wiewel and Perry (2009, p. 318) reinforce this point. In comparing case studies of US universities with international institutions engaged with their communities, they conclude that the main deviation between the two sets of cases is a much greater role of individual leadership in the US and the greater institutionalization found elsewhere. The American traditions of individual leadership, as well as grassroots democracy and local autonomy, clearly create differences in the ways universities operate in comparison with peers elsewhere in the world. While Wiewel and Perry do not use these words, context matters.

Shi and Chow (in Mohrman *et al.,* 2009, p. 314) go on to say that the scope and intensity of strategic thinking are constrained by the context in which they are situated. When metapolicy calls for central control, it is difficult for universities in those countries to articulate an independent vision for regional development, and to manage the interactive relationships between university goals and regional development. The case of China in particular raises a dilemma for many developing countries: How can public universities effectively promote regional development in light of policy constraints? (p. 315).

This point about central control is reinforced by Goddard and Puukka (2008) in describing the OECD study of regional development and higher education:

> *The preceding discussion has implicitly accepted a network*
> *model for moving toward higher education and regional*

development systems. It has not advocated a centralized steering approach whereby the national government directs individual HEIs to undertake particular tasks in specific locations. Nor for reasons partly relating to the problem of appropriate metrics has a market-driven model based on performance or output measures been proposed. Rather the emphasis has been on a bottom up approach of collaborative working where all the partners appreciate the mutual benefits of coming together. Insofar as steering occurs, the approach favoured has been of peer learning through shared practice (p. 37).

The context, then, according to Goddard and Puukka (2008) is a national framework which facilitates conjoint action at the regional or sub-national level and encourages greater direct participation of citizens, businesses, educators and universities. They conclude:

Without this empowerment it is difficult to see how the potential for higher education institutions to actively contribute to regional development can be realized. With the right conditions, regional engagement can become a crucible within which more dynamic and open higher education institutions can be forged, both responding to and shaping developments in the wider society. (pp. 37–38).

Conclusion and lessons learned

The fifteen case studies in *Public Universities and Regional Development* tell fifteen different stories about universities and their involvement in the communities around them. Some of the criteria for analysis are described in the section above but there are also observations and generalizations to be derived from the cases as a group.

Assessment

The case studies illuminate strategic actions by university leaders, examples of creative partnerships, and challenges faced by those involved in regional development activities. It is interesting to note, however, that the case studies often do not address evaluation of the activities in question. In some cases, such as reduction of crime or increased rates of student residency in neighborhoods surrounding the campus, quantitative measures are easy to apply. But more often than not, assessment is limited to activities of engagement rather than their ultimate impact on desired outcomes. And sometimes even those desired outcomes are not clearly defined.

When issues of funding are at stake, however, programmes need more than evidence of activity – they need results. In what ways were the lives of elderly people improved? To what extent can economic development in Chongqing be attributed to the university? How many hurricane victims resumed normal life? Are people more empowered to effect change in their communities? What is the reduction in the levels of pollution in the Ayuquila–Armería river basin? How many people in rural Texas improved their own lives and the lives of their small communities because of the additional education they received? Most of the case studies do not provide real assessment.

Scale and scope

Universities need to be clear about their reasons for becoming engaged in community partnerships and regional development; projects and programmes should be commensurate with the goal. If the desired outcome is poverty alleviation, then the university's commitment must be long-term; if the goal is undergraduate awareness through service learning, then a series of discrete courses may be enough. Too often, though, the stated objective far exceeds the programmatic resources devoted to achieving the goal.

Table 8.1, in outlining levels of commitment to community engagement, implies that *Full Integration* should be the objective. This may not always be the case. A university just beginning its involvement with the community should probably start with small projects to develop expertise and to win the confidence of non-university partners. Without sufficient permanent funding, a university cannot hope to accomplish all that is listed under *Full Integration*. Without infrastructure, even people of good will cannot achieve their goals. The great danger, however, is that people of commitment and good will have high hopes that simply are not realistic.

Leadership and followership

Leaders are usually defined by the positions they hold – president, rector, director, vice chancellor, and so on. The case studies certainly suggest that *Full Integration* is not possible without strong commitment from the top. Mutual and reciprocal partnerships require formal agreements, staffing, financial allocations, but most of all the time and attention of individuals with the power to make commitments on behalf of the university.

But a president cannot wave a magic wand and turn a university into fully integrated community partner. Faculty and staff must be, or become, committed to engagement; they are the individuals who will turn a mission statement into reality. And the direction engagement can flow from the bottom up as well as from top down. Wiewel and Perry (2009) conclude from their international case studies that individual university leaders were not especially important in a set of campus-community real estate development projects. Rather, they reflect, 'What is striking about the present cases is how embedded they appear to be in the structure and institutional relations of their [universities]' (p. 316). Thus commitment from the top may not be essential, although usually quite valuable, to the success of community-university partnerships.

While most of the case studies do not provide full institutional histories, in several instances the university commitment grew out of the personal passion of individual professors and mid-level administrators. Only when the value of involvement with the community became apparent did the senior administration take on the mission of participation in regional development. Leadership can come from many sources, and leadership requires followers who believe in the mission.

The Kellogg Commission report, *Returning to our roots: The engaged institution* (Kellogg Commission, 1999), provides an appropriate ending to this chapter: 'With the resources and superbly qualified professors and staff on our campuses, we can organize our institutions to serve both local and national needs in a more coherent and effective way. We can and must do better.' (p. 3).

The case studies demonstrate the growth in commitment to engagement and provide evidence that many universities are indeed doing better than a decade ago. But engaged institutions are facing ever more complex social, economic, political, national security and technological problems in the 21st century.

References

Beer, A., Maude, A. and Pritchard, A. (2003) *Developing Australia's regions: Theory and practice.* Sydney: UNSW Press.

Boucher, G., Conway, C. and van der Meer, E. (2003) 'Tiers of engagement by universities in their region's development', *Regional Studies* 37(9), 887–897.

Braskamp, L. A. and Wergin, J. F. (1998) 'Forming new social partnerships', in W. G. Tierney (ed.), *The responsive university: Restructuring for high performance* (pp. 62–91) Baltimore: Johns Hopkins University Press.

Brukardt, M. J., Percy, S. L. and Zimpher, N. L. (2006) 'Moving forward along new lines', in Percy *et al.* (eds.), *Creating a new kind of university* (pp. 3–22) Bolton, MA: Anker Publishing Co.

Council on Competitiveness. (2006) *Cooperate: A practitioner's guide for effective alignment of regional development and higher education.* Washington, D.C.: Council on Competitiveness.

Goddard, J. and Puukka, J. (2008) 'The engagement of higher education institutions in regional development: An overview of the opportunities and challenges', *Higher Education Management and Policy,* 20(2), 11–38.

Harloe, M. and Perry, B. (2004) 'Universities, localities and regional development: The emergence of the 'Mode 2' university?' *International Journal of Urban and Regional Research*, 28(1), 212–223.

Kellogg Commission (1999) *Returning to our roots: The engaged institution.* Retrieved 26 January 2010 from the Association of Public and Land-grant Universities database, http://www.aplu.org/NetCommunity/Page.aspx?pid =305. Also http://www.eric.ed.gov/ > ERIC#ED426676 Accessed 28 September 2010.

Kenny, M., Simon, L. A. K., Kiley-Brabeck, K. and Lerner, R. M. (eds.) (2002) *Learning to serve: Promoting civil society through service learning.* Dortrecht: Kluwer Academic Publishers.

Mohrman, K., Shi, J., Feinblatt, S. E. and Chow, K. W. (eds.) (2009) *Public universities and regional development* (Chengdu, China: Sichuan University Press) This book is also available from the University Design Consortium at Arizona State University.

OECD (Organization for Economic Co-operation and Development) (2007) *Higher education and regions: Globally competitive, locally engaged.* Paris: OECD.

Percy, S. L., Zimpher, N. L. and Brukardt, M. J. (eds.) (2006) *Creating a new kind of university: Institutionalizing community-university partnerships.* Bolton, MA: Anker Publishing Co.

Wergin, J.F. (2006) 'Elements of effective community engagement', in S.L.

Percy *et al.* (eds.) *Creating a new kind of university*, 23–42. Bolton, MA: Anker Publishing Co.

Wiewel, W. and Perry, D. C. (Eds.) (2009) *Global universities and urban development: Case studies and analysis.* Armonk, NY: M.E. Sharpe.

Chapter 9

How to strengthen the third mission of the university: The case of the University of British Columbia Learning Exchange

Margo Fryer

Introduction

This chapter provides an overview of the University of British Columbia (UBC) Learning Exchange, an institutional community engagement initiative that has been evolving over the past ten years. The chapter describes some of the major challenges that have been encountered and the lessons that have been learned. The case of the Learning Exchange demonstrates that a commitment to community engagement can take root in the academy. The Learning Exchange experience suggests that this commitment grows as a result of persistent, strategic 'on-the-ground' actions taken within the context of rhetorical and financial support at the institutional level.

The UBC Learning Exchange: From seeds to blossoms to fruit

In 1998, as part of a visioning exercise undertaken by its new President, UBC made a commitment to further the social, cultural, and economic interests of the community beyond the boundaries of its own campus (UBC, 1998). Input from leaders in the local community persuaded the President to begin acting on that commitment by establishing a physical presence in Vancouver's Downtown Eastside, an inner-city community whose seemingly intractable social problems are well-known. The mainstream media focuses on stories about the 'poorest postal code in Canada' that reinforce stereotypes: strung-out addicts injecting drugs on the street, homeless people settling in for the night in the doorways of vacant storefronts, and locals 'known to the police' being involved in late-night assaults in one of the many bars in the area.

When UBC announced its intentions at a press conference in the Downtown Eastside in the autumn of 1998, it was surprised at the reaction. Community activists and leaders of large social service agencies in the neighbourhood were sceptical about this move by the university. What could a large, research-intensive educational institution offer a poor, marginalized community? What were the university's motivations? Acts of resistance such as angry letters to the university's President prompted a major local newspaper to print a front page story with the headline, 'UBC Forced to Cool Outpost Plans' (*Vancouver Sun*, 1999). To its credit, UBC did not abandon the effort, but instead undertook a community consultation to discover what people living and working in the Downtown Eastside thought UBC could contribute and to elicit their advice about how UBC should proceed. That consultation revealed a range of opinion about UBC's proposed initiative: at one end of the spectrum were stories of perceived exploitation by university researchers and declarations that UBC was not welcome in the Downtown Eastside; at the other extreme we found excitement about the resources that could become available and appreciation for the university's willingness to engage with the community. There were enough people and organizations that were at least willing to give the university a chance that UBC decided to proceed with a number of activities that were in line with suggestions made by the community as well as the goals of the university (see Fryer and Lee, 1999).

The UBC Learning Exchange began its work in the autumn of 1999 with the creation of the Learning Exchange Trek Volunteer Program. Thirty student volunteers were placed in eight non-profit organizations and two elementary schools in the Downtown Eastside. In the fall of 2000, we opened a small storefront a few blocks away from the epicentre of the open drug scene and began offering free computer access to local residents.

Students' enthusiastic response to the opportunity to learn while volunteering in the Downtown Eastside resulted in the number of student participants in the Trek Program doubling every year until 2004 when enrolment had to be limited. In 2002, the Learning Exchange began working with faculty members to integrate students' volunteer work into academic course work, an approach to experiential learning called 'Community Service Learning'

(CSL) (For an overview of the pedagogical rationale for CSL see Saltmarsh, 1996; for definitions of CSL and an overview of research on its outcomes, see Eyler and Giles, 1999).

During spring break in 2002, the Learning Exchange collaborated with the University of Guelph to do the first Reading Week CSL project in Canada. A group of 19 students from both universities spent four days in an immersion-type experience learning about community development from activists in the Downtown Eastside while helping the oldest community garden in Vancouver get ready for the spring growing season. In 2006, the UBC–Community Learning Initiative (UBC–CLI) was created, with funding from the J.W. McConnell Family Foundation and UBC, to develop innovative approaches to course-based (curricular) CSL. With the growing integration of students' community-based activity into course work and the focus among many faculties on providing students with research experience, students also began doing Community-Based Research (CBR), which, at minimum, is the conduct of research that addresses questions or issues identified by the community not the academy (Stoecker, 2001).

By the 2009–2010 academic year, the number of students engaging in the community through the Learning Exchange and the UBC–CLI had grown to about 2,000 per year. Students from a variety of disciplines act as literacy tutors, sports coaches, and science or math mentors in inner city schools in Vancouver as well as helping non-profit organizations deliver services in the Downtown Eastside and other parts of the Vancouver region (e.g. providing meals and nutrition education to low-income women). In addition, students from the business school have begun to work with entrepreneurs and business development agencies in small, resource-dependent centres in the province to help these communities diversify their economic base. The success of these CSL initiatives and UBC's increasing emphasis on improving the student learning experience have inspired the university to make the further growth of UBC's CSL and CBR programmes a major strategic priority (UBC, 2009, 2010).

Learning Exchange storefront programmes have also grown substantially since their modest beginnings. The afternoon computer drop-in has been operating at capacity since 2003. We began offering free computer training in 2002 with financial support from HSBC Bank Canada and now train more than 200 people in basic and advanced computer skills every year. In 2004 we started an innovative ESL conversation programme which was designed by graduate students from UBC's planning school in collaboration with local residents who frequented the afternoon drop-in. This programme relies on low-income, English-speaking residents of the Downtown Eastside to act as facilitators of small conversation groups. The facilitators are trained and supported by Learning Exchange staff, with assistance from UBC's English Language Institute. The programme enables immigrants to practice their conversational English in a low-pressure, peer-led environment. In the 2008–2009 academic year, more than 400 immigrants took part in the ESL programme guided by 55 facilitators. Both the computer training and ESL programmes are in very high demand despite the fact that we do no little or no formal advertising. Participants come because of word-of-mouth recommendations from friends, neighbours, family members, and professionals in the community.

In the fall of 2008, the Learning Exchange relocated five blocks south to a larger storefront. This location will make continued growth in our ongoing programmes possible as well as allowing new educational offerings to be developed, including ad-hoc, short-term events. In the past, such offerings have included music appreciation classes, self-advocacy classes, film discussion nights, creative writing workshops led by UBC graduate students, and seminars given by UBC social science faculty.

While this brief description of the growth in Learning Exchange programmes may give the impression that our evolution has been steady and effortless, the reality has been otherwise. Five evolutionary phases, analogous to the development of a garden, can be described. The first phase (1998 to 2000) involved turning the soil and planting seeds. The soil was rocky and the climate inhospitable. The seeds of hundreds of ideas were planted; most of them dried up and blew away. We had to focus on learning about the nature of the environment and how to adapt our tools and techniques. It was sweaty, back-breaking work. The second phase (2001 to 2002) saw a small number of seeds germinate and take root. External donors provided crucial support. Stories about the value of CSL began to spread. We quietly went about our business and did not behave in the disrespectful, exploitative ways the sceptics had predicted. From 2002 to 2005 a third phase, of weed-like proliferation, occurred. The Trek Program, the Reading Week CSL projects, and the storefront programmes were all operating at or beyond capacity. The garden looked like a meadow replete with blooming wild flowers. This rapid, growth led to the fourth phase (2006 to 2007), a time of reflection. We came to realize that we had to bring order to the profusion of blooms and do some judicious pruning and weeding. Between 2007 and 2009, the Learning Exchange was in a regeneration phase. We reconfigured the garden based on a much deeper understanding of the relevant growing conditions, the types of plants that will be most nourishing and beautiful, and the nature of the resources we need to keep the garden healthy.

We have entered the next phase in our evolution: a period of further growth that will be strongly rooted in compost-rich soil, where the existing programmes form the main structural elements of the garden and there is ample room for innovation and experimentation. A strategic plan for the advancement of CSL and CBR at UBC has been completed (UBC, 2010). One of the key goals in the plan is to embed these approaches to community-based experiential learning in the academic fabric of the university. The implementation of this plan will lead to a significant increase in the number of students who engage in CSL and CBR programmes (rising to about 4,000 students or 10 per cent of the student population annually by 2014). The plan aims to inspire a strong focus on the quality of the student learning experience coupled with careful attention to the impacts of students' work in the community. The next stage in the evolution of the Downtown Eastside storefront will take advantage of the trust and credibility that has been built over the past ten years. We will focus on building social capital using community development approaches that emphasize assets and the giving of gifts rather than deficits and the fixing of problems (Kretzmann and McKnight, 1993).

Contributors to success

The Learning Exchange has succeeded because of many factors. We have been very careful to follow the advice we were given during the 1999 community consultation: To work in partnership with organizations that were already active and respected in the community; to avoid duplicating what others were already doing; to avoid competing with existing organizations for funding; and to listen respectfully rather than giving the impression we had all the answers (Fryer and Lee, 1999). The partnerships we have formed with other community organizations (including large and small non-profit social service or health organizations, public schools, advocacy groups, and small businesses) as well as various units within the university have been particularly crucial to our success. This reliance on collaborative relationships is the foundation of our success but, as will be discussed later, it also presents challenges.

Another important contributor to our success has been the enthusiastic response of students to the opportunity to engage in the Downtown Eastside. Students have been effective ambassadors in both the community and the university. In the early years, the energy and skill that students brought to their CSL placements and projects won over many of the sceptics in the community. The stories students told on campus about how their community experiences had brought their theoretical learning alive changed the minds of many of the sceptics in the university (for examples of quotations from students involved in Reading Week projects see http://www.learningexchange.ubc.ca/trek_program/reading/archive.html). The exponential growth in student participation was proof that students were hungry for the opportunity to connect their classroom learning to real-life issues.

We have intentionally enlisted students as allies in the effort to advance CSL at UBC. On occasions when the Learning Exchange has opportunities to talk about CSL with university administrators, prospective donors, media, and student groups, we typically ask students to speak. When we first were introducing the CSL approach to faculty members, we asked students to identify professors they thought would be receptive to the pedagogy. The strategic use of stories and quotations from students, and colourful photographs and videos of students working in community settings managed to, as one colleague put it, 'capture people's imagination.'

One of the primary factors behind the success of Learning Exchange store-front programmes is the nature of the environment that has been created. In a neighbourhood where many people feel they are constantly under surveillance (e.g., by landlords, social workers, health care providers, or police), we have been careful to create an open, respectful space where people can pursue their own learning-oriented activities without having to justify themselves. This does not mean that anything goes. From the beginning, staff have been careful to set an expectation that when people come to the storefront, they come to work on something (e.g., doing Internet research, connecting with family via email, writing poetry or fiction, or working on job searches) and/or they contribute something to the environment (e.g., by engaging in dialogue with other drop-in patrons about current community issues). By now, the patrons themselves do as much to maintain norms around respectful and productive behaviour as the staff do. It has been observed by both patrons and professionals in the community that the Learning Exchange has fewer incidents of problematic behaviour than many settings in the Downtown Eastside. Patrons describe the storefront as 'an oasis' and 'a refuge.' The association with the university is also important. For many patrons, the fact that the Learning Exchange is part of a large mainstream educational institution gives it a cachet. People feel proud to be participants in its programmes. (Fryer, 2007). But it is important not to romanticize the situation. Some patrons seem to have a love–hate relationship with the Learning Exchange. They may be regular visitors at the storefront, but they remain cynical about the university as an institution and are quick to point out instances where they perceive we have been disrespectful or used our power inappropriately.

In addition to being careful about the quality of the learning environments we are creating, the Learning Exchange staff team has followed a set of core practices that have proved to be important. All our programmes have been developed using iterative cycles of planning, action, and evaluation or reflection. We regularly elicit feedback from programme participants and stakeholders and have been doing this long enough that our colleagues are willing to continue engaging in activities like annual evaluation interviews because they know we will make adjustments in our practices and programmes based on their feedback. We also are careful to collaboratively identify shared goals for all our activities and use this sense of shared purpose as a reference point when difficulties arise, as they inevitably do. As part of an institution of higher learning, we consider curiosity to be a foundational practice. As an initiative that crosses many different kinds of boundaries, inclusive dialogue is another core practice.

The other practice that has been crucial to the success of the Learning Exchange is careful risk-taking. This is not a straightforward practice; it is not always easy to determine the appropriate point of balance between risk-taking and caution. But it is an important practice to engage in intentionally, otherwise unredeemable mistakes could be made. The calculation of risk and benefit has been different at different times in our evolution. For example, in the early years, with a small, nimble staff team and many people expecting us to fail, we could pursue ideas, assess their viability, and then abandon them if necessary, and the consequences were minimal. Now, the Learning Exchange has a higher public profile and so we have more to lose by failing. But we also have a strong track record, and so can take risks that we could not take a few years ago (e.g., we can comment publicly on issues in the Downtown Eastside whereas several years ago this would have been seen as presumptuous).

The last factor that needs to be mentioned is perhaps the most important. From the beginning, the Learning Exchange has received strong rhetorical and financial support from UBC's administration. The Learning Exchange was created ten years ago as part of the expression of a new institutional vision. That vision is now in its third iteration. The commitment to the kinds of activities the Learning Exchange has pursued has become stronger with each revisiting of the vision, such that Community Engagement is now one of the key commitments that faculties and administrative units are expected to honour (UBC, 2010). If the Learning Exchange had not been operating within the context of this larger institutional vision and impetus for change, our story would likely be very different.

Building collaborative relationships

As stated earlier, the success of the Learning Exchange is rooted in its working relationships with people and organizations both in the community and within the university. But working relationships are not always harmonious and productive. The source of our strength is also the source of our greatest challenge. In the literature on community-university engagement, it has become a mantra that the work is all about relationships (e.g., Wiewel and Lieber, 1998; Strand *et al.*, 2003; Stoecker and Tryon, 2009). Many authors offer rules and guidelines for building effective partnerships between universities and communities (e.g., Baker *et al.*, 1999; Baum, 2000; Bringle and Hatcher, 2002; Strand *et al.*, 2003; Leiderman *et al.*, 2003; Freeman 2003). Common themes are that the partners should identify shared goals and objectives, clearly define roles and responsibilities, and communicate regularly about successes and challenges.

These guidelines are useful but the Learning Exchange experience indicates that they are not enough. Successful community-university engagement is not only a function of what people do (which can be regulated to some extent by rules and guidelines) but also (and perhaps primarily) it is a function of *who people are*. Does a person's sense of humour, personal style, warmth, openness, and energy level 'fit' with the comparable qualities of a key person in the collaborating unit or organization? If not, no amount of rule-following or references to formal agreements will create a sustainable relationship.

This challenge of achieving a good fit among the individuals involved in community-university relationships is heightened by differences in the cultures of the academy and the community (Bacon, 2002; Freeman, 2003; Stoecker and Tryon, 2009). When working relationships develop smoothly and easily, it is often because the people involved are tacitly playing by the same rules guided by a shared world view. The conclusions we come to about the kind of person someone is and whether we can work with him/her are often influenced by the cultural expectations and norms that we have internalized.

For example, if a professor and the executive director of a mental health drop-in centre need to make a decision about whether to have students lead a field trip to a museum for a group of people with addiction and mental health issues, their analysis may be affected by factors rooted in their different work cultures. The executive director may argue that this would be a great learning opportunity for everyone based on her agency's philosophy of empowerment and capacity-building. The professor may argue that the activity would be too risky based on predominant views in the academy regarding student naivety as well as mainstream cultural stereotypes about people with mental illness and addictions. In keeping with academic norms around how to articulate arguments, the professor may take a lot of time during a meeting with the executive director to explain all the aspects of his concerns and may demand that the decision be delayed until he can think further about the question. The executive director may feel that the professor is being condescending in thinking she needs to hear all the ins and outs of his perspective and assuming that she is blind to the issue of risk or does not know what her clients are likely to do in the context of the activity she is proposing. Working in a culture where decisions need to be made quickly and then implemented, the executive director may be dismissive of the professor's concerns. Both people may come away from this meeting deciding they cannot work with the other. The professor may be judged as arrogant and timid while the executive director is judged to be irresponsible and impatient. In this case, what are essentially cross-cultural differences come to be seen as failings of the person from the other culture. And a great learning opportunity is lost.

While neither 'the academy' nor 'the community' are monolithic, homo-geneous entities, the Learning Exchange experience suggests that the following factors constitute some important differences between community and academic settings:
* propensities for teamwork and collaboration vs. solo effort and competitiveness;
* the meaning of time (e.g., there is often an acute sense of urgency in community organizations that is lacking in the academy) and expectations around the pace of work;
* perception of and tolerance for risk, uncertainty, and error;

- perspectives on the value of different ways of knowing (e.g., indigenous knowledge gained through life experience vs. scientific knowledge);
- perceptions of when it is time for action vs. time for thought or analysis.

Our experience indicates that successful community-university engagement requires an understanding of the cross-cultural dynamics that may be operating in any given interaction as well as the co-creation of 'hybrid' cultural spaces where people can ground their interactions in shared norms, practices, and ways of making meaning. It is not enough to simply follow rules for effective partnerships or hope for the more or less accidental convergence of individuals who easily find common ground. Neither is it reasonable to expect people on one side of the cultural divide to adapt completely to the norms and traditions of the other. In order to rise to this challenge of co-creating new shared cultural spaces, a new guiding metaphor is required.

Community-university relationships as complex adaptive systems

The Learning Exchange experience of the dynamics of community–university relationship-building has prompted us to question the utility of the metaphor that seems to be guiding the field of community-university engagement. The metaphor of 'partnership' evokes an image of relationships where the power dynamics are relatively stable and where there are fixed, clear agreements about roles and decision-making processes. After years of working directly with more than 50 different community organizations of various types, we can confidently say that these conditions rarely exist. Instead, our work is characterized by change, uncertainty, and volatile power dynamics.

As a result of our experiences, the Learning Exchange is moving towards relying on metaphors related to complex living systems for inspiration and guidance. Rather than having the work of the Learning Exchange guided by industrial-era metaphors where structures are rigid and hierarchical and the domains of university and community are conceived as separate, monolithic entities that need to be bridged, we are finding it more fruitful to use metaphors arising from the fields of biology, ecology, and living systems. These metaphors highlight the importance of building strong communication links among actors in the network as a crucial determinant of the network's ability to function and adapt to changing circumstances. Thinking within the framework of these different metaphors generates questions about how to recognize and build on the strengths within each particular network or system with which we engage and what environmental conditions need to be in place to support success in that particular context. These metaphors also stimulate questions about the role of rules in the creation of a network or system (e.g., in complex adaptive systems, effective rules come from the ground up not from the top down) (Kauffman, 1995; Waldrop, 1992; Westley *et al.*, 2006).

Metaphors relating to complex adaptive systems also suggest different ways of thinking about how cultural, organizational, and personal change can occur. For example, rather than expecting that the growth of community–university engagement will occur primarily through the implementation of top-down institutional policies and the work of staff members who act as bridges between the university and the community, the metaphor of complex adaptive systems suggests that change can occur through the contagious influence of individual champions, the creation of fertile conditions for collaboration, including the articulation of context-specific, ground-up rules for engagement, and the co-creation of 'hybrid' cultural spaces. Rather than the focus being on programmes per se, the unit of concern becomes the network of actors engaged in a particular CSL or CBR project or activity. This allows the crucial roles played by students to gain prominence, rather than attention being focused only on the relationships between instructors and professionals from community organizations – those who traditionally hold institutional power and authority. The role of centralized units like the Learning Exchange becomes that of a supportive facilitator of the networks of students, instructors, and community organizations who are doing CSL and CBR rather than being directly involved in planning and implementing these projects.

The overarching value of the complex adaptive system metaphor is that it explicitly acknowledges the diversity and complexity that exists within both the university and the community. This metaphor makes it clear that the terrain of activity is one where change is to be expected and the challenge of adapting to crises and opportunities in the environment needs to be embraced.

The play of power

The kinds of activities that the Learning Exchange has been facilitating tend not to be highly valued in most academic environments. Community outreach programmes, CSL, and CBR and other forms of applied research are seen as marginal activities associated more with the service mission of universities than with their core teaching or research missions. The field of community-university engagement is characterized by attempts to persuade the academic mainstream that universities should be doing the right thing and engaging more with communities to solve the critical social, environmental, and economic problems the world is facing. Advocates strive to bring community engagement into the heart of the academy (e.g., Furco, 2001; Harkavy, 2006) and to have its practitioners recognized according to traditional academic standards including those applied to promotion and tenure decisions (e.g., Checkoway, 2001).

There is an irony in the fact that UBC's entry into the Downtown Eastside brought ideas and intentions which themselves were marginalized within the university into a community that is on the social, economic, and political margins of Canadian society. Despite the fact that power relations are at the forefront of people's minds in the Downtown Eastside, no one in the community seems to be aware that the Learning Exchange itself started out as a marginalized entity or that it has been slowly moving from the margins to the centre. This is true both in relation to its position in the university and its position in the community. This movement has been made possible, not by rhetoric or debate but by action – action that has been consistent and sustained over a significant period of time and action that has brought more and more people into its orbit every year.

There are three obvious lessons here for the field of community-university engagement. First, marginality is relative. No matter how marginalized a community engagement practitioner might feel in the academy, when he/she goes out into the community, he/she carries the power and status of the university. People in poor, marginalized communities are acutely sensitive to perceived (and actual) oppression or exploitation by outside institutions with positional power. Framing an initiative as 'service' in this context would be lethal because of the word's association with the tradition of noblesse oblige. Framing the initiative as an opportunity for engagement and reciprocal learning is an improvement, but the fact that the university has so much more societal status, institutional authority, and financial capacity than its 'partners' in the community cannot be forgotten.

Second, community-university engagement is a messy process that requires perseverance. As noted, UBC's strong institutional commitment and willingness to accept risk has been instrumental to the success of the Learning Exchange. That relationships with communities need to be sustained over the long-term is one of the often-cited rules of the community engagement game. In practice, this means there is a constant tension between consistency and adaptability. As with complex adaptive systems, there are times when community-university engagement initiatives hover in the space at the edge of chaos. This space is full of power but is uncomfortable.

This observation is linked to the third lesson: There may not be positional power at the margins but there is enormous emergent power. In order to move the field of community-university engagement forward, this power needs to be recognized, embraced, and mobilized. For community engagement to move from the margins to the centre of the academy, many aspects of academic culture and practice will need to change. But there are allies waiting to be enlisted. Community organizations and students can be effective champions for community-university engagement. More attention should be paid to the question of how to mobilize these untapped resources. While advocates for community engagement have concerned themselves with the question of how to legitimize or institutionalize community-based activities such as CSL in the academy (e.g. Butin, 2006; Hollander *et al.*, 2001; Stoecker, 2008), the field seems not to have recognized that the issue of legitimacy is as relevant in the community as it is in the academy. Researchers in the field have only recently begun to respond to the call issued by authors such as Cruz and Giles (2000) to redress the neglect of community perspectives and concerns (e.g., Stoecker and Tryon, 2009).

This lack of attention to the need to build support for community-university engagement within communities and among students and the concomitant neglect of the dormant power residing in these two stakeholder groups is the Achilles heel in the community-university engagement body. Not only does this inattention make us vulnerable to charges of hypocrisy but the hubris at its root puts the whole movement at risk. We who practice and advocate for community-university engagement must examine our own assumptions about power and knowledge. We must shift the focus from traditional forms of positional power (including our own) and learn to catalyse the emergent power of the collaborative networks we seek to create. Only then will the enormous transformative potential of community-university engagement be ignited.

References

Bacon, N. (2002) 'Differences in faculty and community partners' theories of learning', *Michigan Journal of Community Service Learning*, 9, 34–44.

Baker, E.A., Homan, S., Schonhoff, R. and Kreutner, M. (1999) 'Principles of practice for academic/practice/community research partnerships', *American Journal of Preventive Medicine*, 16(3S), 86–93.

Baum, H. (2000) 'Fantasies and realities in university-community partnerships', *Journal of Planning Education and Research*, 20, 234–246.

Bringle, R. and Hatcher, J. (2002) 'Campus-community partnerships: The terms of engagement', *Journal of Social Issues*, 58(3), 503–516.

Butin, D. (2006) 'Disciplining service learning: Institutionalization and the case for community studies', *International Journal of Teaching and Learning in Higher Education*, 18(1), 57–64.

Checkoway, B. (2001) 'Renewing the civic mission of the American research university', *The Journal of Higher Education*, 72(2), 125–147.

Cruz, N. and Giles, D. (2000) 'Where's the community in service-learning research?' *Michigan Journal of Community Service Learning*, Special Issue, 28–34.

Eyler, J. and Giles, D. (1999) *Where's the learning in service-learning?* San Francisco: Jossey-Bass Publishers.

Freeman, N. (2003) *A meeting of minds: A handbook for community-campus engagement*. Seattle: Community–Campus Partnerships for Health.

Fryer, M. (2007) 'Moving from the ivory tower to the community', *Academic Matters*, 14-15.

Fryer, M. and Lee, B. (1999) *Challenge and promise: Report of summer student community consultation*. The *University of British Columbia's Downtown Eastside Initiative*. Vancouver: University of British Columbia.

Furco, A. (2001) 'Advancing service-learning at research universities', *New Directions for Higher Education*, 114, 67–78.

Harkavy, I. (2006), 'The role of universities in advancing citizenship and social justice in the 21st century', *Education, Citizenship and Social Justice*, 1(1), 5–37.

Hollander, E. L., Saltmarsh, J., and Ziotkowski, E. (2001) 'Indicators of engagement', in M. E. Kenny *et al.* (eds.) *Learning to serve: Promoting civil society through service-learning*, 31–49. Dordrecht: Kluwer Academic Publishers.

Kauffman, S. (1995) *At home in the universe: The search for laws of self-organization and complexity*. New York: Oxford University Press.

Kretzmann, J. P. and McKnight, J. L. (1993) *Building communities from the inside out*. Chicago: ACTA Publications.

Leiderman, S., Furco, A., Zapf, J., and Goss, M. (2002) *Building partnerships with college campuses: Community perspectives*. Washington DC: The Council of Independent Colleges.

Saltmarsh, J. (1996) 'Education for critical citizenship: John Dewey's contribution to the pedagogy of community service learning', *Michigan Journal of Community Service Learning*, 3(1), 13–21.

Stoecker, R. (2001) A report to the Corella and Betram F. Bonner Foundation and Campus Compact: Community-based research: The next new thing'. University of Toledo.

Stoecker, R. (2008) Challenging institutional barriers to community-based research. *Action Research*, 6(1), 49–67.

Stoecker, R. and Tryon, E. A., with Hilgendorf, A. (2009) *The unheard voices: Community organizations and service learning*. Philadelphia: Temple University Press.

Strand, H., Marullo, S., Cutforth, N., Stoecker, R., and Donohue, P. (2003) *Community-based research in higher education*. San Francisco: Jossey-Bass.

UBC (University of British Columbia) (1998) *Trek 2000: A vision for the 21st century*. Vancouver: The President's Office, University of British Columbia.

UBC (University of British Columbia) (2009) *Place and promise: The UBC plan*. Vancouver: The President's Office, University of British Columbia. http://strategicplan.ubc.ca/

UBC (2010) *Strategic plan for the advancement of community service learning and community-based research*. Vancouver: University of British Columbia, www.csl.ubc.ca, *Vancouver Sun*, 1999 (exact date unknown).

Waldrop, M. (1992) *Complexity: The Emerging science at the edge of order and chaos*. New York: Simon and Schuster.

Westley, F., Zimmerman, B., and Patton, M. (2006). *Getting to maybe: How the world is changed*. Toronto: Random House Canada.

Wiewel, W. and Lieber, M. (1998) 'Goal achievement, relationship building, and incrementalism: The challenges of university-community partnerships', *Journal of Planning Education and Research*, 17, 291–301.

Chapter 10

The university-based researcher in indigenous communities: Participatory research as a dialogue for redefining the 'other' in university-community relations

Seth A. Agbo

Introduction

The academic view that has increasingly dominated research is that indigenous communities are 'Others' who dwell in educational 'borderlands'. Quinnan (1997) describes significant 'Otherness' as 'a nameless, faceless attribute forced on disadvantaged groups different from the majority because of race, ethnicity, gender, class, or age' (p. 33). Similarly, hooks (1990), describes the concept of the 'Other' as follows:

> No need to hear your voice when I talk about you better than you can speak about yourself . . . only tell me about your pain. I want to know your story. And then I will tell it back to you in a new way. Tell it back to you in a way that it has become mine, my own. Re-writing you, I write myself anew. I am still the author, authority. I am still the coloniser, the speak subject, and you are now the centre of my talk. (p. 153).

Similarly, speaking to relations of domination, Giroux (1994) describes Western culture as 'a one-dimensional Eurocentric academic canon, the autonomous subject as the sovereign source of truth, and forms of high culture which maintain sexist, racist, homophobic, and class-specific relations of domination' (p. 30).

From its birth in twelfth century Italy and France to its colonization of the modern developing world, the university maintains a tenacious endurance over time with a stubborn resistance to change in spite of external pressures and internal transformations (Altbach, 1992; Perkin, 1984). By tradition as an elite institution, the university strives to remain protected from external interference and therefore unwilling to break the cultural mystique and behavioural codes built over time. One of such mystiques is to maintain some form of social differentiation, with some parts of society valued or rewarded than others. The degree of such differentiation and its significance for the way research is conducted varies dramatically across research populations and within research paradigms. Moreover, there are many different bases or criteria for such differentiation. Among the most common are age, race, ethnicity, regional origin, sex, lineage, and income (Quinnan, 1997). Both across and within research populations and paradigms, there is considerable variation in which one of these, or which set of them, is most powerful as a determinant of how research is conducted.

Similarly, the implications for the objectification of indigenous 'other' cultures in university-based research can be clearly derived from views of the university as a traditionally elite institution. According to Palmer (2000), the university's strong element in the pursuit of theoretical rationality is rooted in the empiricist tradition that emphasizes the detachment of the subject from the object as the key role in the progressive unfolding of knowledge and that anything practical is ultimately not an embodiment of worthy knowledge and rationality.

> *Academic culture holds disconnection as a virtue ... Intel-lectually, the academy is committed to an epistemology, a way of knowing which claims that if you don't disconnect yourself from the object of study—whether it's an episode in history, or a body of literature or a phenomenon of the natural world—your knowledge of it will not be valid ... For a century and more, we have venerated 'detached scholarship' while disciplines that require close encounters between the knower and the known— art, music, dance, and the like—have been pushed to the bottom of the academic totem pole* (Palmer, 2000, p. 3).

Furthermore, up to the last quarter of the last century, research was based to a substantial extent on the tenets of positivism and an objectification of indigenous 'other' cultures in which forms of theory, data, and analysis fail to measure themselves against the needs of indigenous peoples (Creswell,

2008). Set against this backdrop of research culture, it is clear that indigenous societies are accorded a marginal status, that is, the status of the 'Other'. The point of view that will help to restore some balance to the picture for a renewed confidence between university-based researchers and indigenous communities should be a paradigmatic shift.

The main purpose of this chapter is to clarify the place of indigenous culture and epistemology within academic research. Concentration upon the general theme of this book – 'Service to the community' – enables the place of indigenous knowledge to be examined within the third mission of the university. Such an examination clarifies what is distinctive to indigenous knowledge as a major part of academic research. The analysis, hopefully, is to hone awareness of the intentions and the effects of the changes that are possible in enhancing relationships between universities and indigenous communities.

This paper describes a three-year collaborative study between university-based researchers and aboriginal communities to investigate key aspects of aboriginal knowledge and culture that communities see as reflecting the curriculum needs of aboriginal students, as well as the effective digital tools that would enhance and extend the delivery of the curriculum. The paper closely examines how participatory research can be utilized as a dialogue in redefining indigenous other cultures and rejects research paradigms embedded in positivistic constructs that prevent adequate consideration of the epistemology of indigenous 'other' cultures.

Participatory research as a dialogue for redefining the 'other'

Traditionally, university-based research is positivistic, objective, and has the potential to deform the capacity for open dialogue with other cultures. It does not provide a base for mutual reciprocal relations between cultures, particularly those of ethnic groups. Gadamer's (1986) concept of fusion of horizons negates the notion of objectivity and absolute answers in favour of an open dialogue in which each party accepts that the understanding of each other as well as understanding themselves is considerably variable. Similarly, in searching for an acceptable as well as legitimate way of dealing with the 'other' Freire's (1970) concept of dialogue and problem posing is significant for collaboration between the university-based researcher and indigenous communities.

> *Since dialogue is the encounter in which the united reflection
> and action of the dialoguers are addressed to the world which is
> to be transformed and humanized, this dialogue cannot be
> reduced to the act of one person's 'depositing' ideas in another,
> nor can it become a simple exchange of ideas to be 'consumed'
> by the discussants* (p. 77).

Freire further argues that 'Without dialogue, there is no communication and without communication, there can be no true education' (p. 81). Thus, in the terms of Freire, dialogue encourages critical thinking and action. This study involves the mobilization of community people to pose problems and find solutions to them. The research process should, therefore, be flexible to accommodate all the necessary viewpoints of participants. As Freire writes of problem-posing:

> *Problem-posing education, as a humanist and liberating praxis,
> posits as fundamental that men subjected to domination must
> fight for their emancipation. To that end, it enables teachers and
> students to become subjects of the educational process by
> overcoming authoritarianism and alienating intellectualism; it
> also enables men to overcome their false perception of reality.*
> (p. 74).

Therefore, the objective of this project is to collectively build a group ownership of information as we move from creating the 'other' where the cultural traditions of a less powerful group are suppressed by the agenda of research and simply observed as objects of study, to portraying the views of the indigenous people. In this process, our conception of research hinges on participatory research that we find to be of greater analytical importance than positivistic, scientific theories that paralyse the ability to engage with the goals and aspirations of the people who are the objects of the present study. In this context, participatory research is an important goal for the selection of criteria and the formulation of corresponding research goals for indigenous societies.

Participatory research is useful in helping dominated, exploited, and minority groups to redefine old problems, propose fresh alternatives and take action in solving the problems (Kemmis, 1991; Maguire, 1987; Participatory Research Network, 1982). Hall (1981) defines participatory research as a social action process that meshes the activities of research, education and action. Therefore, participatory research provides an arena for collective empowerment that helps to deepen knowledge about social problems and helps to formulate possible actions for their solution. Similarly, Creswell (2008) defines participatory research as a social action process that meshes the activities of research, education and action by 'incorporating an emancipatory aim of improving and empowering individuals and organizations' (p. 555). According to Park (1993) 'Participatory research is emerging as a self-conscious way of empowering people to take effective action toward improving their lives' (p. 1). Torres (2002) also argues that participatory and action research 'offer a practical alternative to positivism, and are particularly useful to enhance the degree of participation of the 'studied' populations in policy and planning' (p. 378).

Participatory research is increasingly tied to and powerfully influenced by the concern with power and democracy and provides important social learning networks that are critical to issues of gender, race, ethnicity, sexual orientation, physical and mental abilities, and other social factors, and therefore leaves no room for the suppression of indigenous 'other' cultures (Agbo, 2006). Thus, the present study does not merely describe social reality, but radically tries to change it by combining the creation of knowledge about social reality with actual action in that reality. The common ethos of the project consists of an emphasis on the voices of First Nations with 'insider' cultural experiential knowledge not found in texts to be included in the knowledge production. In what follows, the analysis proceeds with the background and the origin of the issues.

Background and origin of the issues

One of the challenges facing aboriginal education in Canada is how to enhance aboriginal students' achievement through culturally responsive pedagogies (Agbo, 2005). The issue involved is not merely that of methods of teaching and learning but of acquiring the necessary tools for shaping and implementing a socially and culturally oriented curriculum that recognizes aboriginal local resources in context and reinforces and maximizes their use in education to make school learning an integral component of the social and cultural context of aboriginal children's heritage (Battiste and Henderson 2000; Hampton, 1995).

The education of aboriginal youth has been one of the responsibilities of the Canadian government inherited from the British Crown as part of the Terms of Confederation. The Department of Indian Affairs established residential schools to assimilate aboriginal people into mainstream Canadian society, culminating with the Indian Residential Schools, the last of which closed in 1980. The literature indicates that education in residential schools isolated aboriginal people from their language, culture, beliefs, and attitudes, and taught them to resist aboriginal values and culture (Agbo, 2005; Battiste and Henderson, 2000; Lomawaima, 1994). Concurrently, researchers have used radically reviewed and evolving concepts to examine the residential education system and its effects on First Nations (Battiste and Henderson, 2000; Lomawaima, 1994). It is accepted that the residential schools were adept in isolating First Nations children from their mother tongue, traditions, culture, beliefs, and attitudes, and that the 'academic disciplines and educational systems were complicit with Christian domination and religious oppression' (Battiste and Henderson, 2000, p. 97).

Existential changes in aboriginal communities have brought critical attention to the fundamental reformulation of the boundaries between aboriginal cultures and Eurocentric education (Agbo, 2002). The changes are particularly connected with the information and communication technologies. The current orientation towards a more comprehensive and less parochial form of education for aboriginal people has thrown up the latent challenges to utilize modern technologies in aboriginal communities. One of the most important of such challenges is the question of student achievement of schooling in aboriginal communities, a problem that the Canadian Government expected to be solved by means of assimilating aboriginal students into the mainstream, but which has been intractably resisted.

Meanwhile in Ontario's far north, many of the students sent out to high schools in urban centres drop out to return to their communities. Those who return home carry with them a variety of social problems including drug and alcohol use. The communities lack the resources to deal with the problems of the drop out students. In response to the growing numbers of dropouts back in their communities, the Keewaytinook Okimakanaka, (KO) the Northern Chiefs Council, a tribal council serving six First Nations in Ontario's far north established the Keewaytinook Internet High School (KiHS) in 1999. The chiefs mandated the creation of a pilot project to determine whether the Internet could be an effective tool to deliver education. The purpose of the project, as directed by the KO chiefs, was to find a way for grade nine and ten students to remain at home in their community while learning accredited high school courses.

Community service based on wishes of local inhabitants

Arguably, part of the reorientation that participatory research has brought about in social science research is the emphasis on the process and criteria of entry into the research site. Participatory research principles require that researchers should 'put themselves out to be requested' from the community rather than traditional forms of social science research that have depended on object-like relations between the inquirer and that which is to be researched (Agbo, 2003, 2006; Maguire, 1987). To provide a base for mutual reciprocal research relationships and to develop intercultural relations that advantage neither party and protect the interests of both the university researcher and the community, research relationships need to be negotiated with the wishes of the local inhabitants (Agbo, 2005, 2006). In participatory research terms, this amounts to the researcher preparing the grounds for invitation from the community, that is, exploring the potential for developing new forms of working relationships that are based on mutuality and the development needs of the community (Agbo, 2006; Park, 1993).

In contrast to traditional social science research paradigms that allow little or no space for the culture and protocols of the host community, participatory research acknowledges community cultures and protocols in equal terms with the research agenda. Accordingly, for real community service to occur, researchers cannot enter into communities simply as objects to be studied, controlled, and manipulated, however well meaning. Genuine community service projects need to be negotiated and implemented with the invitation and wishes of the local inhabitants. This project is therefore a collaborative study designed to advance digital online education as it is used in First Nations communities in Ontario's Far North.

Research communities

The present study was conducted in several small First Nations communities in Northern Ontario. Access to most of the communities from outside is by plane. The Wasaya Airlines provide daily flights from Thunder Bay, Sioux Lookout, and Red Lake to all the communities in northwestern Ontario, while Air Creebec provides daily flights to communities in the James Bay area. The main aircraft that ply the routes are Beech 99s and Cessna 180s. The communities also make considerable use of float- and ski-equipped aircraft for trapping and hunting trips and travelling to other communities. During winter months, communities construct winter roads that usually officially open in February until the end of March. The supplies of diesel fuel, foodstuffs and building supplies also heavily depend on the winter roads. Communities along the Hudson Bay receive heavy equipment and supplies by barge.

With populations between 200 and 3,000 residents, unemployment is relatively high in the communities. Most of the full time employment in the communities is at the Band Office, the School, the Northern Store, and the Nursing Station, with a few more positions becoming available with road, electrical, airstrip, water and sewerage, and telephone services. The only non-First Nations residents of the community are teachers, nurses, and Northern Store workers and construction workers who visit periodically to undertake repairs of the community facilities. In many of the communities, members participate in seasonal economic activities that include periods of wage earning and periods of hunting, fishing and gathering to sustain themselves and their families. More and more community members are employed in the service economies that are springing up. There are also seasonal employment opportunities such as tree planting, forest fire fighting, fishing and hunting guides and in construction. A growing number of community members are securing employment working in the mining and forestry industries, especially in the Red Lake and James Bay areas.

Non-science, indigenous research and technology: Building praxis

Participatory research rejects the idea within academia that the best way to enhance the development of indigenous communities is to do research *for* the communities, where communities' cultural traditions are suppressed by the agenda of positivistic, scientific methods. The ideology of strategic rationality where the slavish imitation of the natural sciences overwhelms the cultural authenticity of indigenous communities prevents adequate consideration of who should be the beneficiary of research in indigenous communities. In contemporary times, collaborative research in indigenous communities finds its strongest justification in recent discussions of consumers of change and technology.

Social informatics scholars (Bishop *et al.*, 2003; Kling, 1999, 2000; Star *et al.*, 2003; Van House, 2004) argue that technology and the social are insepar-able and mutually constituted: responsive, well-designed technologies empower users. Research indicates that conventional Eurocentric notions as the basis for educational design in digital systems for educational purposes in indigenous communities may be inadequate and that both technological and curricular designs need to support community determination, flexible cultural interpretations, and adjudication of cultural values across social boundaries. Digital environments such as KiHS hold the promise of richer curricula, enhanced cultural pedagogies, more effective organizational structures, stronger links between schools and community, and the empowerment of disenfranchised learners and groups when programmes are negotiated and their implementation tested against the needs and wishes of the local inhabitants (Bishop *et al.*, 2001; Behrmann, 1998; Trotter, 1998). The emphasis on science and scientific ideology virtually always pay little or no attention to questions of cultural differences, or the politics and ethics of cultural interaction.

University outreach and community engagement

The university team comprised two professors and two doctoral students from the education faculty who travelled to the communities to interview community people and to conduct workshops to ascertain community priorities for schooling and ways to put the priorities into action projects. Prior to the commencement of the project, the university team reviewed aboriginal ethnographies, community histories and documents, reports and school records, along with provincial and local curriculum themes and materials as an introduction to the issues affecting First Nations education. These materials were analyzed by delineating the attitudes, values and implicit patterns that demonstrate community perspectives and priorities of schooling on reserves.

It will be noted that 'power relations' has been placed at the head of the list of those factors affecting university-based researcher–community interaction and perception. In other words, one of the arenas within which to best test university-based research in indigenous communities is that of power relations. Participatory research is concerned with the reorientation of research so as to highlight the implications for cultural interaction and the mutual reciprocal relations between indigenous communities and the university-based researcher. Thus the significance of the power relationship between the university and the community brings with it a tendency for university researchers to adhere strictly to community protocols (Agbo, 2006). Emphasis upon how the university team conducted the community outreach is interpreted below. The interpretation merely predicates the mutual reciprocity by which the outreach was conducted.

The most significant phenomenon of the outreach is the dynamic relationship that co-exists between the university and the community. This relationship is maintained through praxis and dialogue (Freire, 1970). In thinking of the dialogical process in participatory research, for example, a remarkable way in which dialogue is embodied in research is through group discussion workshops. In the present project, the university team utilized group discussions to engender the value of unity and harmony and to promote a sense of personal and collective responsibility in the research process. According to the Participatory Research Network (1982), 'Group discussions are probably the most widely used method in participatory research. They occur throughout the process, and are often used together with other methods' (p. 6). The network suggests small groups of between 8 and 25 people who meet to solve problems by sharing experiences, information and support. This study targeted groups of community people in each of the participating communities who are active on school affairs, to act as an advisory or reference group for the project. Basically, this group advised on what to do in the course of the project. Participants were encouraged to present and talk about their own ideas especially about what changes they required for the Internet high school in the community. An example of how group discussions were used as a dialogical process in the present study may be relevant.

The university team (two professors and two doctoral students) flew into each of the communities and spent three days conducting interviews of community elders, teachers, students, and parents. After the interviews in each of the communities, participants from all the participating communities were invited to Sioux Lookout and Thunder Bay respectively for the workshops. Participants' airfares and boarding and lodging were covered and each participant was offered a daily honorarium of $100. Each of the workshops began on a Monday as a travel day and ended at noon on Thursday. For the workshops, an invitation was extended to as many as 45 people from all the participant communities. Attendance at the workshops ranged between 25 and 32 participants. These people were composed of the school teaching and support staff, directors of education, the Local Education Authority (LEA) members and some community people. During each of the workshops, there were four groups with an average of six to eight people in each group. A group was made up of education directors, teachers, parents and band council workers, who constituted a research team that worked together under a secretary. The group worked on one of three themes (research questions) of the study. For example, in one of the workshops, the first group identified problems associated with the status of aboriginal language and culture in the Internet high school; the second group discussed how non-aboriginal teachers could be culturally prepared to teach First Nations students; and the third group worked on priorities for developing descriptors that would form the components of a culturally responsive curriculum. At the workshops, the university-based researchers acted as facilitators and joined in various group discussions. After the whole of the morning was spent discussing issues in groups, the groups broke up for lunch and came back in the afternoon to discuss group results in a plenary session. At these sessions, group secretaries presented their reports for comments.

The discussions generated conditions under which people felt comfortable and free to speak. We used the group discussions to build a sense of trust, support and cooperation as a group of people who shared the same ideas or problems. Our discussions allowed us to sustain communication among us and also acted as productive interviews (Participatory Research Network, 1982). The arrangement seemed to work very effectively as participants indicated that they found the exercise very interesting. Sometimes, disagreements that resulted in arguments made it necessary for participants to take votes on issues. If participants agreed, the secretary documented the discussions and tape-recorded them to ensure that important remarks were not overlooked. After the discussions, summary reports were produced and distributed to all participants for their perusal and feedback. Sometimes participants drew attention to any issues that were missed in the report.

A few main points emerge from the foregoing discussion on outreach to communities. First, as universities seek answers to effective community engagement, they must remember that effective service to the community lies in outreach, indeed, but in an outreach that is based on an agreement of equals, based on mutual respect and the recognition that each group has particular strengths that complement each other. Both the university and the communities should benefit and build capacity. Second, the university must establish connections that engage community members such as chiefs and council members, educators, teachers and teaching assistants, parents, and students. Third, for a sustained participation by community members in university projects, it is important for the university team and community members to collaborate and develop research and training plans that allow for the training of community members to carry out research work in their own communities.

This project sustains relationships that are based on the efforts of community-based researchers who live and work in their communities. This embedded research is creating a new dynamic and dialogue between university-based researchers and community-based researchers and their respective cultural and intellectual traditions. Fourth, for successful participatory adaptation, community members have to become co-decision makers at every stage of community service projects. Too often, techno-logical design and evaluation are characterized by features that are detrimental to the education of those outside the social, Eurocentric mainstream (Warschauer, 2003). Indigenous communities have their own research protocols, and it is important for outsiders to respect and adhere strictly to the protocols. Finally, university researchers must base projects on community consultation to make certain that ongoing community knowledge is reflected in every aspect of the project.

Conclusion

The order in which the analysis proceeded was, inevitably, arbitrary and therefore concealed some fundamental connections. These may now be clarified. I began this paper with the claim that indigenous communities are rejecting forms of research based on an objectification of indigenous 'other' cultures in which forms of research fail to measure themselves against the development needs of indigenous communities. Cultural suppression in indigenous societies has been licensed by the hegemony that dominant cultures' exercise in providing political, intellectual, scientific and ideological symbols to subordinate groups of which the realities of culture are often suppressed within social science research methodologies (Agbo, 2005; McLaren, 2007; Welch, 1993). As a consequence, there is a reaction against university-based positivistic or scientific methods of research in indigenous communities. The premise for this call is that scientific modes of research in indigenous communities fail to come to grips with the cultural reality of the people who figure in the research (Welch, 1993).

In order to restore some balance to the picture for a renewed confidence between university-based researchers and indigenous communities a paradigmatic shift is required. The implication of meaningful and relevant research relationship between indigenous communities and university-based researchers are that decisions, data collection, data analysis and action projects should be based on genuine attempts at developing mutual understanding rather than the university-based researcher playing the cult of the 'expert' with an objectified analysis of the indigenous cultures. Genuine and authentic research projects should be collaborative and decisions need to be negotiated and their implementation carried on with the wishes of community members.

The effectiveness with which university-based researchers fulfil their mission in indigenous settings depends upon their understanding of themselves and those cultural environments in which they operate, and upon their acquiring the competencies necessary for them to function as effective collaborative researchers. In a departure from much previous work in research, participatory research removes the concept of research in indigenous communities from its current Eurocentric and scientific constraints to a collaborative, differentiated, and specialized referent, partly based on *praxis* and dialogue (Freire, 1970; Gadamer, 1986). The argument implies a need to turn the tables on the sort of mindset implicit in academic research and on many similar reflections on indigenous knowledge. One of the main issues that should face university-based researchers in the 21st century is adherence to the third mission of the university and provision of service to society. The implications for a meaningful and relevant service to the community are that cultural analysis necessarily begins with an examination of the degree to which research is negotiated and implemented with the wishes of indigenous societies rather than continuing to rely on objective academic knowledge and a scientific outlook that downplays indigenous epistemology.

Acknowledgement

This study was made possible by a grant from the Social Sciences and Humanities Research Council (SSHRC) of Canada. I wish to acknowledge SSHRC for sponsoring this project.

References

Agbo, S. A. (2003) 'Changing school–community relations through participatory research: Strategies from First Nations and teachers', *The Canadian Journal of Native Education* 23(1) 25–56.

Agbo S.A (2005) 'Perspectives on local control of education with a future orientation: A view from First Nations', *Journal of Educational Thought,* 39(3), 287–321.

Agbo, S. A. (2002) 'Unstated features of cultural deprivation or discontinuity: Culture standards for administrators and teachers of Aboriginal students', *EAF– The Journal of Educational Administration and Foundations* 16(2), 10–36.

Agbo, S. A. (2006) 'Changing school–community relations through participatory research: Strategies from First Nations and teachers', in J. A. Winterdyk, L. Coates and S. Brodie (eds.), *Quantitative and qualitative research methods reader: A Canadian orientation*, 78–98) Toronto: Pearson.

Altbach, P.G. (1992) 'Patterns in higher education development: Toward year 2000',in R. F. Arnove, et al. (eds.), *Emergent issues in education: Comparative perspectives*, 39–55. Albany: State University of New York Press.

Battiste M. and Henderson, J. Y. (2000) *Protecting indigenous knowledge and heritage: A global challenge.* Saskatoon, SK: Purich.

Behrmann, M. (1998) 'Assistive technology for young children in special education', in C. Dede (ed.), *Learning with technology. 1998 Yearbook of the Association for Supervision and Curriculum Development*, 73–93. Alexandria, VA: ASCD.

Bishop, A. P., Bazzell, I., Mehra, B., and Smith, C. (2001) 'Afya: Social and digital technologies that reach across the digital divide', *First Monday*, 6(4) http://www.firstmonday.org/issues/issue6_4/bishop/index.html

Bishop, A. P., Bazzell, I., Mehra, B., and Smith, C. (2003) 'Participatory action research and digital libraries: reframing evaluation' in A. P. Bishop, N. A. Van House, and B. P. Buttenfield (eds.), *Digital library use: Social practice in design and evaluation*, 161–189) Cambridge, MA: MIT Press.

Creswell, J. W. (2008) *Educational research: Planning, conducting, and evaluating quantitative and qualitative research* (2nd Edition). Upper Saddle River, NJ: Pearson Education.

Freire, P. (1970*) Pedagogy of the oppressed*. New York: Seabury Press.

Gadamer, H. (1986) *Truth and method*. New York: Crossroads Publishing.

Giroux, H.A. (1994) 'Living dangerously: Identity politics and the new cultural racism', in H.A. Giroux, and P. McLaren (eds.), *Between borders: Pedagogy and the politics of cultural studies*, 29–55. New York: Routledge.

Hall, B.L. (1981) 'Participatory research, popular knowledge and power: A personal reflection', *Convergence: An International Journal for Adult Education*, 14, 6–17

Hampton, E. (1995) 'Towards a redefinition of Indian education', in M. Battiste and J. Barman (eds*.*), *First Nations education in Canada: The circle unfolds*, 5-46. Vancouver: UBC Press.

hooks, b. (1990) *Yearning: Race, gender and cultural politics*. Boston: South End Press.

Kemmis, S. (1991) 'Critical education research', *Canadian Journal for the Study of Adult Education,* 5(3), 94–119.

Kling, R. (1999) 'What is social informatics and why does it matter?' *D-Lib Magazine, 5*. Retrieved from http://www.dlib.org/

Kling, R. (2000) 'Learning about information technologies and social change: The contribution of social informatics', *Information Society*, 16(3), 217–232.

Lomawaima, K. T. (1994) *They called it prairie light. The story of Chilocco Indian School*. Lincoln: University of Nebraska Press.

Maguire, P. (1987) *Doing participatory research: A feminist approach*. Amherst: The Center for International Education, University of Massachusetts.

McLaren, P. (2007) *Life in schools: An introduction to critical pedagogy in the foundations of education* (5th edn). Boston: Allyn and Bacon.

Palmer, P. J. (2000) 'Learning communities: Reweaving the culture of disconnection', *Washington Center News* (Spring), 34.

Park, P. (1993) 'What is participatory research? A theoretical and methodological perspective', in *Voices of Change: Participatory research in the United States and Canada,* P. Park *et al.* (eds.), 1–19. Westport (CT): Bergin and Garvey.

Participatory Research Network 1982. *An Introduction to participatory research*. Toronto: ICAE.

Perkin, H. (1984) 'The historical perspective', in Clark, B. (ed.) *Perspectives on Higher Education: Eight disciplinary and comparative views*, 16–55. Berkeley: University of California Press.

Quinnan, T. W. (1997) *Adult students 'at risk': Culture bias in higher education.*

Westport, CT: Greenwood Publishing Group Inc.

Star, S. L., Bowker, G., and Neumann, L. (2003) Transparency beyond the individual level of scale: convergence between information artifacts and communities of practice', in A. P. Bishop, N. A. Van House, and B. P. Buttenfield (eds.) *Digital library use: Social practice in design and evaluation*, 241–269. Cambridge, MA: MIT Press.

Torres, C.A. (2002) 'The state, privatization and educational policy: A critique of neo-liberalism in Latin America and some ethical and political implications', *Comparative Education*, 38(4), 365–385.

Trotter, A. (ed.) (1998) 'Technology counts 1998: Putting school technology to the test (special report)', *Education Week*, 18(5), October. http://www.edweek.com/sreports/tc98/ Accessed 4 October 2010.

Van House, N. (2003) 'Digital libraries and collaborative knowledge construction', in A. P. Bishop, N. A. Van House, and B. P. Buttenfield (Eds.) *Digital library use: Social practice in design and evaluation*, 271–295. Cambridge, MA: MIT Press.

Warschauer, M. (2003) *Technology and social inclusion: Rethinking the digital divide.* Cambridge: MIT Press.

Welch, A.R. (1993) 'Class, culture and the state in comparative education: Problems, perspectives and prospects', *Comparative Education*, 29, 7–27.

Chapter 11

Community engagement and citizen education: The case of the Rural Mexico Program

Hugo Gutierrez and Nora Guzman

Introduction

Mexico's private universities have not distinguished themselves as generators of social change. But now that we are faced with the reality that the Mexican government has been less than effective in reducing poverty, these institutions have a unique opportunity to participate in generating the social cohesion that is needed to face national and global challenges.

Graduates of the Monterrey Tech System occupy very influential positions in society. In 2008, 22 per cent of its alumni held positions of higher management in the 153 largest companies in the country, 22 per cent of state governors were alumni, 78 per cent were partners or owners of a company 20 years after graduation, and 3 per cent were in the field of higher education (ITESM: President´s address to the board of trustees, 2009.)

Consequently, an understanding of the complex national reality is essential. These challenges are not the responsibility of a single institution. One can argue that it is the government's responsibility to solve the issue of poverty. But that ignores the fact that there is an economic class who accepts a national strategy of low wages and a culture of limited citizen participation.

What are the options? We suggest that by universities framing issues and asking questions we can better address the conditions of the more vulnerable elements in society. An example of such action is the Mexico Rural Program, run by Tecnológico de Monterrey (Monterrey Technological Institute of

Superior Studies) in the northern state of Nuevo Leon. This programme works with children in rural communities who have limited educational opportunities and need to be better prepared to deal with the challenges their generation will face.

This programme provides an ample range of possibilities through 'professional social service' (servicio social professional), which is based in federal law. This law requires college students from both private and public institutions to work 480 hours in 'professional service projects'. While the intent of the law is admirable, the lack of guidelines makes application inconsistent.

This chapter will show how community engagement programmes such as this can be used as a formative tool for the students to become engaged citizens. In the first part we will give some background information and basic facts about the country and the practice of social service itself. The second part will focus on two concepts that give basis to the practice: social citizenship and civil society. The last part will talk about the case of Tecnologico de Monterrey's strategies on forming socially conscious citizens through community engagement. Finally, we'll analyse the case of the Mexico Rural (Rural Mexico) programme, a community engagement programme that is aimed at tutoring children from poor rural areas.

Background

According to Mexico's National Institute of Geography and Statistics (INEGI) the country has a population of about 108 million people with 29.7 per cent living in the main urban areas of Monterrey, Guadalajara, Mexico City and the central cities of Puebla and Toluca. With a GDP per capita of about $7,000 and a GINI index of 47.5 (2006) (CONEVAL, 2007) 50.6 million Mexicans cannot afford to pay for basic health care, education, public transportation, shelter, and dress needs, while 19.5 million don't have enough income to buy food to satisfy their basic nutritional requirements.

Education

Article three of the 1917 Mexican constitution specifies the right to receive an education that is free, secular and mandatory. In spite of this, the national schooling average is 8.1 grades. In 2006, education spending represented 6.9

per cent of the national GDP (INEGI, 2007). However, the country scored well below the OECD members' average in reading, math and science skills at the Programme for International Student Assessment of the same year. (OECD, 2007). It also mandates that State guarantees availability of educational services. In order to comply with this legislation, the Secretariat of Public Education was created for the purpose of designing the strategies, methods and actions needed to educate the country's population.

Fundamental to this mission was the philosopher, Jose Vasconcelos (1882–1959), who throughout his participation in public life advocated the development of education and culture in Mexico. He was named President of the Universidad Nacional de México (National University) in 1920. A year later he designed the framework that would foster and promote national development in the educational field. Starting with literacy, native education programmes and education from the elementary level to higher education, he created the Secretariat of Public Education. His memoirs, letters and essays reflect his ideas centred on the relationship between education and social realities. When he assumed the aforementioned deanship he stated the following:

> *When I say education I refer to the direct teaching by those who know something in favor of those who know nothing; I refer to the teaching that is useful in increasing the productive capacity of each hand that works, of each brain that thinks . . . Let us take the field-hand under our safe-keeping and teach him to multiply his productivity by a hundredfold thorough the use of better tools and methods. This is more important than distracting them with verb conjugations, since culture is the natural fruit of economic development . . .* (Vasconcelos, 1950, p. 11).

With these ideas, the Secretariat of Public Education (SEP, its Spanish acronym) developed as an institution focusing on education, as a social equalizer. Mexico has established education from first through ninth as basic, and has the mandate to make it available to the population. Thus, 90.7 per cent of students in those grades attend public schools and 9.3 per cent go to private schools (SEP, 2008).

Regarding higher education, 2.3 million 19–23-year-olds go to either public or private universities, that is 25 per cent of the population in that age group. Of these, 33.3 per cent go to private universities while 66.6 per cent go to public institutions (SEP, 2008). These statistics show that college students are a privileged sector of the population. We suggest that this puts them in a position to serve the less privileged.

Social service: A brief history

Vasconcelos was a promoter of what was later known as 'social service', a project that emerged in Mexico in the mid 20th century. It arose from a need to improve social welfare and development; hence it was determined that university students, given their specific competencies, could favourably affect society by putting into practice certain abilities and knowledge that university life had fostered and nurtured.

Social service is therefore an activity that is carried out by Mexican students in compliance with a federal law enacted from 1952. This law stipulated that all university students pursuing a professional degree without distinction must provide social service as a degree requirement.

Until 1952, the law was a determining factor in all professional degree programmes. Little by little, more legislation was created and different structures were created, until finally in 1973 the mandatory nature of social service was formulated through the Federal Education Law for all citizens and beneficiaries of education in Mexico.

Since then, there have been increasing efforts to organize and structure the practice of social service. In 1978, the Federal Social Service Coordinating Commission was created for students in institutions of higher education. Its primary objective was to organize social service on a national level.

The commission's most important contribution was establishing a long-overdue definition of the objective of social services. As a result, they came up with three objectives:
1) to develop in the student a conscience of solidarity and commitment towards society;
2) to establish an alignment of the activities with national priorities; and
3) the need for the social service project to contribute to the academic formation and training of the future professionals.

Today, there are a series of principles which have been articulated in the different pieces of legislation that affect social service. Among these principles, the following stand out:

- respect for community initiatives;
- participation and organization of the community;
- a shared responsibility between those involved in each programme.

(Maldonado, Hoyo, García de Alba and Martínez, 2005, p. 51)

Social service

In practice, each institution is free to manage social service as they see appropriate. NGOs, foundations, government offices, and different institutions request students for their social service projects. Universities usually have their own projects in which students can take part. Some universities, such as ITESM have rigorous vetting processes in which students can be involved.

While the law defines social service, there are no sanctions in place for those institutions that don't comply with the regulation. This lack of control opens the door to different acts which could be construed as less than ethical. The process defining social service needs to be more explicit, for this activity can be used as a very powerful tool in teaching students about good citizenship practices.

Social citizenship and civil society: A practical conceptualization

Citizenship plays a crucial role in making democracy work. Alain Touraine (1995, pp. 99–100) points out that first citizens must feel that they belong to a specific political collective, he establishes citizenship as one of the fundamental elements in order for a completely democratic society to exist.

The concept, as analysed by Touraine, does not limit itself to the legal definitions granted by the state: citizenship has to be exercised, for it is a right. However such an exercise is carried out from a call for social integration, which in itself is founded on autonomy (p.100).

Thus, the concept of a passive citizen who waits for the state to give him or her certain rights is not in itself a useful one. A citizen must recognize in others the rights that he or she demands, and must assume responsibility in the exercise and defense of such rights. For he or she lives within a community and acquires a stake in its sociopolitical processes.

T.H. Marshall established a concept during the 1950s called 'social citizenship'. A social citizen is one who sees his or her first- and second-generation rights protected. First-generation rights have to do with the individual liberties, such as freedom to assemble peacefully and freedom of expression (Marshall, 2006, pp. 30-31).

As mentioned previously, the concept of citizenship involves action. Citizenship is exercised, and that action is carried out in the public sphere, the sphere in which civil society exists. In practice, civil society has organized itself to work on topics of fundamental importance such as healthcare, education, economic development and environmental issues.

Colleges and universities may not be a part of what one might call civil society but their impact is inarguable. In third world countries such as Mexico, their studies are taken into account when talking about public policy (as an example of this, see the document 'Políticas públicas para el Crecimiento y la Consolidación Democrática' edited by the School of Public Administration and Policy at ITESM), State, Federal and Local Governments are counting on universities to come up with projects that will help their constituents.

The more traditional and formal role of colleges and universities has always been the creation and transmission of knowledge which, ideally, contributes to the development and wellbeing of humanity. It is no accident that students, professors and scientists are the first ones to be repressed and/or controlled by authoritarian governments (see the cases of Cambodia, Bangladesh, Chile, Argentina, Myanmar, etc).

This exchange of ideas helps to frame the minds of future professionals, helping them to develop positions on different issues, as well as ways to assume a role in the creation of solutions to social, political and economic problems. A way in which such institutions can play a role in forming conscientious and ethical citizens is through projects that go beyond a classroom setting, thus allowing for a more comprehensive and integral education. For it is very difficult to try and change that which is not truly known.

Popping the bubble: Education in citizenship

As was previously stated, universities which have been most influential as agents of social change in Mexico have been public institutions. The clearest example of this is the National University, although the University of Sonora and others have also played a fundamental role.

We cannot identify private universities in Mexico who have facilitated social service projects. One hypothesis already established in this paper is the fact that, simply put, these institutions need the economic elite in order to exist, and the elite can, from time to time, dictate the focus of the university. If we add the church hierarchy to the mix, the reality becomes even more interesting and complex.

One can argue that private universities cannot and will never be elements of change simply because they are, for the most part, in charge of educating the elite which has been brought up in that reality and has benefited from it. But one could also argue that those members of elite economic groups are precisely the ones who are in a position to change things from within, especially in the most immediate future.

How, then, must one move 'the elite' toward the kind of change and social cohesion that is needed to move forward? A first approach is precisely popping the protective bubbles with which the middle and upper classes have surrounded themselves. One way of doing this, is to have students in private universities witness other realities and make them aware that they will play a key role in shaping the country's future.

ITESM has developed an integral strategy in their formative efforts. An important distinction is that ITESM does set limits by establishing organizations in which a student may do his or her community service. It specifies the reason for the activities, as well as which actions count as social service.

We can say that there are different ways of defining service. There are a wide range of activities that can be defined as social service. Donating clothes, food or money for the needy – all are commendable. But if not accompanied by a strategy for development, they are prone to perpetuating the cycle of poverty as they do 'to' others rather than work 'with' others.

Activities that have an element of participation and inclusion are better described by Brazilian educator, Paulo Freire, with the concept of 'dialogue'(1970, p.27). He points out that the meeting of people through dialogue is not only necessary, it is vital – both get to listen, both get to speak. All involved in social projects must be co-participants and co-owners of these projects, because, as long as all of the stakeholders are involved; they all grow.

In order to show a small example of these efforts to 'pop the bubble', we will describe the Mexico Rural Program, which is part of the Department of Social Development and Citizenship at the Monterrey Campus of ITESM. We start with a description of the programme's organization.

Education in citizenship and social engagement: ITESM's strategies

To achieve these goals ITESM has designed various strategies. One of them is social service through various models. The formative and social service modality that the Tecnologico de Monterrey uses is a multi-component construction that includes:

- An induction workshop, in which students are prepared to enter community work. The social service induction workshop helps students to become aware of the relevance of participating in social service (ITESM, no date).
- Social service focused toward work in marginalized com-munities. This includes at least 240 hours of social service. Students must provide this service between the third and eighth semesters of their undergraduate programme.
- The Rural Mexico Program, the central theme of this essay, also responds to a special academic concern: how to bridge the gap between teaching the concept of citizenship and direct civic action. It has been considered particularly important for the study plan of each academic programme to integrate the concept of citizenship throughout the curriculum in addition to offering specialized courses in each discipline, such as 'Society, Development and Citizenship in Mexico'.
- Other social service programmes include 'Friends of Nature' (Amigos de la naturaleza) and 10X10. The first one looks to provide people with environmental competences and community development.

As part of the required courses, students of all programmes in ITESM have to take a course on citizenship. This course also offers the opportunity for them to register in the Rural Mexico social service programme. In this way, theory influences their social service as well as their roles as agents of change and their commitment to national development.

Mexico is a country with an approximate population of 103 million people and although the Human Development Index places it in a relatively high position, (# 53), poverty has increased in recent years. President Felipe Calderon acknowledged that during his government the number of Mexicans experiencing dietary poverty increased from 14 to 20 million. On average they live on less than $2 a day, mainly because of the economic crisis and the rise in food prices. (Herrera, 2009, p. 20)

Due to this situation, acts of engaged citizenship are called for, especially by those who are privileged enough to have received a college education. In 2008 a total of 2,778,856 students were enrolled in higher education in Mexico in both public and private universities. The development of civic consciousness in Mexico has been slow after having lived through a political regime in which a single party ruled for over 70 years. Mexican society has been characterized by a strong lack of democracy and political culture.

Civic participation is at transition point between private and public life in which social service will provide the community work needed to positively impact social development in the country. Amartya Sen states that 'development can be conceived as an expansion process of the real freedoms an individual enjoys' (Cortina, 2007, p.26).

Since the Rural Mexico Program is an educational project, its objectives are designed to provide a liberation and emancipation of sorts. Let us consider that knowledge nourishes the spirit and is an important principle of critical thinking that in turn generates choices and opportunities.

Civic consciousness is not obtained easily. It is a road that implies learning and practising on a day-by-day basis, in a conscientious and practical manner. From the standpoint of conscience, assuming a role of commitment toward others is critical. The researcher, Rosa Mari Ytarte, concludes that:

> *Citizenship education, aside from the realms of status and rights, assumes an open pedagogy . . . citizenship is the competency of education and it deals primarily with guaranteeing full*

access to the social sphere of each and every one of the subjects of education, but also of building, of creating this common sphere through culture. (Ytarte, 2007 p. 190)

We consider that the first step toward sensitivity is through fieldwork. Experiencing first-hand the real needs of the country allows students to follow up with action, commitment and reflection.

We expect that, through the practice of citizenship, some of these competencies might be acquired. Social service has traditionally been a problematic issue in Mexico for various reasons: chief among these, aside from the lack of competencies, are the lack of civic culture, lack of administration and a bureaucratic requisite to obtain a professional degree.

Because of this, a large proportion of students still do not value the implications, significance and relevance that this social commitment entails. Nevertheless, we consider that a social formation project, articulated within an academic sphere and with an administrative structure, a follow-up process, a diverse number of actors involved with specific and differentiated roles, all striving for a common goal, may lead to an improved impact on social development. In the following analysis, we will examine a case study with positive results.

University student testimonials reflect the change that takes place within them and their growing awareness as citizens. Veronica Michelle wrote in May 2009:

> *... It's an important sense of responsibility which I developed as the sessions progressed ... They needed a person to learn security and self-reliance from, a person who would convey the sense of studying and learning ... Your vision and expectations for them are enormous and the time to accomplish it is short.*

Students experience different learning processes when encountering children who approach them without any hesitancy and address them as 'professor'. Discovering their social realities, in some cases, is very different, since it provokes reflection within students. By the end of the term, they are aware that they provided their knowledge, time and skills for these children's development.

In the 21st century, Mexico's challenge is to attain a democracy based upon civic involvement. We consider that the practice of social service is a formative action that involves competencies and that it will lead to more widely held democratic values. The population that is aware of existing problems will become involved and participate actively in the social development of the country.

The Mexico Rural Program: Community engagement and citizenship in action

The case we will be analysing in this chapter, the Rural Mexico Program, corresponds to a fully developed activity in the Monterrey Tech System (ITESM), a private university founded in 1943. It currently includes 33 campuses throughout Mexico, with approximately 81,672 students and 8,418 professors. In its mission statement it states principles that seek to encourage students to become more committed to their communities.

Although having an aggressive scholarship programme, many of the students come from upper middle class and privileged families, and, as we have previously shown, are very likely to be in positions of power, and influence, both in the private and public sectors.

Program mandate

Mexico Rural started in March of 1998 as one of the first efforts of the institution to institute a strategy of deeper involvement of the academic world in social service actions. Its two goals are twofold. For the students it encourages the development of society through student participation in rural educational programmes. Communities strengthen their processes of academic and human development.

The programme works within the so called 'Citric Region' in the northeastern state of Nuevo León. At present, Mexico Rural participates with close to 500 children in 14 communities; each semester 280 students carry out their social service there. Each student works at the sites during at least three weekends, and during these visits he or she participates in activities that contribute to the goal towards the community, mentioned above.

How is it that these visits contribute in a concrete way to the stimulation of social awareness and good citizenship among ITESM's students? To measure their effect, we would like to refer to some of the answers that the students have given to a questionnaire they are asked to fill out by the end of each semester, that illustrate the impact that their experience has had on them.

The methodology for this study is based on David Coopperrider's Appreciative Inquiry (AI). AI stipulates that, if in an organization people do more of what works, what doesn't work tends to disappear. The questions asked by AI are designed to lead the person into what Cooperriders calls the first 'D', Discovery, a stage in which stakeholders discover the best of what is, as opposed to the problem solving approach, that leads people into thinking about what isn't. (Cooperrider et al., 2005).

A question that is especially interesting is 'How has the programme contributed to your formation as 1) a professional 2) a citizen 3) a person? The answers fluctuated in three main aspects: on the one hand, some students pointed out that what they learned from the experience was to be more appreciative of what they have, whereas others went a little bit further on the subject by adding that going to the rural communities gives them a different perspective on life. One student sums it up by writing, 'I used to see having a house and being able to study and go to college as something normal, but now I see that is not true'. That is, they see their lives as the norm but, by looking at other realities, their concept of normality is challenged and they see these other realities as normalcy for the people in the communities.

Another group based their testimonies on their experience as college students and future professionals, and they feel motivated to work to create businesses, jobs and 'generate opportunities'. This phrase jumped right off the page because it has been used by Mexican President Calderon and is a reminder of the federal government's flagship social programme 'Opportunities', which is basically a programme that pays poor people in exchange for them sending their children to school and gives the family a basket of basic foods to satisfy the children's nutritional needs on the condition that they will take the children to government offices in order for social workers to corroborate that the children are getting the food. In spite of the official-sounding language, the testimonies reflect a clear sensitivity on the part of the student toward the needs of others. As one student put it, 'As a future professional I feel that the things we do must not only be to produce money (for ourselves) but to effect social change and help others'.

Yet another group of students says that they feel that they are more sensitive toward the needs of others and other realities, but they don't mention specific commitments or action plans. Some members of this group add that the programme gave them the conviction that we must all work to improve education in the country.

And then there are those students that came out deeply transformed. One of them, a female student, talked about the struggle she went through in order to comply with the social service as a requirement for graduation. Her first reaction was taking the pragmatic road, choosing a project which didn´t take up a lot of her time. She heard the programme was on weekends and linked to a course she was taking. Working with also seemed enjoyable. In the end she realized she wasn't concerned with the institutional requirement. What mattered most was to commit herself to the development of the country and its children. She ends her testimony by saying, 'I hope to go on paying back the favor with more children, more communities, more education and more value to exercise this humanity that is expressed in citizenship.'

Conclusions

It is here where we can establish that social service programmes like Mexico Rural, in which students are exposed to realities different from their own, have very clear value in the formation of civic consciousness and establish objectives to address it.

Nevertheless, these programmes by themselves are not enough. They must be accompanied by academic courses connected to the programmes, such as 'Society, Development and Citizenship.' in which students undertake a historic, economic and sociological analysis of Mexican society and the development of the country. This course includes the continuing reflection of what it means to be a citizen, establishing a more integral strategy that is not infallible and is in a process of constant improvement.

Furthermore, the experience of being a part of an institution of higher learning has to mean something more than the simple transfer of knowledge to foster professional development. We must find ways in which we can better prepare the students to work beyond self development. Tools such as community engagement programmes expose the student to realities that may be very different from their own, but that is just the first step. The next step is making them aware they can make the philosophy and practice of community engagement part of their personal and professional lives.

All of this may sound idealistic, but in reality is part of a conscientious design and application of methods that are supported by clearly defined educational goals and formation of intentions. Such a design cannot and should not leave out the needs, talents and abilities within the community. On the contrary, it should help strengthen them, as we provide the context for future work.

In sum, programmes such as Mexico Rural are only an initial set of strategies established to form the citizens today's society so urgently needs. Providing opportunities for increased civic participation supports generations that are more inclusive when decisions must be made and acted upon – generations that can see each other.

References

CONEVAL (2007) *Informe ejecutivo de la pobreza en México* (Executive Report on Poverty in Mexico) URL: http://www.coneval.gob.mx/contenido/info_public/1778.pdf Accessed 2 October 2010.

Cooperrider, D. Kaplin D. and Whitney D. (2005) *Appreciative Inquiry: A positive revolution in change.* San Francisco: Berret-Koehler.

Cortina, A. (2007) 'Ciudadanía: verdadera levadura de transformación social' ('Citizenship: True yeast of social transformation') in N. Guzman (ed). *Sociedad desarrollo y ciudadanía en México.* (*Society, development and citizenship in Mexico*) México: Limusa.

Freire, P. (1970) *Pedagogía del oprimido.* (*Pedagogy of the oppressed*) México: Siglo XX Editores. (20th Century Publishers).

Herrera, C. (2009) *Hay ya 20 millones en pobreza alimentaria, reconoce Calderón (Calderón aknowledges there are 20 million in extreme poverty) La Jornada* (October 3rd, 2009) Mexico City: Mexico.

INEGI (2007) Indice general, INEGI (General Index, INEGI). Retrieved 12 October 2009 from: http://www.inegi.org.mx/inegi/contenidos/espanol/acerca/inegi324.asp?c=324.

ITAM (No date) 'Programas de servicio social-externo', *Dirección Escolar ITAM* ('External social service programmes') Retrieved 25 October 2009, from http://escolar.itam.mx/serviciosocial/programas_externo.html.

ITESM (2007) 'Reglamento general de servicio social para alumnos del Tecnologico de Monterrey', IDESS.('General rules of social service for ITESM students') Retrieved 2 October 2009, from http://www.itesm.mx/vds/dfs/doctos/reglamento_ss_2007.pdf.

ITESM (2010) President's annual report to the Board of Trustees.

ITESM (No date) 'Taller de induccion al Servicio Social Monterrey', Tecnológico de Monterrey. ('Induction to social service workshop, Monterrey Tech) Retrieved 2 October 2009, from http://www.itesm.mx/vds/dfs/SSC/tinducc.htm.

Maldonado, Hoyo, García de Alba and J. Martínez, (2000) *El servicio social: Institución para el desarrollo municipal. (Social service: An institution for municipal development)*. México: SEDESOL, ANUIES.

Marshall, T. (2006) *Class, citizenship and social development essays.* New York: Doubleday and Co.

Michelle, V. (2009) *Testimony.* Encuesta semestral México Rural, Tecnológico de Monterrey ('Mexico Rural Quarterly Survey'). ITESM: Mexico.

Sen, A. (2001) *Development as freedom.* Oxford: Oxford University Press.

SEP (2008) *Recursos para investigadores (Sources for researchers)* Retrieved 1 October 2009, from: http://www.sep.gob.mx/wb/sep1/investigadores.

Touraine, A. (1995*) ¿Que es la democracia? (What is democracy?)* México: Fondo de Cultura Económica (Economic Culture Fund Publishers).

UNDP (2009) Human development report 2009. Retrieved 17 October 2009, from http://hdr.undp.org/en/reports/global/hdr2009/.

Vasconcelos, J (1950) *Discursos: 1920–1950. (Speeches: 1920–1950)* México: Botas Editorial. (Boots Publishing).

Ytarte, R. M. (2007) *Culturas contra ciudadanía: Modelos inestables en educación (Culture versus citizenship: Unstable models in education).* Barcelona: Gedisa.

Chapter 12

Community-based research as community engagement: Tales from the field

Shauna Butterwick and Penny Gurstein

Introduction

This chapter focuses on the power relations inherent in community-based action research (CBAR) with particular attention given to building mutually respectful and beneficial relationships between universities and community members. We also consider the connection between CBAR, knowledge-creation and mobilization, and policy-making. We are faculty members working in two different academic fields: Adult Education and Community and Regional Planning at the University of British Columbia. We bring a feminist orientation to CBAR and a commitment to social justice, raising questions about how, by whom, and for what purpose research is undertaken. As Maguire (2001) points out, 'feminist and action researchers both seek to unsettle and change the power relations, structures and mechanisms of the social world and social science research' (p. 65). We hope these explorations offer a kind of 'power sensitive conversation' (Haraway, 1988, p. 590). CBAR, we believe, has great potential for taking practical action on the gendered nature of inequality (Nussbaum, 2006) and that this approach can help to 'unsettle questions, texts, and collective struggles; to challenge what is, incite what could be, and help imagine a world that is not yet imagined' (Fine, 1994, p. 25).

While CBAR with a feminist perspective situates itself in a social justice framework, it cannot be assumed that such an understanding of 'community engagement' is the same for research funding agencies, university administrations and policy-makers. Community engagement is often seen as a strategy to win support for the aims and goals of the academy. Furthermore, while CBAR has much to offer policy decisions, given the contextual specificity of knowledge generated, it is an approach not yet fully embraced by policy-makers who question its validity and generalizability (Flyvbjerg, 2001). The potential for CBAR to support social justice goals is, however, evident in the strategic plan of the University of British Columbia (UBC):

> *UBC exists for the communities it serves: local, provincial, national, and global. An integral part of those communities, the University enters into relationships where decisions about means and ends are made collaboratively, costs and benefits are shared, and learning is reciprocal. Beginning with interest and outreach and moving through engagement and empowerment, UBC recognizes degrees of commitment and nurtures relationships along the full spectrum. In its highest form, community engagement casts the community partner in the leading role with the University acting in support.* (Place and Promise: The UBC Plan, 2009, p. 14)

While the commitment of the university to its communities can be far-reaching and encompassing, it is in the direct engagement of academics and community members that relationships and power sensitive conversations are created and nurtured. In many situations, it is individual faculty members who enter into relationships; in other cases, it is whole units or departments that are engaged. There is great diversity in these forms of engagement, many of them occurring long before community engagement became part of the official discourse or identified as a key component of the university's plan. Much can be learned from analyzing examples of CBAR as cases that explicate the politics of community engagement, how we might theorize such interactions, as well as considerations about the practical, on-the-ground, issues to be addressed. Telling practice stories helps to illuminate the complexities and intricacies of these relationships.

Community-based action research as community engagement

CBAR is a research orientation that supports democratic, participatory and collaborative processes and power sharing. As Ibàñez-Carrasco and Riaño-Alcalá (2009) state:

> *CBAR engages communities and individuals as agents (not subjects) of activities, products, and knowledge production; it strives to implement transparent, flexible, and trustworthy processes in communities and between individuals. CBAR strives to make the individuals it involves accountable to one another and to use systematic research practices and knowledge production to advance an understanding of an issue and its implications for policy, practice, program delivery, and planning.* (p. 3)

CBAR is *not* simply about academic researchers consulting with community members, nor is it a process that focuses only on community deficits, rather it recognizes assets and capacities of communities. Furthermore it is not simply academic research conducted in a community setting. CBAR is not only about generating important information and data, thus contributing to knowledge, but it is a process that can also mobilize knowledge and involve taking action. The CBAR projects outlined in this chapter are part of a family of research approaches also known as participatory action research or PAR. As Wadsworth (1998) points out PAR 'is not just research which is hoped will be followed by action. It is action which is researched, changed and re-researched, within the research process by participants'. (p. 15)

While CBAR is a powerful process that can bring about change, this approach to research has not been fully embraced by research intensive universities who tend to compartmentalize theory and action. Levin and Greenwood (2000) argue that this approach 'will not benefit universities over the long run. Society at large requires approaches to knowledge creation and application to help [them] become environments for continuous learning and ongoing adaptation to highly dynamic political, economic and social conditions'. (p. 112)

CBAR and the politics of recognition

To this discussion of CBAR, we bring Nancy Fraser's (1998) ideas about the politics of redistribution, recognition and representation as a frame for thinking about community engagement as a central mission of universities and about CBAR as an expression of community engagement. Fraser is centrally concerned with matters of social policy and how it should address inequalities and injustices. One of the dimensions of inequality is economic wherein some groups, communities and institutions have access to resources, while others do not. To address this requires the redistribution of resources.

The second dimension of Fraser's model focuses on recognition and respect for differences. Fraser's third dimension (2001) focuses on the politics of representation and the creation of mechanisms for equal political voice. Community engagement can be thought of as a kind of politics of redistribution undertaken by universities because it involves the sharing of academic resources with non-academic communities. It can also be viewed as a way to recognize community groups and their needs and capacities, as well as different forms of scholarship.

Four cases of CBAR with which the authors have been involved are highlighted below. They have been selected to illustrate the politics of redistribution, recognition and participation as outlined above. While all of the cases involved partnerships between academic researchers and community members and groups, some were initiated by the community, while others were started by academics. While the specific foci and the context of each of these cases vary, they all speak to both the value and the challenges of CBAR. While using a CBAR approach proved to be highly effective in generating important knowledge, these cases also point to the different priorities and capacities for knowledge mobilization of both universities and community groups, and to how the qualitative research can be dismissed as anecdotal within the academy.

Tales from the field

The politics of misrecognition

The first case to be explored illustrates a form of university-community engagement that was initiated by academic researchers, building on their own experiences as feminist activists, who, once funding was obtained from UBC, engaged in outreach to the community to identify interested participants. This CBAR project generated a great deal of interest and engagement by community members which led to significant insights into particular issues. Priority was given to sharing the results of this project with the community through day long workshops. This form of knowledge dissemination was greatly appreciated by the community; however, these initial forms of distribution or knowledge mobilization were devalued and discounted as real research by the university.

In 1998, the professor of Adult Education partnered with a colleague in the Theatre department to submit a proposal to an internal UBC fund to conduct a community-based research project on exploring feminist coalition politics using popular theatre processes. The focus of this research grew out of experiences with feminist coalitions (particularly the conflict that arose in relation to race, class and other differences). The project sought to explore the power of popular theatre to tell community stories, reflect on those stories and identify sites of struggles, and outline possible actions to be taken which could then be rehearsed through theatric activities with the larger community (Prentki and Selman, 2000).

The research process involved several stages. The first stage took several months in which workshops were held and a small group of women (fourteen) were recruited. The second stage occurred over a period of four months; weekly meetings were held during which various theatre processes were used to tell stories and examine issues. The third stage took another two months; in this stage, the larger feminist community was invited to day-long workshops where participants learned about popular theatre processes through participatory activities and were then shown several theatrical scenes which depicted coalition struggles, scenes which had grown out of the weekly explorations. During this stage, outreach was also made to individual women's groups and members of the project ran popular theatre workshops where issues were explored using theatre processes. Many of the participants wanted to continue with the project for another year and so a second year of activities occurred with similar stages. Overall this CBR project lasted just under three years.

Later when the Adult Education professor was going through the tenure process, the community performances were discounted and not recognized as 'products' of research. Questions were raised and critiques made about research productivity. While tenure and promotion was eventually granted, this occurred only after a protracted process which involved the creation of additional documents that involved reframing of CBAR for evaluation by traditional notions of scholarship. New reviewers also had to be secured. While many articles about this project were later published in peer-reviewed journals (e.g. Butterwick, 2000; Butterwick and Selman, 2003, 2006, 2009), the community-based dissemination strategies which held to the principles of CBAR and PAR (to involve community in all stages of the research) remained outside academic standards. Such knowledge mobilization, even if recognized by the university, was not regarded as crucial to the research, but, rather, existing outside the academic sphere of productivity.

In this case, the sustained participatory process that characterized the community-university partnership shifted resources from the academy to the community, thus CBAR contributed to a redistribution of resources. Furthermore, the theatre activities proved to be powerful mechanisms that engaged with the politics of recognition, as the lived experiences of participants were effectively captured through dramatic form. Resources were further distributed when community theatre workshops were employed to share the results of the study with the larger community. This community commitment, however, was not recognized by the academy as within the realm of scholarship. This case speaks of the risks of engaging fully with the principles of CBAR given the narrow vision of research productivity held by universities.

Speaking truth to power
In the second case, the ambivalent outcomes of CBAR and community engagement are also evident. While the 'products' or knowledge generated through CBAR and PAR were highly valued by the community and led to increased community mobilization and politicization, the results of CBAR were devalued in certain policy contexts.

This project was a partnership between the Adult Education professor and the National Alliance of Philippine Women of Canada (NAPWC), an umbrella organization formed in 2002 representing a variety of Filipino women's and youth organizations in Canada. This group was undertaking a project entitled 'Filipino community and beyond: Towards full participation in a multi-cultural Canada'. Funded by Heritage Canada, the three-year project focused on using participatory action research (PAR) to further explore issues and mobilize community members. The main focus of activities was examining the processes and policies that maintained Filipino women's and youth's economic and racial marginalization. Another key aspect of the project was policy engagement and developing a more vibrant form of participation in Canada's multicultural society. The role of the academic partner was partly consultant and partly evaluator, and involved regular meetings with the steering committee and participation in national events. Formal evaluations were submitted to the funder by the academic partner; these assessments were also shared with the project participants at the annual consultation meetings. The partnership between the academic researcher and NAPWC grew out of prior experience both parties had with each other.

Among the many activities undertaken in the NAPWC project was policy engagement. As a result of the PAR process the lived reality of many Filipino women working as nannies under the Live-in Caregiver Program (LCP) was made evident including their vulnerability to abuse by employers, their lack of rights as migrant workers, and overall, the structural barriers created by immigration policy. This knowledge was shared in briefs written and presented to parliamentary committees, and at meetings held with policy-makers. The NAPWC also developed skills in working with the media. Based on their research, the NAPWC called for the dismantling of the Live-in Caregiver Program (LCP) and a return to an earlier policy framework under which Filipino women could enter Canada, not as migrant workers with temporary visas, but as new immigrants who could bring their families, work in their professional fields, and apply for landed immigrant status. The NAPWC pointed to the racism and sexism underlying the LCP programme and its restrictions which leads to family disintegration and economic marginalization. Members of the NAPWC and local Filipino organizations have worked continuously on bringing their research about the problems of this programme to policy-makers with limited success. The results of their PAR studies have shown the details of women's everyday lives under the LCP, and how this programme contributes structurally to gendered, raced and classed exploitation.

The lived experiences of LCP workers as revealed through PAR projects was however, often challenged by policy-makers who wanted quantitative evidence of the extent of the problem. Undertaking such a large scale survey would take resources not available and surveys would not reveal the contextual specifics of participants' struggles. It is also very likely that LCP workers would not feel safe to answer truthfully about their situations, given their economic dependence on their employers. Some limited policy engagement successes have occurred, however, when current LCP workers have participated in these policy meetings and shared their experiences. Their testimonials seem to at least open some areas of question for policy-makers, but they undertake these endeavours at some risk. There have been recent changes to the LCP, but many of the fundamental restrictions apply, so the policy engagement work of groups, like the NAPWC, are continuing.

As with the first case, this example illustrates the paradox of CBAR. On the one hand, participatory research generated important knowledge about the everyday lived reality of Filipino domestic workers, shedding light on how specific policies were creating structural barriers to achieving equality. The CBAR process politicized community members and thus redistributed resources in relation to civic engagement. On the other hand, this kind of engaged research is very resource-intensive and the results, because they cannot be generalized, are often not recognized as legitimate by decision makers.

Conducting research in the midst of policy change

Community-university linkages can be fraught with complications from outside these partnerships that affect advocacy and mobilization. The 'Income Assistance Project,'[1] a five-year research project that the Community Planning professor was involved with, intended to advance understanding of the environment in which single mothers with young children live when they receive income assistance (IA), or 'welfare,' and how their lived experiences were affected by government policy changes over time.

Key government policy changes were enacted in 2002 in the Province of British Columbia on income assistance (IA) and employment assistance (EA). These changes affected eligibility for assistance (e.g. single mothers were required to find work when their youngest child turned three), rates, benefits and delivery of service. This fluctuating environment seriously affected the respondents of the study leaving them with less funding, less services to rely upon, and a complex reporting structure, resulting in continuing challenges to provide basic necessities of food, housing, and childcare for their children.

The research site in northern BC was particularly affected by government restructuring on multiple levels. Provincial cuts to income assistance levels and increased surveillance for welfare fraud combined to make income assistance recipients very nervous about participating in a study that intended to examine ways they were surviving. Internal government restructuring affected economically depressed rural areas disproportionately and many families lost their last remaining wage-earner through job cutbacks. Some service providers who would have helped in recruitment left the region because of unemployment. As well during the study time period, the Ministry for Children and Families, with responsibility for child protection and community service contracts, was being split into aboriginal and non-aboriginal authorities, creating a great deal of instability, affecting potential participants as well as community members and service providers.

The Income Assistance community partners were two community research and policy organizations.[2] While neither of these organizations have core operational funding from the province, both do work that responds to the changing policy context. The community partners did receive release time to participate in the project, but it was not sufficient in releasing them from their ongoing work commitments as the course releases for the academic partners were.

Both the academic and community partners were committed to advocacy and mobilization, but the funding for the project did not include this component, as is the case with most academic funding. The role of 'advocacy' is not a core mission of the academy as actions that could lead to influencing decisions is considered beyond the purview of 'objective' academic research (Fine, 1994; Hall, 2000). Still, a policy report (Gurstein and Goldberg, 2008) was prepared that was released by one of the community partners and a dialogue has been started with the Provincial government on the implications of the study. While considerable data was generated and, in addition to the report, a number of chapters (Gurstein and Vilches, 2009), journal articles (Kershaw *et al.*, 2008; Fuller *et al.*, 2008), as well as forthcoming chapters and articles have been produced, the advocacy component which the community partners have the expertise in was not as fully realized as was initially contemplated. Until strong arguments are generated on why advocacy should be a logical extension of community-based research the funding and organization of such research will continue to preclude these activities.

Negotiating university and community roles in research

The fourth project, which is ongoing, to be discussed is one where the Community Planning professor is involved. The Climate Justice Project[3] seeks to identify and develop economic and social policy options that lead to aggressive action on climate change with broad-based public support. The project addresses climate policy from a social justice perspective considering the social and economic effects of climate change, and that climate change affects people differently, depending on their position in society. The project has both a community and academic director, and it is administered through the community partner.[4] The considerable experience of the community partner in advocacy and mobilization through their published and online reports, editorials, and press releases, as well as several dedicated positions in communications at the organization, makes them highly effective in getting research findings disseminated to a wide audience thus becoming part of the public debate on issues. The community partner also links with a number of labour and environmental organizations, which furthers extends their reach.

Research partners in this project include a multidisciplinary team of academics from three BC universities, along with researchers and advisors from BC trade unions, environmental non-government organizations, First Nations and social justice groups, and other research institutes. The project is strategically designed to build linkages across these groups, and to translate results into policy actions and knowledge mobilization activities through national and international networks, in academic and popular formats. The project's research will be used to develop educational materials for a citizen engagement process, the results of which is intended to inform a long-term and multi-faceted policy strategy for BC.

As the primary community partner is a research and policy advocacy organization, the roles between researcher and community are intermingled. While this can have many positive benefits in terms of focusing research to areas that will have the most policy benefits, it has also resulted in tensions when the university researchers' timetables and priorities are different than the community researchers. Community researchers may not see the benefit of doing theoretical research that can set frameworks for future research. Their focus is on policy relevant research. Academic researchers are not used to reporting research in a popular format and to a tight deadline. While the community research organization does peer review for all of their publications, there is not the same importance on peer-reviewed publications as in the academy. As well, since the community partner is administering the project and setting the budget, funding for students is not as high a priority as it would be if administered by an academic. Nevertheless, the community partner has a good grasp of the socio-political context of the issues surrounding climate change and extensive linkages to both environmental and social justice organizations, providing the academics with entrees into these groups that might be difficult to make otherwise.

Conclusion

Barriers to collaboration on advocacy and mobilization
In the discussion of the cases above we have identified a number of barriers that prevent the translation of community-based research to further social justice. The first case, points to the ambivalent relationship universities have with community engagement. CBAR projects may be funded, but they face risks if the results, findings, or 'products' do not meet traditional university expectations of scholarship. The second case also shows a tension. PAR approaches can bring to the surface evidence of structural inequalities, but the findings of these projects are rendered suspect by policy-makers who regard such studies as, at best, anecdotal. What is valued and recognized in many decision making arenas is quantitative research, the qualitative accounts of participants rendered less worthy (e.g. Risk, 2000).

The last two cases illustrate the differing roles, responsibilities and perspectives of the community and university partners. Collaborations shift during different phases of the research process resulting in various administrative and other barriers to collaboration. There needs to be recognition of issues pertaining to funding, timing and dissemination of information to relevant audiences. In order to move forward on research collaborations between university and community partners, funding and time constraints and the differing mandates of community and university institutions needs to be understood and supported. Community partners cannot participate beyond what is financially supported and within the mandates of their organizations. University partners are also hampered by their university responsibilities and its expectations. Although the goal of CBAR is to involve all parties equally, their unequal ability to be involved highlights the need to recognize that there are inequities and that each partner needs to be supported in a way that suits their restrictions.

We have found that in some CBAR projects the community and university partners are not as explicit with each other as they could be about what they hope to get out of a project. There is often a tension in trying to be explicit without being doctrinaire, as the nature of research is meant to produce an outcome that is not easily predicted, and community contexts change, sometimes dramatically, in the course of research on policy-related issues. However, there is an opportunity for learning between the community and university by sharing challenges, and addressing unpredictable occurrences and needs. The challenges can contribute to an understanding of research focus, and may help clarify some of the practice challenges as well as identify the many voices in a collaborative process.

Whether academic researchers should engage with advocacy is a long-standing debate, as Ladwig and Gore (1994, p. 234) note, 'the paradox of academic activism is a failure to think clearly about the relationship between the audience for the research and the context that is supposedly opened up for change'. And there is often a disjuncture between the aims and resources available in a project that limits the ability to do advocacy and mobilization. While academic and community partners may agree on the importance of these activities they are difficult to accomplish without appropriate and sufficient resources. Academic funders do not provide on-going funding for mobilization activities, and little or no funding for reporting of findings through community avenues. Even if they do provide funding, these community-based dissemination strategies are not recognized as legitimate 'products' of research. Furthermore, academic funding guidelines are also not realistic in terms of release-time stipends for community partners to undertake work on these projects. Community organizations do not have access to public funding to cover a share of the research stipends as universities have. Furthermore, funding agencies are reducing, or eliminating, the release-time stipends for both academic and community partners.

In trying to address disjunctures in collaboration, there need to be realistic expectations on what can be accomplished in a research project to influence policy changes. Available resources need to match these expectations. Community partners need to play a pivotal role in influencing policy as they often have the expertise in advocacy and mobilization. In academic models of policy research, it is the expert researcher(s) and senior officials in government who meet with the policy-makers (politicians/cabinet members) who then move policy based on the best available evidence. There is no, or a limited role, for community input. This, as portrayed in Figure 12.1, is a 'triangle' that needs to be redesigned as a 'diamond' where communities become active participants in the influencing of policy through research.[5]

The diamond of policy change shown in Figure 12.1 is offered as a re-conceptualization of the relationship between community, university and policy-makers, whereby the community, researchers, senior officials and politicians are all involved in affecting policy change. This recommendation is made considering Fraser's politics of recognition, noting the dominant

Figure 12.1 Diamond of policy change

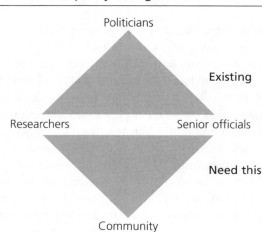

224

orientation of policy-makers (and it could be argued academic tenure review committees) to research is very much to maintain the status quo. As Nutley *et al*. (2007) point out, policy-makers respond to research where the methodology is relatively uncontested, where results support existing ideologies and are not contentious to the powerful, where research findings have strong advocates within the existing political structure, and are endorsed by opinion leaders.

The politics of recognition

By offering several examples of CBAR projects, another point has been raised, perhaps a more substantive and controversial one; the discussion of how scholarship and research is understood, recognized, and evaluated. As Saltmarsh *et al*. (2009) argue, in a report on university-community engagement activities, to fully take up the challenge of community engagement, universities and colleges cannot continue with the status quo. They noted there was 'widespread evidence of innovative engagement activities across higher education' (p. 1). However, they reference a 2004 conference report on community university engagement prepared by Brukardt *et al*. (2004),) which notes that: 'few institutions have made the significant, sustainable, structural reforms that will result in an academic culture that values community engagement as a core function of the institution' (p. 5). Referring to another author (Cuban, 1988), Saltmarsh *et al*. (2009) call for 'second order' changes in 'the fundamental ways in which organizations are put together' (p. 12). Reconsideration is needed in relation to how research and scholarship in general, particularly CBAR and PAR approaches, are understood and regarded in key moments of evaluation such as tenure and promotion.

These four cases illustrate how conducting mutually beneficial and respectful forms of community engagement through CBAR takes time: time to build relationships, time in the field, and for many projects, a long term commitment. This temporal dimension of community engagement must be taken up front and centre in discussions that seek to promote a larger involvement with such initiatives. A project may take several years to establish trust and build relationships with community groups, conduct the actual research itself, and share the results of that engagement. As the above authors note, to really have community engagement become central to university culture, then there needs to be an understanding and recognition of the value of different forms of scholarship beyond traditional articles in academic peer reviewed journals. There are different ways of knowledge dissemination, of sharing the results of CBAR with communities and the wider public (such as community forums, theatre and other arts-based methods). What counts as peer review needs to be reconsidered. The principles of CBAR challenge the traditional academic notion of peer review; community partners bring important perspectives to bear on review of the research process and its outcomes. Their contributions and assessment of the validity and relevance of the research are rarely recognized in any significant way in the academy. Academic researchers engaging with these alternative understandings of research, research productivity and value, face the risk of their hard work being undervalued or at worst considered irrelevant to the work of a research intensive university. If community engagement is valued then this needs to be evident in all sites of evaluation from the review of proposals to the granting of tenure.

In closing

We have sought to emphasize three key points in this chapter. First, we draw attention to the challenges of academic–community research partnerships and call for recognition of the different material and political contexts which have bearing on the research possibilities and orientations of academic and non-academic researchers. Second we want to note how CBAR, when conducted in mutually respectful and beneficial ways for both academic and community participants, is not only about generating important information and data, thus contributing to knowledge, but it is a process that can also mobilize knowledge and involve taking action. The third point is that CBAR, which involves building partnerships with community groups and making the knowledge generated from research more widely available, is a form of public pedagogy and a significant aspect of policy engagement, especially in those circumstances where change of repressive policy is needed.

CBAR and university-community partnerships are central to universities moving forward, and learning from, community engagement processes. This requires reflexivity on the part of both universities and their community partners to recognize and overcome the barriers to this engagement.

In the beginning it was noted our research and specifically our approach to CBAR was informed by a feminist sensibility and a commitment to social justice and contributing to what Haraway (1988) has called 'power sensitive conversations'. This attention to power, particularly gender inequality, was central to the four cases discussed in this chapter. Whether in the context of feminist organizing and coalitions, the experiences of Filipino domestic workers, the repressive policy reforms that diminished the lives of single mothers on social assistance, or ways in which the public debate about climate change must be broadened in order to recognize its links to social and gender injustice, issues of power permeate every case.

In this chapter attention was also drawn to the power relations which shape CBAR and community engagement, specifically the question of what counts as knowledge and scholarship. Fraser's framework that considers the politics of redistribution, recognition and participation helps to illustrate how much work remains to be done so that community-centred knowledge dissemination principles of CBAR, including the importance of advocacy, are valued and funded, and acted upon.

References

Brukardt, M.J., Holland, B., Percy, S. and Zimpher, N. (2004) *Calling the question: Is higher education ready to commit to community engagement.* A Wingspread statement, available at www.uc.edu/president25/documents/wingspread.pdf Accessed 2 October 2010.

Butterwick, S. (2002) 'Your story/my story/our story: Performing interpretation in participatory theatre', *Alberta Journal of Educational Research*, 48(3), 161–177.

Butterwick, S. and Selman, J. (2006) 'Embodied metaphors: Telling feminist coalition stories through popular theatre', in D. Clover and J. Stalker (eds.) Special Issue: 'The art of social justice: Re-crafting activist adult education', *New Zealand Journal of Adult Learning*, 34(2), 42–58.

Butterwick, S. and Selman, J. (2003) 'Intentions and context: Popular theatre in a North American context' in *Convergence*, 36, 51-66.

Butterwick, S. and Selman, J. (2009) Shaking the belly: Laughter as 'Good Medicine' in anti-oppressive work', *Educational Insights,* 3(2) http://ccfi.educ.ubc.ca/publication/insights/v13n02/toc.html Accessed 2 October 2010.

Cuban, L. (1988) 'A fundamental puzzle of school reform', *Phi Delta Kappan,* 69(5), 341–342.

Fine, M. (1994) 'Dis-stance and other stances: Negotiations of power inside feminist research', in A. Gitlin (ed.) *Power and method – Political activism and educational research*, 13–35. New York: Routledge.

Flyvbjerg, B. (2001) *Making social science matter – Why social inquiry fails and how it can succeed again*. Cambridge: Cambridge University Press.

Fraser, N. (1998) 'Social justice in the age of identity politics: Redistribution, recognition and participation', Paper presented at the Wissenschaftszentrum Berlin Fur Sozialforschung, Berlin, Germany. Retrieved from http://www.ISSENSGELLSCHAFT.org.

Fraser, N. (2001) 'Social justice in the knowledge society: Redistribution, recognition and participation', Paper presented at the *Wissenschaftszentrum Berlin Fur Socialforschung*, Berlin, Germany. Retrieved from http://www.WISSENGELLSCHAFT.org.

Fuller, S.; Kershaw, P. and Pulkingham, J. (2008) 'Constructing "active citizenship": Single mothers, welfare, and the logics of voluntarism', *Citizenship Studies,* 12(2) 157–176.

Gurstein, P. and Goldberg, M. (with Fuller, S.; Kershaw, P; Pulkingham, J. and Vilches, S.) (2008) *Precarious and vulnerable: Lone mothers on income assistance.* Burnaby: SPARC.

Gurstein, P. and Vilches, S. (2009) 'Re-visioning the environment of support for lone mothers in extreme poverty', in M. Cohen and J. Pulkingham (eds.), *Public policy for women: The state, income security, and labor*, 226–247) Toronto: University of Toronto Press.

Hall, B. (2001) 'I wish this were a poem of practices of participatory research', in P. Reason and H. Bradbury (eds.) *Handbook of action research – Participative inquiry and practice,* 171–178. Thousand Oaks: Sage.

Haraway, D. (1988) 'Situated knowledges: The science question in feminism and the privilege of partial perspective', *Feminist Studies*, 14(3), 575–97.

Ibàñez-Carrasco, F. and Riaño-Alcalá, P. (2009) 'Organizing community-based research knowledge between universities and communities: Lessons learned', *Community Development Journal* doi: 10.1093/cdj/bsp041.

Kershaw, P.; Pulkingham, J. and Fuller, S. (2008) 'Expanding the subject: Violence, care and (in)active male citizenship', *Social Politics: International Studies in Gender, State and Society,* 15(2), 1–25.

Ladwig, J.G. and Gore, J. M. (1994) 'Extending power and specifying method within the discourse of activist research', in A. Gitlin (ed.), *Power and method: Political activism and educational research*, 227–239. New York: Routledge.

Levin, M. and Greenwood, D. (2001) 'Pragmatic action research and the struggle to transform universities into learning communities', in P. Reason, and H. Bradbury (eds.) *Handbook of action research – Participative inquiry and practice,* 103–113. Thousand Oaks: Sage.

Maguire, P. (2001) 'Uneven ground: Feminisms and action research', in P. Reason, and H. Bradbury (Eds.) *Handbook of action research – Participative inquiry and practice,* 59–69. Thousand Oaks: Sage.

National Alliance of Philippine Women in Canada. http://www.napwc.org/ Accessed 2 October 2010.

Nussbaum, M. C. (2006) 'Poverty and human functioning: Capabilities as fundamental entitlements', (Chapter 3) in *Poverty and inequality* (pp. 47–75) Standford, CA: Stanford University Press.

Nutley, S.; Walter, I. and Davies, H. (2007) *Using evidence: How research can inform public services.* Bristol, UK: Policy Press.

Prentki, B. and Selman, S. (2000) *Popular theatre in political culture: Britain and Canada in focus.* Bristol, UK: Intellect Books.

Razack, S. (1998) *Looking white people in the eye.* Toronto: University of Toronto Press.

Risk, R.C. (2000) 'Influencing the policy process with qualitative research', in N.K. Denzin and Y. S. Lincoln (eds.), *Handbook of qualitative research*, 2nd edn, 1001–1017. Thousand Oaks: Sage.

Saltmarsh, J.; Hartley, M, and Clayton. P. (2009) *Democratic engagement white paper.* Boston, MA: New England Resource Centre for Higher Education.

Wadsworth, Y. (1998) 'What is participatory action research?' *Action Research International*, 2, Downloaded 31 January 2020 from http://www. scu.edu.au/schools/gcm/ar/ari/p-ywadsworth98.html.

Notes

[1] The Income Assistance Project, a study funded through CHILD (Consortium for Health, Intervention, Learning and Development), a SSHRC MCRI (Social Science and Humanities Research Council Major Collaborative Research Initiative) project, is a qualitative longitudinal study that investigates how low-

income, lone-mother families are affected by provincial policy changes that have reduced social assistance and enforced paid work obligations for assistance recipients.

[2] The community partners were Social Planning and Research Council of BC (SPARC BC) and Canadian Centre for Policy Alternatives of BC (CCPA).

[3] The Climate Justice Project, a project funded through the SSHRC CURA program (Social Science and Humanities Research Council Community-University Research Alliance) is a large project with four major streams of research and many small funded studies. See: http://www.policyalternatives.ca/projects/climate-justice-project/about Accessed 2 October 2010.

[4] This is a partnership between the CCPA and UBC. The Community Planning professor initially was the Co-Principal Investigator on the project but is now one of the stream leaders.

[5] Developed by Michael Goldberg, former Research Director at the Social Planning and Research Council of BC, and community partner on the Income Assistance project. Presented at the Community Campus Partnerships in Health 10th Anniversary Conference, Toronto, 2007.

Chapter 13

From service to engagement: Moving margins to the centre

Paul Crawford, Anne Kaplan and Diana Robinson

Introduction

University professionals committed to the practice of engagement must be willing to work in the interstices where prized traditions confront the need for adaptation. This work combines boldness and delicacy and, if done well, produces a 'productive zone of disequilibrium' that can yield innovation (Heifetz *et al.*, 2009, p. 29). Universities are odd organizations: on the one hand they guard important cultural traditions; on the other hand, they question existing forms of knowledge and practice. Such dialectical work is their *raison d'être*. However, it's not unusual for universities to chafe when their forms of knowledge and practice are called into question.

This chapter describes how Northern Illinois University (NIU), a large public regional university in America's heartland (100 km west of Chicago, Illinois), has been reframing its approach to regional service in response to fundamental shifts in demography, economics and public policy. These shifts have been felt across the entire higher education landscape but particularly by public higher education institutions (HEIs) sharing geographic space with other institutions striving to meet the economic and workforce development needs of their common region. As the landscape reorganized itself, key adaptations were necessary for NIU to sustain its relevance as a regional university.

This account focuses on the Division of Administration and University Outreach (NIUO) and its response to factors – internal and external – shaping its capacity for 'third mission' work. The division took strategic steps to mobilize a culture of engagement. As a change agent, NIUO conducted 'in-reach' *and* 'out-reach' work designed to move marginal practices to the centre of university strategic design and conduct. The process of creating holding environments where successful engagement can occur is delicate, and often political (Heifetz, 1994).

Background

The W.K. Kellogg Foundation's 1996 study on the future of public universities in the United States warned that '[Institutions] ignore a changing environment at their peril . . . [and] risk becoming . . . irrelevant in a world that has passed them by' (Kellogg Commission, 1996, Introduction, para. 3). These words implicitly questioned third mission models which emphasize unilateral, episodic or issue-centred service. Such approaches are giving way to engagement practices that create 'collaboration between higher education institutions and their larger communities (local, regional/state, national, global) for the exchange of knowledge and resources in a context of partnership and reciprocity' (Carnegie Foundation, 2010, Community Engagement Section, para 1). Engagement practices accept and assert responsibility for the well-being of regions by sharing leadership that pursues sustained, regional prosperity (Alliance for Regional Stewardship *et al.*, 2006).

The northern quarter of Illinois, anchored by Chicago, contains roughly 80 per cent of the state's population and occupies at the heart of a robust global economic region (Florida *et al.*, 2007). NIU is a public doctoral/research-extensive university with a regional mission to serve the Chicago metropolitan area, expanding suburbs, traditional manufacturing cities, and smaller rural communities. Surrounding Chicago are several 'collar counties' without a local public university in their midst. Most NIU students come from this region and remain for employment.

From its beginnings in 1895, NIU has possessed a clear regional mission – joining sibling institutions serving southern, eastern and western regions in Illinois. In terms of its continuing education function, however, the university oscillated between centralization and decentralization from the 1930s through the 1990s. Between 1992 and 2001, the university built two education centres in the collar counties, and a third in Rockford to the northwest, prompting consideration of new economic and community development activities. To proceed effectively, greater coherence among previously dispersed units was needed to create a shared understanding of engagement practices. Following a strategic planning process, a contextualized vision took shape guided by three questions.

- What is unique about our situation?
- What can we be the best at?
- What can we do to integrate engagement activities across the institution?

The strategic planning process yielded business plans aligned with the division's vision, mission and priorities; branding and identity standards were formed; and a performance-management process was implemented. The results of this learning process included the integration of engagement into departmental, unit and individual activities; a framework for responding to questions regarding the university's regional impact; and a narrative for integrating engagement practices across the university.

Figure 13.1 was developed to represent the division's relationship to its external environment and illustrate concepts driving engagement efforts. The overlapping circles place NIUO within NIU, and NIU within the region. The

Figure 13.1

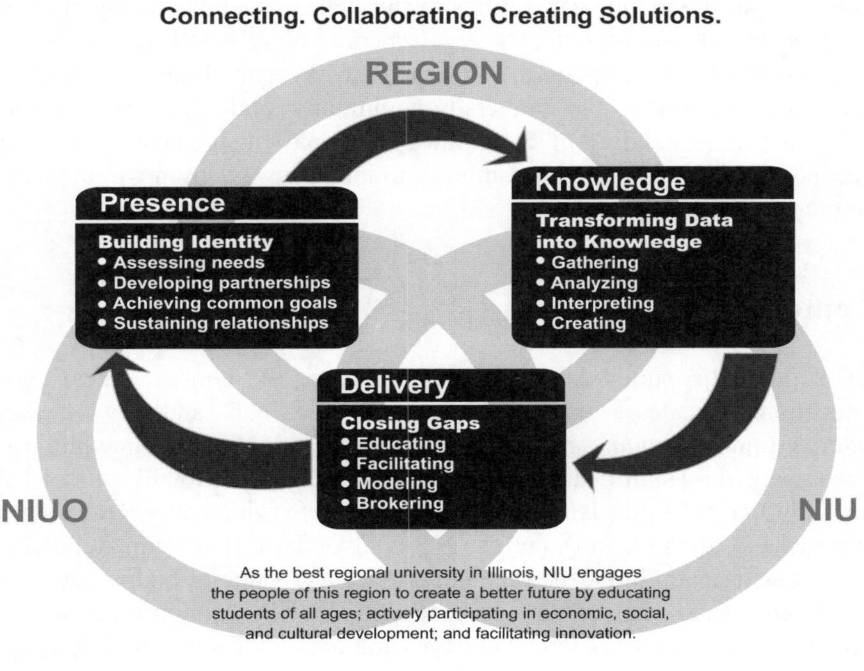

Connecting. Collaborating. Creating Solutions.

REGION

Presence
Building Identity
- Assessing needs
- Developing partnerships
- Achieving common goals
- Sustaining relationships

Knowledge
Transforming Data into Knowledge
- Gathering
- Analyzing
- Interpreting
- Creating

Delivery
Closing Gaps
- Educating
- Facilitating
- Modeling
- Brokering

NIUO

NIU

As the best regional university in Illinois, NIU engages the people of this region to create a better future by educating students of all ages; actively participating in economic, social, and cultural development; and facilitating innovation.

boxes labeled 'presence,' 'knowledge' and 'delivery' represent objectives. Whereas most universities have discrete units charged with such activities, NIUO now provides an organizational home to the following operations, combining educational delivery, applied research and economic development, and information technology services:

- Association Resource Center
- Broadband Development Group
- Center for Governmental Studies
- Center for P-20 Engagement (P-20 is the pre-school through postgraduate education continuum)
- Community College Relations
- Conferencing Services
- Education and Training
- eLearning Services
- Information Technology Services
- PASCAL International
- Rural Health Resource Services
- Northern Public Radio

Simply gathering talent is insufficient; a common understanding of engagement practices is needed to consolidate units which might not comprehend the unique capabilities of their closest neighbors. By engaging each other, opportunities for synergy emerge. What is still in progress for NIU Outreach, however, is the 'in-reach' work of integrating engagement practices throughout the university-community and facilitating a more extensive understanding of the value of regional engagement for first and second mission work. NIUO continues to identify ways to move the margin to the centre.

Context

Like all public policy-dependent enterprises in the United States, higher education navigates a macroeconomic sea which ebbs and flows between interventionism and *laissez-faire* capitalism. Major national policy initiatives accompanied by significant public resources – e.g., the Morrill Acts of 1862 and 1890 establishing land-grant colleges, the Servicemen's Readjustment Act of 1944 (the G.I. Bill), and the National Defense Education Act of 1958 – have historically broadened the importance and value of higher education. In recent years, however, a preoccupation with economic crises and competing priorities has forced colleges and universities to find independent solutions to demographic and economic fluctuations. At present, HEIs are being forced to manage twenty years of public disinvestment. State and federal support has contracted as the nation's need for an educated workforce and related services is at an all-time high. A popular public argument is that HEI costs are too high and accountability too low. As the public grapples with important issues of national security, health care, social security and tax relief, higher education seems to be pushed to the side and perceived as ineffectual in those areas that count most.

Asserting a coherent and relevant vision of university engagement is essential to reclaiming public support for the role of HEIs in society. That such impulses do not come naturally to many HEIs reflects a division of intellectual labour that creates boundaries both within and among HEIs. Organizations like NIUO cannot unilaterally make the case for public support of higher education, but they are the units in closest contact with a university's varied public constituencies. Engagement operations can and should reflect the best of what a university has to offer to the wider public by way of third mission outreach. One of these offerings involves carefully naming the challenges that face the wider public.

Articulating societal challenges, and providing warrants in support of those descriptions, is a political undertaking. For example, following a series of partnerships with individual community colleges, NIUO offered an analysis of three well-established cities in its primary service region (Northern Illinois University, 2005). This report described issues facing each community and several opportunities for collaboration among the HEIs serving these locales: NIU and three community colleges. A meeting of these HEIs was scheduled to discuss the NIU-identified issues: readiness for higher education, innovation, industry clusters and workforce development, and population growth and diversity. While there was general agreement among the participants regarding the identified concerns, consensus regarding multilateral collaboration failed to germinate. One institution expressed interest, but the others indicated the reluctance of their Boards of Trustees to support work benefiting communities outside their defined service boundaries. If nothing else, this meeting showed that something else was needed to mobilize collaboration. The fact that NIU prepared the initial report on its own, rather than through a joint process, might have sent the wrong message.

Community college engagement: lessons learned

Following construction of the aforementioned regional education centres, NIU had begun to consider new opportunities for collaboration with the twenty community colleges sharing the region. Such geographic density of two-year institutions is unusual in the US, but these HEIs were often taken for granted: a high proportion of associate's degree-bearing students would inevitably transfer from the community colleges to NIU, so a kind of *laissez-faire* symbiosis prevailed.

Figure 13.2 The Northern Illinois region, NIU and surrounding community colleges

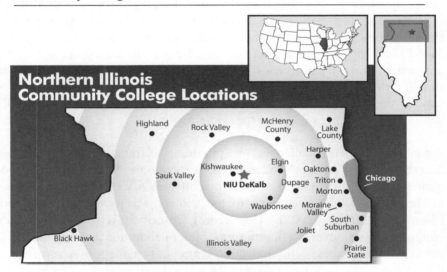

Note. Concentric circles indicate 40 km increments from DeKalb, IL.

Over the past several decades, approximately 40 per cent of NIU graduates have begun their academic careers at community colleges. But, as the competitive landscape changes, private and profit-oriented proprietary institutions are achieving significant success in delivering marketable degrees for place-bound working adults who often purchase higher education on the basis of convenience rather than cost. As this new majority of nontraditional students (25 years of age and older) eclipses the traditional 18–22-year-old demographic, the 'what, where and how' of higher education has become increasingly commoditized (Kaplan, 2004). How can a public university, with a deep and abiding commitment to academic traditions, adapt without compromising core principles?

To better understand these issues, we differentiate in Table 13.3 between technical and adaptive challenges (Heifetz, 1994), a distinction that illuminates the dynamic tension between inherited traditions and the need for innovation. Technical problems represent interruptions or gaps resolved with existing knowledge or by appeal to authorities with expertise. Such tradition-reinforcing authority might reside in manuals, scholars, regulatory agencies, or even politicians. By contrast, adaptive problems require stakeholder learning as existing knowledge is insufficient or absent.

Table 13.3. Technical and adaptive problems

Technical problems	Adaptive problems
Easy to identify	Easy to identify; easy to ignore
Lend themselves to cut-and-dried solutions	Require changes in values, beliefs, roles, relationships and approaches to work
Often solved by an authority or expert	People with the problem do the work of solving it
Require limited changes, often contained within a single organization	Require change in numerous places, often across organizational boundaries
People are generally receptive to technical solutions	People often resist acknowledging adaptive challenges
Solutions often implemented quickly – even by edict	Solutions require experiment and discovery; they can take a long time to implement and must be voluntary

Note: Adapted from Heifetz and Linsky (2002).

Adaptive challenges fall into four general categories (Heifetz *et al.*, 2009). The first involves *a gap between espoused values and actual behaviour*. For example, HEIs might speak in terms of providing access to underserved populations while using disproportionate levels of endowments to recruit high-achieving students with multiple enrollment options. Secondly, HEIs might wrestle with *competing commitments*, such as research vs. public service. A third challenge involves *institutional resistance to difficult or unspeakable issues* that lie below the surface but silently influence decision-making. Finally, *work avoidance* is evinced by systematic diversions or deflected responsibility. Knowledge of these patterns should inform the interstitial work of engagement, both internal and external.

Resolution of adaptive challenges often requires a change in ideals, attitudes and behaviours – although such changes need not mean jettisoning essential values. Engaging people, organizations and communities in this work is difficult because the *status quo*, even when it is no longer effective, is called into question. The engagement process takes on heightened significance because the work of adaptation involves adjudicating what is essential and what can be modified or discarded as no longer effectual (Heifetz *et al.*, 2009). This work is particularly hard in the academy where the professional ethos often stands in opposition to such factors as marketplace rationality.

Boundary-spanning practitioners engaged in mobilizing adaptive work need to understand the political nature of their work. The dangers and opportunities are real, most particularly the tendency for individuals and organizations to treat adaptive challenges as technical problems. Engagement practitioners who instigate and/or modulate provocative work will encounter predictable forms of resistance, including diversion, marginalization and seduction by the status quo or outright attack (Heifetz and Linsky, 2002).

Returning to the topic of NIU's engagement with its neighboring community colleges, some additional background is necessary. Generally, the highest academic credentials awarded by community colleges are two-year associate's degrees. But, as the higher education landscape shifts, this inherited model of what constitutes a normative division of labour among community colleges and baccalaureate institutions is called into question. For example, the Carnegie Classification of Institutions of Higher Education system in the United States now has a category for 'associate's college' because some states authorize community colleges to award baccalaureate degrees (Carnegie Foundation, 2010). These community college baccalaureates are predominantly designed to create progression pathways for individuals with two-year applied science degrees in career and technical fields (Townsend *et al.*, 2008). Career and technical education programmes are to associate of applied science (AAS) degrees what traditional transfer programmes are to the associate in arts (AA) or associate in science (AS) degrees.

Using the International Standard Classification of Education system (UNESCO, 1997) to facilitate international comparison, the AAS degree is a credential (Level 4B) that does not provide access to tertiary programmes (Levels 5 and 6). As such, the AAS has been considered a terminal degree in the United States (Cohen and Brawer, 2010) and is typically dismissed by baccalaureate degree-granting HEIs as something other than higher education. However, as marketplace and workforce development needs change, universities have noticed that AAS degrees account for a large portion of the two-year degrees awarded by community colleges: 38 per cent in Illinois during 2009 (Illinois Community College Board, 2010). As the community college baccalaureate movement gained momentum in the United States (Floyd *et al.*, 2005), Harper College (a northern Illinois community college named for University of Chicago founder William Rainey Harper, one of the nation's earliest community college advocates) initiated a call for state-level legislative change to garner authority to 'offer a pilot program under which the district may offer bachelor's degrees' (Illinois General Assembly, 2009). NIU and other public and private universities opposed this legislation. At the same time, however, NIU's Center for Governmental Studies (CGS) co-produced a *State of Working Illinois* report which argued that a baccalaureate degree was the most important factor in boosting a worker's wage-earning potential (Gleeson *et al.*, 2008).

Harper College – one of NIU's top transfer-student producing community colleges – wanted baccalaureate degrees formulated in response to documented workforce development needs in their service district, particularly in areas related to homeland security professions, such as police and fire officers, a politically attractive goal. NIU offered to deliver existing programmes which it considered relevant, but Harper demurred, indicating a lack of match with the needs-assessment data garnered through environmental scanning and employer interviews. Following a protracted public relations contest and an associated legislative battle, the two sides eventually came to an accord (Pohl, 2009). But getting to this point was far from easy, given conflicting internal interpretations regarding what Harper wanted and what the university could fairly do while retaining as much of the *status quo ante* as possible. The university did not possess a single perspective on this matter: NIU Outreach had one perspective, University Relations another and the faculty a third. More importantly, it was hard to get the right representatives together for the right conversation.

Had this baccalaureate access issue not been turned into a legislative contest it is hard to predict how the institutions might have achieved resolution. When the demand for education is strong and the options more than sufficient, as was the case in Illinois during the 1950s and 1960s, opportunities for self-serving growth outpace collaborative impulses. However when the marketplace tightens, as it has since the 1980s when enrollments tapered off, issues of identity, mission and strategy are called into question.

NIU's collaboration with community colleges to develop a new academic programme was experimental rather than instinctive. On one hand it broke the traditional baccalaureate mold in order to serve AAS degree-holders, which is what Harper and other community colleges were seeking. But on the other, it brought faculty together in a collegial manner that enabled both sides to see that there was a shared interest in serving students without sacrificing core baccalaureate principles. Collaboration of this sort required both internal and external faculty engagement before a constructive inter-institutional conversation could take place. A kind of ethnographic learning was called for. Completing this work helped both sides become intelligible to one another and generated a holding environment where innovation could occur. In the end, a new, very practical baccalaureate programme was developed through joint needs assessment, cooperative planning and shared leadership. To facilitate this adaptive work, NIU Outreach had to navigate a number of inter- and intra-organizational boundaries, preserve fragile social capital, and find ways to pace the work so that the level of disequilibrium did not exceed individual or organizational tolerance before a resolution was possible.

Overzealous attention to what makes institutions different from one another – an unfortunate consequence of classification systems – can also impede the development of a collaborative imagination. In the United States, the term 'articulation' describes the process of comparing academic courses during a student's inter-institutional transfer process. More broadly, articulation provides a metaphor for examining NIU's relationship with its neighbors. Far too often, certain HEIs consider other institutions to be unintelligible and see no reason why a forced relationship will be anything other than disjointed. Such defensive assessments are typically made as a function of preserving an institution's core values. In the case just presented, AAS degrees were not being articulated; they did not correspond to existing models of progression and the arguments made by HEIs advocating for their significance in the higher education system were hard to grasp. In the end, the strongest impetus for institutional change in the face of the Harper Bill was the political situation, which did help bring the right people to the table. Together, the institutions developed new ways of articulating degrees and co-created high-quality baccalaureate-completion programmes for previously marginalized audiences. NIU was able to adapt to the changing environment because it learned how to listen to the needs of the region according to terms that the region articulated. It moved from a position of providing service to a position of being an engaged partner willing to share teaching, learning and leadership.

At the heart of any adaptive learning process is diagnosing the challenge. Consider a gathering of college and university presidents to discuss sharing institutional talent in order to solve vexing problems that outstrip their independent problem-solving capabilities. Each president in such a discussion represents multiple constituencies (faculty, administrators, accreditation agencies, service regions, tax payers, funders and donors). Additionally, each president arrives with some pre-understanding regarding the issue. Finally, as an interlocutor, each president has notions regarding ideal outcomes, key values that must be upheld, and a list of potential losses that will need to be managed if adaptive change is indeed necessary. Each of these elements, if disturbed, can create disequilibrium in the status quo. On the one hand, disturbances and disequilibrium signal where the work of engagement must take place. On the other hand, too much disequilibrium can outstrip an individual's (or an organization's) ability to work through the adaptive challenge. Engagement professionals need the social capital, and the interpersonal skills, that sustain this boundary-crossing work. Further, they must pace the work so disturbances can be resolved within a safe holding environment. In short, the engagement challenge involves managing disequilibrium so that it becomes productive.

As the Harper Bill episode played out, the Illinois Board of Higher Education (IBHE) launched an initiative called the Illinois Public Agenda for College and Career Success. Goals associated with this initiative included increasing educational attainment, expanding college affordability, developing more post-secondary credentials to meet the demands of the economy and global society, and improving integration of Illinois' educational, research and innovation assets (Illinois Board of Higher Education, 2009). At the heart of the agenda was a push to develop new regional partnering habits. As the IBHE agenda was taking shape, NIU was introduced to PASCAL International, an independent not-for-profit global organization dedicated to promoting the exchange of best practices in place management, social capital, and learning region development (see also Chapter 1, the introduction to this volume). Following a period of mutual investigation and discussions, NIU's interests in regional engagement seemed to mesh with PASCAL, so the university agreed to become both a member and the North American administrative partner.

As the PASCAL Universities Regional Engagement (PURE) initiative took shape in 2008, NIU approached the region's community colleges in hopes of capitalizing on the growing emphasis on regional collaboration. Since PURE was designed to investigate the role of HEIs in sustainable regional development, and NIUO was determined to establish a new model for collaboration, the institution's leadership jointly convened a meeting with regional community college presidents to discuss the PURE initiative at a community college campus. In order to set the right tone, this meeting utilized a consensus-building approach that involved as much listening as speaking.

Whereas the previous community college meeting, which took place in 2005, did not create the kind of leverage hoped for, it provided lessons that helped the university modify its posture. This time, the institutions did agree on a collaborative effort to formulate a comprehensive, demand-driven strategy for responding to existing and projected workforce development needs in the northern Illinois region, and to find ways to open higher education opportunities for people in poverty. In short order, the institutions also assigned high-level decision makers to a PURE project work team.

As the next set of PURE meetings commenced with these newly assigned participants, additional collaborative, trust-building work had to be replicated – a slow but valuable and necessary process. At the conclusion of the first phase of the PURE project, a set of regional themes took shape in alignment with the founding charge. Each theme would require shared, cross-regional learning among the HEIs and other regional partners rooted in the founding charge of workforce development and increasing access to higher education for economically marginalized residents.

Four projects were identified:
1. Expanding access to the baccalaureate for career and technical professionals, based on collaborative regional assessment to determine workforce development needs; and, investigating the most effective modes of instruction and delivery to enhance affordable accessibility for place-bound adult learners.
2. Creating shared regional outreach to Latino audiences, with a focus on enhancing 'higher education literacy' among families; and, identifying best practices for establishing cooperative linkages between community-based organizations, community colleges and four-year institutions to create coherent pathways into higher education.

3. Turning regional data into practical information to efficiently shape economic and workforce development practices; determining the types of data, e.g., current/projected demographics, economic, labour market, entrepreneurship, and business-related, needed by HEIs and affiliated enterprises; and, developing a web-based portal to disseminate information.
4. Gathering regional HEIs together to streamline student transfer and progression between community colleges and baccalaureate institutions, particularly in teacher education programmes.

Although much of the initial energy for these efforts came from NIU, a major focus of the second phase of PURE (still in progress as of this writing) is rebalancing ownership of the projects. Each of these four projects was selected because it was important to a majority of the partners, and a litmus test of the project's value will be whether partnerships continue in meaningful ways over the long run.

Conclusion: toward a necessarily uncertain future

One of the most valuable roles a public university can and should play is that of a convener, creating holding environments where adaptive challenges can be productively engaged. To be effective in this role, HEIs must first tackle their own adaptive challenges and be willing to creatively engage tension (internal and external) associated with balancing traditions and calls for innovation. By re-examining its core commitments and pursuing institutional learning, NIU is creating a new engagement paradigm. Most recently, the university's involvement in international comparative research has provided additional opportunities to recast its relationship with regional partners and constituents, some of whom had been left on the margins. New boundary-dissolving networks are developing, linking NIU with provocative enterprises concerned with the vitality of northern Illinois. The success of this work – internal and external; local and global – will verify NIU's ability to be a fully engaged partner in the educational, social, cultural, political and technological future of its region.

Effective boundary spanning, in service of creating social capital and generating collaboration, combines elements of art and science. Williams (2002) summarizes research on boundary spanning traits, including sophisticated networking skills, entrepreneurial and laterally innovative thinking, as well as a high tolerance for ambiguity and otherness. Such individuals and organizations are cultural brokers (Sydow, 2000) whose stock-in-trade is building inter-relational trust rather than hierarchical power (Heifetz *et al.*, 2009).

At a policy level, higher education in Illinois is, and is likely to remain, highly politicized as it responds to financial constraints and demands for evidence that warrants its value. Providing public value is particularly acute as higher education finds new ways to illustrate the impact of its work and argues for the investments needed to achieve transformational results. While teaching is the primary role of all but a few narrowly focused research institutions, public institutions, especially public regional institutions, must take every opportunity to assert a role for higher education that goes beyond instruction. Allowing legislators and the public to dismiss, overlook, or devalue the other core competencies of an engaged HEI will undermine the comprehensive role these institutions play in developing vibrant regions that can compete in the global marketplace.

NIU's engagement with community colleges provides an indication of how instructional issues (e.g., baccalaureate-completion programmes for marginalized audiences) capture the public's imagination. But there is more to the story as the intellectual capacity that produces instruction can serve many other purposes. Higher education's second mission, which is oriented to research and the creation of new forms of knowledge, is the most obvious of those uses and the one most familiar to university faculty. But in the current climate, many public officials view research as a task that should be the purview of a limited number of private universities and flagship publics. To survive in the 21st century and to make appropriate, effective and innovative use of the intellectual capital available on its campus, a regional university must become part of the fabric, the culture and the vitality of its service area. This engagement, in turn, feeds research – making it increasingly relevant to a public that demands accountability.

NIU's willingness to create new baccalaureate degrees in partnership with its community college neighbours demonstrates an adaptive leap forward. Extending engagement as a basic operational commitment across the wider university, however, is another matter. Boundary-crossing skills are needed within the institution where much needs to be done relative to integrating engagement practices within other university functions. Building internal working relationships is as complex and as political as working with external communities and groups.

In the current economic and political climate, public universities in general, and divisions like NIU Outreach in particular, face a future that looks less and less like the past. The shift in demographics, with more adult students seeking university courses and degrees, presents an opportunity to make the case for the value of a comprehensive regional university. Outreach units willing to adopt the complex, boundary-spanning practices of engagement are better positioned to make the case for universities relative to economic and workforce development, education reform, social welfare, and other policy issues occupying legislators. As public funding for higher education diminishes, universities need innovative ways to demonstrate their public value. Enterprises founded in principles of robust engagement have much to contribute to regional prosperity if they are integrated into the broader imagination of the university. At NIU, this work is in progress.

References

Alliance for Regional Stewardship, American Association of State Colleges and Universities and National Center for Higher Education Management Systems. (2006) *Tools and insights for universities called to regional stewardship.* Denver, CO, Washington, DC, and Boulder, CO: Alliance for Regional Stewardship.

Carnegie Foundation (2010) *The Carnegie classification of institutions of higher education.* Retrieved from http://classifications.carnegiefoundation. org/.

Cohen, A. M. and Brawer, F. B. (2010) *The American Community College* (5th edn.) San Francisco, CA: Jossey-Bass.

Florida, R., Gulden, T. and Mellander, C. (2007) 'The rise of the mega region', *Cambridge Journal of Regions, Economy and Society*, 1(3), 459–476. doi:10.1093/cjres/rsn018.

Floyd, D. L., Skolnik, M. L. and Walker, K. P. (eds.) (2005) *The community college baccalaureate: Emerging trends and policy issues.* Sterling, VA: Stylus Publishing.

Gleeson, R.E., Sobol, A., Soe, H., Taylor, S., Bisacky, T., Kaslow, Y., Mancini, C., Martire, R. and Kleppner, P. (2008) *The state of working Illinois, 2008.* Chicago and DeKalb, IL: Center for Tax and Budget Accountability, Center for Governmental Studies (Northern Illinois

University), and Office for Social Policy Research (Northern Illinois University).

Heifetz, R. A. (1994) *Leadership without easy answers*. Cambridge, MA: Harvard University Press.

Heifetz, R. A. and Linsky, M. (2002) *Leadership on the line: Staying alive through the dangers of leading*. Boston, MA: Harvard Business School Press.

Heifetz, R. A., Grashow, A., and Linsky, M. (2009) *The practice of adaptive leadership: Tools and tactics for changing your organization and the world*. Boston: Harvard Business Press.

Illinois Board of Higher Education. (2009) *The Illinois agenda for college and career success*. Retrieved from http://www.ibhe.org/masterPlanning/materials/070109 PublicAgenda.pdf.

Illinois Community College Board. (2010) *Annual student enrollments and completions in the Illinois community college system, fiscal year 2009*. Retrieved from http://www. iccb.org/pdf/reports/09enrollmentrpt.pdf.

Illinois General Assembly. (2009) *House bill 0656*. Retrieved from http://www.ilga.gov/legislation/96/HB/PDF/09600HB0656lv.pdf.

Kaplan, A.C. (2004) 'Outreach in the twenty-first century: Survival strategies for a unique environment', *Continuing Higher Education Review*, 68, 117–128.

Kaplan, A.C. (2010, February 10) 'The U.S. perspective on current challenges for universities and regions', opening plenary session comments presented at the PASCAL consultative development group visit to the Thames Gateway region, Eland House, London, England.

Kellogg Commission. (1996) *Taking charge of change: Renewing the promise of state and land-grant universities*. Washington, DC: W. K. Kellogg Foundation.

Northern Illinois University. (2005) *Shared challenges, collaborative responses – three river towns: Aurora, Elgin, Rockford*. DeKalb, IL: NIU Outreach and Administration.

Pohl, K. (2009) 'Harper, NIU strike deal that puts quest for 4-year degrees on hold', *Daily Herald*. Retrieved from http://www.dailyherald.com/story/?id=329984.

Sydow, J. (2000) 'Understanding the constitution of interorganizational trust', in Lane, C. and Bachman, R. (eds.) *Trust in and between organizations: Conceptual issues and empirical applications* (revised edn.), 31–63. Oxford: Oxford University Press.

Townsend, B. K., Bragg, D. D. and Ruud, C. M. (2008) *The adult learner and the applied baccalaureate: National and state-by-state inventory.* Retrieved from http://occrl.illinois.edu/sites/occrl.illinois.edu/files/Projects/ lumina/ Report/AppBaccInventory.pdf Accessed 25 February 2010.

UNESCO (United Nations Educational, Scientific and Cultural Organization) (1997) *International standard classification of education, 1997.* Retrieved from http://www.uis.unesco.org/TEMPLATE/pdf/isced/ ISCED_A.pdf.

Williams, P. (2002) 'The competent boundary-spanner', *Public Administration*, 80(1), 103–124.

Chapter 14

Faculty reward systems and the third mission of colleges and universities

Melvin Hill and LaVerne Williamson Hill

The public and the political systems which govern, support and monitor institutions of higher education in the United States have become increasingly more demanding in their expectations of both how those institutions operate and the results of those institutions' efforts. As societal problems become increasingly complex in both content and scope the public turns to universities and colleges for assistance in addressing those problems. The late Dr Ernest Boyer, former president of the Carnegie Foundation for the Advancement of Teaching, emphasized the great 'intellectual hope and civic progress' present in the many outstanding colleges and universities in the United States, visualizing them as 'partners' in the on-going search for solutions to society's most critical problems (Boyer, 1996, p. 11). This same sentiment was echoed in 2000 in the Penn State Uniscope 2000 project. 'The Information Age with its rapidly evolving technology demands a highly knowledgeable workforce and a civic culture of involvement and creativity. The 21st century presents major challenges and increased opportunities for University scholarship. We need to address the need for disseminating and applying state-of-the-art knowledge throughout society' (Alter, 2000, p. ix).

However Boyer noted in 1995 that, despite their considerable growth, America's colleges and universities also suffered from a disturbing decline in public confidence and a general belief that they were no longer the vital centres of important societal work they were intended to be. Institutions, and the faculty within them, can too often become self-absorbed and isolated from the communities which surround them. Political leaders often perceive institutions and faculty as living and working only within their campus enclaves, out of touch and unconcerned with the 'real world' or 'real world problems.' This sentiment was echoed by Dr Fred Davison, a former president of the University of Georgia, who once said that he felt that one of the most important responsibilities he had as president was to maintain a 'centrifugal force' in the organization, since the natural tendency at a university was 'centripetal.' He said that the sponsoring society expected no less and that there was an obligation on the part of the university to ensure that its sights were directed outward and not inward (Hill, 1999).

Boyer proposed that the academy must become more vigorous partners in a 'scholarship of engagement' (Boyer, 1996, p. 11). It was this 'scholarship of engagement' which offered the strongest possibility that institutions could give back to the public and political systems which created and supported them, which allowed them to utilize their intellect and talents to assist in the solutions to the problems plaguing modern society.

Boyer did not suggest replacing the traditional teaching and research missions of colleges and universities. Rather his 'scholarship of engagement' concept became a third mission of the institution, equal in importance to the other two, and important to the overall health and success of any institution of higher education and the community within which it existed.

In the years following Boyer's observations supporters of the concept of the scholarship of engagement, both inside and outside the academic community, have promoted this ideal. Examples of successful initiatives include the excellent work of the Community-Campus Partnerships for Health (www.ccph.info), Campus Compact (www.compact.org), the National Outreach Scholarship Conferences (www.outreachscholarship.org), and the member institutions of the Higher Education Network for Community Engagement (www.henceonline.org). Other scholars began to focus research and teaching in Boyer's area of inquiry, colleges and universities added units devoted to service work, policy-makers proposed working more closely with academic groups, etc.

In 1995, concerned that the United States and its land-grant institutions were facing significant structural changes, the National Association of State Universities and Land-Grant Colleges sought the financial support of the W.K. Kellogg Foundation to examine the future of public higher education. The project, spanning four years, examined all aspects of institutional function – values, accountability, costs, access, etc. and produced a set of detailed reports and recommendations. The Commission's recommendations included the following:

Institutions and academic leaders should:
- *transform their thinking about service so that engagement becomes a priority on every campus, a central part of institutional mission;*
- *develop an engagement plan;*
- *develop incentives to encourage faculty involvement in the engagement effort;*
- *secure stable funding to support engagement, through reallocation of existing funds or the establishment of a new Federal-state-local-private matching fund.*

(Kellogg Commission, 2001, p. 17)

The report went on the conclude that 'among the significant problems facing society today are challenges of creating genuine learning communities, encouraging lifelong learning, finding effective ways to overcome barriers to change, and building greater social and human capital in our communities. Engagement in the form of service-learning, outreach, and university–community partnerships can help address these problems' (p. 17).

The Commission's work was instrumental in further promoting the service concept among colleges and universities throughout the United States. But while the concept and mission of public service and engagement has indeed been accepted by institutions debate remains within and among universities as to its importance within the institutional community, how it should be defined, to what extent faculty should engage in this mission, and, in particular, how much weight faculty work in this effort should be given in the employment, promotion, and tenure process. It is this final factor which most directly affects the actual success of the mission itself, since it is the lack of a clear-cut evaluation and reward system which discourages faculty involvement in public service and engagement.

Historical issues

Ward (2003) identifies five major eras in the development of the system of higher education in the United States: Colonial College (1636–1770), Denominational College (1770–1860), Research University (1860–1945), Mass Education (1945–1975), and the Contemporary Era (1975–present). Higher Education is influenced by numerous important societal factors and changing social, cultural and political patterns, institutions of higher education reflect those changes overtime. In the United States the system of higher education has evolved from one which served a small number of economically privileged students to one which provided increasing access for many economic, social and cultural groups. As student and faculty populations became more diverse, research interests and agendas expanded to encompass issues more common to public and political interests. The public service mission gained support in the university/college setting.

'The research university era perhaps more than any other time in history solidified the explicitly public service mission of higher education' (Ward, 2003, p. 50). As Ward notes, the land-grant movement legislated and solidified relationships based on service between higher education and the public. Higher education institutions were no longer limited to educating students but were also committed to providing technical expertise to the growing nation. 'This time period firmly established the triumvirate mission of teaching, research, and service so commonly held in higher education today' (Ward, 2003, p. 50). During the contemporary era, however, many institutions moved away from the mission of service that once seemed so important. The Service Mission, having been incorporated into so many institutional mission statements as the all important third mission, has lost much of the ground gained in earlier years and often receives far less attention than its teaching and research counterparts. This problem seems due in large part to issues related to the difficulty of defining the service mission and assessing its importance as it relates to its sister missions.

Defining engagement and service

In 1996 the Kellogg Commission on the Future of State and Land-Grant Universities stated that the notion of engagement referred to redesigned and re-envisioned teaching, research, extension and service functions that are sympathetically and productively involved with the communities that campuses serve however those communities are defined (Ward, 2003, pp. 1–2). D. David P. Moxley suggested that 'the purpose of many institutions of higher education is to engage in research and, in particular, research for the common good, or to use a somewhat out of fashion word, for the commonwealth' (Moxley, 2004, p. 235).

While the term 'service' or 'public service' or even 'community service' could be considered positive activities in an institutional context, what do they actually mean? Teaching is clear. Research is clear. When these terms are used, college and university administration, faculty and staff understand what they mean, regardless of discipline. But what is service? How does the service mission of a university translate to the faculty role? While most colleges and universities reference service in their mission statements, and usually in their faculty promotion and tenure criteria and guidelines, few define specifically what they mean by 'service.' Perhaps even those who draft those statements have only a vague idea of what they mean by the term. Does it mean service to the institution? To the community? Which community – local, state or global? Will 'service' mean the same thing in one discipline as in another? Will the term have the same meaning in one department as another? As in one school as another?

Perhaps it is the many possible definitions or interpretations which have actually led to institutions' nebulous descriptions of service. This lack of clear definition is, in itself, a serious problem in promoting the service mission among faculty and within the institution as a whole. 'Because service is vaguely understood and defined, it is often viewed as less meaningful and important than for the more easily defined (and rewarded) roles of teaching and research' (Ward, 2003, p. 2). Faculty resist the 'rhetoric of civic responsibility' in their scholarship because of a concern for 'how it counts' or how this type of work will be viewed in a traditional promotion and evaluation system (Moore and Ward, 2008, p. 5). Faculty are unlikely to support or engage in the service role if they are uncertain as to where it fits in their own work agendas and/or how it is to be professionally recognized and rewarded (Ward, 2003). Current promotion and tenure evaluation systems which dominate the academic world demonstrate a clear preference for the research and teaching roles and either ignore outreach scholarship or show an outright prejudice against it in the evaluation process. For example, faculty may be advised by administrators that efforts in the service area will be labeled as volunteer work rather than professional work or will not be credited as part of their professional portfolio for evaluation for promotion or tenure. More often than not service has been viewed as more 'charity' than scholarship and thus not a priority in the academic environment.

It is true that the service mission is more difficult to define than its teaching and research mission counterparts, but it is no less important to define. The complexity of the definition process is found in both where the service is performed and who benefits from the service. 'Service' may be defined along two axes – internal vs external and professional related vs community related. Internal service may be defined as work done by faculty members within the institutional context and which is ultimately beneficial to the entities within the institution, such as service on committees or on faculty governance bodies. In external service activities faculty may represent their institution, in whole or in part such as departments or with schools, or with community associations. Using the professional related vs. community related axis, the service is either related to activities that are strictly associated with professional associations, such as the American Association of University Professors or a national accrediting organization for institutions or particular disciplines. Also included in this category are community associations to which faculty members may lend their expertise, such as initiatives to study poverty, health or education issues important in the local, state or national community. It is this final category in which the faculty member has the least to gain personally or professionally, the community has the most to gain, and resources are most needed.

Moxley notes that the degree to which this type of service is even needed will vary with the type of community in which an institution is situated. While institutions located in more affluent communities may serve as a source of cultural and intellectual enrichment for that community, those located adjacent to poor communities may experience higher demands as community members look to the institution as a source of healing or recovery for the social ills they face. In either case the actions of the institutions will impact the very quality of life of the community itself (Moxley, 2004, p. 236).

There is, of course, the potential for overlap within these definitional categories, and it must be noted that each of these types of service is important to the faculty member and to the institution. Each facet of the definition should be recognized in the discussion as to how best to define the service role. Some form of weighting would be inevitable. The simple use of the word 'service,' with no explanation as to what that term means to the institution and for the faculty member, is an inadequate approach. To continue in this way will lead to the same result as in the past – service will be largely ignored and undervalued. But since mission statements are universally and mercilessly brief, where can a complex definition of this nature be explored? The answer is in the faculty and institutional assessment systems which universities and colleges utilize to measure their own and their faculty members' professional progress and determine advancement.

Service and assessment

A 1989 survey conducted by the Carnegie Foundation for the Advancement of Teaching found that 69 per cent of research university faculty respondents agreed with the statement that their institution needed better ways beside publications to evaluate scholarly performance of faculty. Boyer argued that the full range of all faculty talent must be more creatively assessed (Braskamp, 1994). In continuing difficult economic times colleges and universities are increasingly being expected by policy-makers and the public at large to demonstrate their worthiness as recipients of public funds. Assessment and evaluation provides information for this purpose. Even private institutions generate such information in annual reports and recruitment literature as contributors and potential students and their parents must make choices. The involvement of institutions in service activities has increasingly become a potential measure of note for both citizens and policy-makers alike. Faculty members may seek more meaningful use of their own expertise, thus seek out more service oriented dimensions to their teaching and research interests. How can these societal, institutional and personal needs be accommodated in assessment systems?

Assessment strategies for faculty must be effective for the individual faculty member but also, if we are to encourage and promote service activities, address the complexities of the service definition. In other words, a broad repertoire of assessment methods is needed. While Braskamp and Ory note that 'the ultimate test of assessment is whether it advances faculty and institutional development,' specific goals for effective faculty assessment should be addressed in any effective system.

1. Assessment should address both individual and institutional goals.
2. Assessment should address the complexity of faculty work.
3. Assessment should foster faculty members' uniqueness and promote career development.
4. Assessment should clearly communicate institutional goals and expectations.
5. Assessment should promote faculty collegiality.

(Braskamp and Ory, 1994, p. 20)

Institutions should be free to design their own evaluation methods and it would indeed to impossible to design one system for all institutions. But it is important to stress that outreach scholarship must be respected and valued *before* any appropriate evaluation can begin. As noted in the Penn State Uniscope report: 'Outreach scholarship suffers because it has been judged a secondary activity or has been considered too difficult to assess' (Alter, 2000, p. ix). Work done in the Penn State Uniscope 2000 effort, the University of Alaska Southeast faculty handbook and a few other institutions has shown that work activities in the academic realm in outreach scholarship can be as quantified in the same way it has been in teaching and scholarship. But such an effort takes time, commitment and thoughtful discussion between disciplines, faculty and administrators. The Uniscope and Alaska efforts noted above are particularly good examples of how detailed evaluation systems can be developed in outreach scholarship when faculty and administration are committed in a joint effort to do so.

Further issues for discussion

Certainly a number of important factors must be considered. Research to date on evaluation systems shows major differences among institutions based on institutional size and among public and private institutions. Much of this difference may be related to funding sources and the clients with which public and private institutions work. Differences regarding approach to the service mission exist between disciplines, as some disciplines adapt more easily to participation in the service role than others. For example, the Social Sciences typically have access to a broad array of service opportunities for field work while Classical Literature may find the design of service opportunities more challenging. Differences may also exist among faculty level, rank and experience regarding a faculty member's willingness or interest in moving beyond teaching and research to the service role. Perhaps this exercise in itself can be considered a challenge in creative thinking!

However, if institutions of higher learning are to give the service mission the equal status that it deserves attention must be paid to the evaluation component. While there is no specific evaluation formula which must be followed in order to promote service, the following guidelines can provide some structure:

1. Institution administration must express unqualified support for the service mission equally with the teaching and research mission and this must be communicated throughout the institution, to all levels of administration, and all faculty and staff. This support can be expressed symbolically through communication and in a more realistic sense by providing those faculty members who are largely engaged in service functions the same salary, promotion and tenure benefits currently available to non-service faculty. If hiring qualifications are largely the same, as they are on most campuses, promotion and tenure options should be the same for teaching, research and

service faculty. It would also be beneficial to remove artificial communication barriers between service and non-service faculty and units on campus. Opportunities for joint projects should be explored, particularly if those projects involve bringing together faculty members from multiple mission areas with students and with policy-makers and related groups from the 'real world.' Great opportunities for synergy are lost when such win/win/win connections are not made. The positive political benefits for the institution can be an unexpected bonus.

2. Faculty must be involved in the design of the evaluation system, including faculty from all discipline areas (Arts and Sciences, Business, Education, etc.) to insure that drafted language is as clear as possible and that there is sufficient 'buy-in' by the faculty.

3. Faculty must have flexibility in the contract/hiring process so that they will be able to negotiate, by percentage, their time as devoted to each mission area. This can be negotiated between the institution/department and the faculty member according to need and can indeed be renegotiated each year as needed, but must be clear to the faculty member so that he/she will know exactly how he/she will be evaluated at the end of each contract period.

Other problems which will need to be addressed include:
1. What types of service will be accepted?
2. Will paid consulting work be accepted?
3. Will service in public office be accepted?
4. How will possible legal liability for the institution be addressed?
5. How much movement between service, teaching and research is to be allowed?

Perhaps the most immediate problem to be faced is that the institution will, in fact, have to have a systematic evaluation system in place. Not all institutions do. Reviews for promotion and tenure vary dramatically even among public institutions from formal portfolios to informal individual meetings to individual check sheets to promotion and tenure granted by one department (reportedly) 'by surprise.' A systematic assessment of work does require a system. The most serious issue remains the need for support for outreach scholarship as a legitimate mission and concept within the academic community. This support must come before any evaluation system will have any success.

Successful steps

Unfortunately, few institutions to date have developed and implemented an evaluation system with sufficient detail. The University of Alaska Southeast is one exception. Approved by the faculty senate, its system provided a detailed chart, divided by faculty rank and university and public service, with specific lists of activities which would be considered appropriate for evaluation purposes. Similar charts developed under the Uniscope 2000 Penn State Community of Scholars Project provided even greater detail for service scholarship (as well as research and teaching), including specific examples of activities and how such activities should be documented for evaluation. Despite the success of the Uniscope effort, its result has not met with broad acceptance in the academic community. Once again, the issue of acceptance of the importance of the service mission looms large. The promotion of the service mission by administrators, consistently and in the evaluation process, has repeatedly emerged throughout faculty discussion of the issue as an important determinant of the success of outreach scholarship. Unfortunately, in times of budget austerity faculty devoted entirely to the service mission remain prime targets for budget cuts and the third mission can be easily weakened.

Concluding comments

As Braskamp and Ory wrote over a decade ago, 'A well-defined campus mission is becoming more important in academe. As resources become more scarce, more priority goal setting is needed' (Braskamp and Ory, 1994, p. 55). These words are even more true today. Campus administrators, at least in theory, have made it clear that service is a part of the mission of college and university campus. Indeed college and university presidents have elevated service to the third mission. But that mission does not receive the respect and attention its placing would seem to indicate.

As communities needed the expertise and talents of their institutions a decade ago, they need them even more today. And institutions also need communities. Communities provide the raw materials that give meaning to the long neglected service function of institutions. It is a symbiotic relationship.

Faculty members get involved in public service and outreach for a number of intrinsic reasons – personal history and values, a sense of responsibility, the nature of their discipline, a feeling of belonging in the community, a sense of purpose in their work and extrinsic reasons – job description, grants, release time, cash awards, recognition, enhanced reputation (Colbeck and Weaver, 2008, p. 8). Whatever their reasons for being interested in service work, the lack of extrinsic reward – the failure of the university or college system to provide a reliable evaluation system which recognizes service participation – is cited as the reason why more faculty are not involved in the service mission (Colbeck and Weaver, 2008). This is a disturbing, if understandable, explanation for lack of involvement in such an important endeavour. It is a correctable problem. How much untapped expertise and creativity is waiting in our institutions of higher education to solve the important societal problems we face today? How many of those problems may go unsolved for lack of a realistic evaluation system for outreach scholarship, or due to a system's failure to recognize the value of expertise or creativity used to solve the problem outside the walls of academe? To be overwhelmed by a problem because a solution cannot be found is tragic but understandable, but to be overwhelmed by a problem for which a solution could have been found but was not because the engaged scholar was not encouraged to work on the problem is a strong indictment of any system of higher education.

References

Alter, T. (Keystone 21 Project Director) (2000) *Uniscope 2000: A multidimensional model of scholarship for the 21st century*. University Park, Pa.: The Uniscope Learning Community.

Boyer, E. L. (1996) 'The scholarship of engagement', *Journal of Public Service and Outreach*, 1(1), 11-20.

Braskamp, L., and J. C. Ory. (1994*) Assessing faculty work: Enhancing individual and institutional performance.* San Francisco: Jossey-Bass Publishers.

Colbeck, C. and L. D. Weaver. (2008) 'Faculty engagement in public scholarship: A motivation systems theory perspective', *Journal of Higher Education Outreach and Engagement,* 12(2), 7–32.

Hill, M. B. Jr (1999) 'At the juncture of the academy and the community: the story of the Carl Vinson Institute of Government', *Metropolitan Universities: An International Forum*, 10(1), 69.

Kellogg Commission. (2001) *Returning to our roots: Executive summaries of the reports of the Kellogg Commission on the Futures of State and Land Grant Universities.* Available online at http://www.aplu.org/NetCommunity/Page.aspx?pid=305.

Moore, T. L. and Ward, K. (2008) 'Documenting engagement: faculty perspectives on self-representation for promotion and tenure', *Journal of Higher Education Outreach and Engagement*, 12(4), 5–27.

Moxley, D. P. (2004) 'Engaged research in higher education and civic responsibility reconsidered: A reflective essay', in T.M. Soska and A. K. J. Butterfield (eds), *University-community partnerships: Universities in civic engagement.* New York: The Haworth Social Work Practice Press.

Ward, K. (2003) *Faculty service role and the scholarship of engagement.* Washington, D.C.: Jossey-Bass Publishers.

Chapter 15

Community engagement and collective agreements: Patterns at Canadian universities

James E. Randall

The increased emphasis towards community engagement by universities is reflected in many ways. These include prominent mention in the installation addresses of presidents and chancellors, presence in mission statements and strategic plans, creation of new centres and institutes dedicated to community-university engagement, as well as the establishment of high-profile administrative posts such as Vice Presidents – External Relations (e.g., Australian Universities Community Engagement Alliance, 2006; Mohrman *et al.*, 2008; Tornatzky, 2005). However well-intentioned and effective these initiatives may be in shaping the institutional culture of a university or college, they are not the only, nor perhaps the most significant, means of influencing the working lives of faculty members on campuses. Collective agreements, as legally binding documents setting out terms and conditions of employment, may serve to be more effective and direct means of reflecting and conveying the importance of community engagement to faculty members. With this as a setting, the first objective of this paper is to describe the multiple ways in which community engagement or community service is reflected in the language of collective agreements at Canadian universities. The second objective is to assess the relationship, if any, between these codified representations of community and the other contextual characteristics of these universities and the communities within which they are located.

Background

Whether as a function of increased public accountability, a corporatization of academia, or constraints on funding, administrators at Canadian, American, Australian, and UK universities have become more vocal in articulating the local/regional engagement of their universities (e.g., Bond and Paterson 2005; Chatterton 2000; Jackson and Meyers, 2000). This has increased the level of acceptance of service-related activities among faculty and students on campuses across North America (Zlotkowski, 1996). Beginning with their installation addresses, chancellors and presidents have spoken passionately about the role of their universities in addressing the social, economic and environmental challenges facing their surrounding communities. As only one of many examples, in his 2008 installation address at the University of Manitoba, David Barnard defined greatness at the university to include, '. . . strengthening its linkages with the community, and increasing its impact on the province's economic, cultural and social development.' It is the rare president who does not use her or his installation address as an opportunity to extol the importance of community engagement as one of the core activities of the university.

Given the prominence accorded these very public pronouncements, one would expect the sentiment to be internalized within the universities in the form of policies, institutional structures and rewards. In fact, in an analysis of the twelve most engaged research universities in the United States, Tornatzky (2005) and Tornatzky *et al.* (2002) found a high degree of concordance between the public emphasis placed on community engagement by senior academic leaders and other features associated with the 'engaged university', including individual rewards and recognition, such as tenure and promotion criteria, the language contained in mission statements, visions and strategic academic plans as well as offices and senior administrative positions dedicated to fostering external linkages. However, the relationship between administrator rhetoric and the level and nature of community engagement is not as simple and linear as suggested above. Holland (1997) accurately captures this complexity by stating that, 'Even though the rhetoric of service is similar at many institutions, a cursory glance at campus literature, professional publications, and conference presentations makes it obvious that engagement in service-related activities is playing out differently across institutions, and the level of involvement in and the commitment to service takes many different forms.' (p. 30). Clearly, as Holland and Gelmon (1998) note, senior administrators cannot '. . . unilaterally create and sustain partnerships or mandate faculty and student involvement.' (p. 5)

Several researchers in the United States have attempted to categorize the level of community engagement by universities according to a set of characteristics or dimensions. For our purposes the most applicable is that undertaken by Holland (1997) and her colleagues, using a case study approach of 23 American universities.

In a summary matrix created to describe and categorize seven dimensions and four levels of institutional commitment to service, one of the dimensions is described as 'Promotion, Tenure, Hiring'. At the lowest level of institutional commitment or 'Low relevance', service to campus committees or to the faculty member's discipline is the only aspect of service linked to faculty evaluation. Conversely, the highest level of institutional commitment to service within this category (i.e., Level 4, 'Full integration') would see community-based research and teaching as key criteria for hiring and rewards. Holland suggests that only a few of the universities she analysed had even attained Levels 3 or 4.

Much of the literature on university engagement with community is focused on service learning, defined as a course-based, credit-bearing educational experience in which students participate in and reflect on a service activity within the community (Bringle and Hatcher, 2000). Furco (2002) undertook an analysis similar to that of Holland (1997) in examining the components associated with the presence of service-learning at a set of 43 American universities and colleges, where one of the 18 components was 'Faculty incentives and rewards'. His framework identified three sequential levels of institutionalization, including 'Critical mass building' (Level 1), 'Quality building' (Level 2), and 'Sustained Institutionalization' (Level 3). At the first level there are few if any incentives provided to faculty to engage in service-learning and service-learning was not recognized in promotion, tenure or review. It was only at the third level that one finds service-learning consistently represented in the process for faculty review, tenure, and promotion. Moreover, it was found that embedding service-learning in the tenure, promotion and review processes was the second strongest predictor (behind developing a critical mass of faculty involved in service-learning initiatives) associated with the overall institutionalization of service-learning at these institutions. The results by Holland, Furco and others should not be considered too surprising. As Ward (1998) states, 'University missions are translated through symbols and systems, particularly the curriculum and faculty reward structures' (p. 73).

Within the institution, individual faculty members and the president may be highly engaged in the community. In the case of faculty, this occurs as a function of their project-specific links with colleagues in the private and public sectors on specific research or teaching projects. In the case of Presidents, engagement with the local and regional stakeholders is one of the core functions of the position. However, as pointed out by Goddard and Puukka (2008, p. 29), there may be little connection between these two actors and the customs of the institution may act as barriers to systematic university engagement. Although there are many indicators of an engaged university (e.g., the Kellogg Commission report of 1999), analysing language within Collective or Faculty Agreements is arguably one of the best means to gauge the institutional importance accorded community engagement by individual faculty members. Collective agreements are the formal terms and conditions of employment between faculty members and the universities. As such, they govern the policies and procedures surrounding the definition and assignment of faculty workload, duties, and responsibilities as well as criteria for evaluation. They reflect the negotiated priorities of university management and faculty membership and, with few exceptions, are not subject to radical change over time. Therefore, an examination of these documents may tell us much about the collective institutional attitudes towards community engagement. Moreover, examining the collective agreements of universities allows us to link the characteristics we might associate with 'community engagement' to the geographical context associated with these universities.

The discussion above shows that there is a growing body of research describing the characteristics associated with universities and colleges that are engaged with their communities. However, very little of this work has examined university collective agreements systematically and comprehensively with a view to developing an understanding of the ways in which community engagement or service is reflected in these documents. The analysis which follows takes this step using Canadian universities. It also interprets the findings in the context of the characteristics of these universities and the communities in which they are located.

Method

Collective agreements for almost all Canadian universities and university colleges are compiled and updated in a searchable database by Faculty Bargaining Services (FBS) (www.caubo.ca/community/faculty-bargaining). A branch of the Canadian Association of University Business Officers (CAUBO), FBS includes 59 degree-granting universities and university colleges in Canada. The searchable database includes current and archived collective agreements for most of these institutions. The most current collective agreements for all FBS member universities were searched for the key words *'community'* or *'communities'*. The articles associated with these keywords were then examined in more detail to evaluate the significance of the word(s) in the context of the overall article and agreement. Although this database has some limitations, these are not considered significant for the purposes of this research.[1]

Analysis and results

The words 'community' or 'communities' are used in a variety of different ways in collective agreements, not all of which pertain to the relationship between the university and society. In some cases, these words are used in reference to the internal academic group that constitutes the university or university-college, in whole or in part. Examples of this application include, '. . . contributions to the university-community' or '. . . rights of other members of the UNBC community'. 'Community' is also used to refer to faculty members' disciplinary-specific or professional affiliation, as in, 'Staff members are encouraged to participate in the activities of the wider professional community associated with their discipline, profession or specialty.' Finally, the term 'community' is used in reference to the relationship between an individual faculty member, an academic unit or the institution as a whole and the broader external city, region, or general society. It is this latter usage that is the focus of the research discussed in this paper.

The words 'community' or 'communities' are found somewhere in the collective agreements of almost all of the 54 English-language universities in the FBS database. Fifteen of the agreements used 'community' only in the first or second context noted above (i.e. in reference to the internal academic or disciplinary-specific community). This group of 15 universities is not homogenous by any means. It includes several of the largest and most research-intensive universities in Canada, including the University of Toronto, McGill, McMaster, Alberta, Saskatchewan and York University, as well as a contingent of medium-sized, regionally oriented universities (e.g., Guelph, Trent, Memorial), and a group of primarily undergraduate universities and university-colleges, for example Thompson Rivers University, Mount Saint Vincent, Kwantlen, Vancouver Island University and Athabasca. Although there are no clear distinguishing features of this group, it does include several of the largest, most metropolitan universities in

Canada. A more careful reading of the agreements of these universities suggests that reference to 'community' is more often associated with the national or international research mission at these universities and less so with the local urban area or region immediately surrounding these campuses.

Community service may be less well represented at research universities because many of the more common representations of community service are associated with pedagogy and the academic curriculum (Furco, 2001). Given that research-intensive universities emphasize research over undergraduate teaching, they are '. . . less inclined to have a concerted, campus wide effort to promote the advancement of a particular pedagogy.' (Furco, 2001, p. 67). At the large, research-intensive universities, this phenomena may be a function of the Germanic roots of many of these American [and Canadian] institutions, where the focus was on '. . . pure research that was 'wholly unconstrained by narrow utilitarian considerations' (Lucas, 1994, p. 171, as quoted in Furco, 2001). This is also linked to a persistent view of scientific enquiry as 'placeless'. In speaking to the nineteenth century continental European universities, Bender (1998) refers to this as the *denial of place*. Goddard and Puukka (2008) suggest that modern research universities, striving for universalism and a scientific claim to truth that transcends time and place, have established missions that transcend their actual locations.

The collective agreements of the remaining 39 universities in the dataset do use the word 'community' in their agreements to refer to the relationship between the university or the individual faculty member and the surrounding city or region. Examination of the multiple ways in which 'community' is used within this group of 39 universities is the focus of the next step in the analysis.

A number of the collective agreements contain preambles that communicate the academic objectives of the university. Although not strictly linked to terms and conditions of employment, these preambles are akin to institutional mission statements. The principle of community engagement is contained within many of these preambles. For example, the preamble to Wilfrid Laurier University's agreement (2005 to 2008) contains the following, 'The Parties recognize that the objective of the University is the attainment of high standards of academic excellence in the pursuit and dissemination of knowledge for the benefit of students and of the academic and wider communities.' (Article 1).

One-third of the 39 universities use the words 'community' or 'communities' in their preambles. Although reference to the external community in a preamble has no direct consequence for the professional lives of faculty members, it does represent one additional indicator of the role that universities and their faculty members believe they should play in their surrounding communities. Despite the fact that all universities point to teaching, and most point to scholarship, as fundamental core functions that link them to broader society, not all of them articulate community engagement as a formal third element of university life.

Almost all university collective agreements have one or more sections that articulate the roles and responsibilities, duties, activities or workload expected of faculty members. These sections constitute the second major area in which the word 'community' is expressed. Of the 39 collective agreements, 19 of them (49 per cent) incorporate the words 'community' or 'communities' in this manner. For example, the University of Manitoba's Agreement states that faculty members '. . . have the right and responsibility to engage in community service when related to and appropriate to their discipline and field of expertise.' (Article 19.A.2.4.3.3). It is not uncommon to see reference to community as part of a list of Academic Freedoms. For example, at Dalhousie University this is articulated as, 'Academic freedom . . . implies protection of Members by the Board and the Association from pressure intended to hinder or prevent them from pursuing their scholarly and research interests and communicating the results thereof to students, colleagues and the community at large.' (Article 3.03). Rarely is community engagement binding on faculty members when stated in this manner. However, the level of specificity that is associated with being listed as a responsibility, activity or freedom does suggest a greater and more formal significance to the role of community in the professional lives of the faculty members and in the institutional culture.

Arguably the most important elements of university collective agreements are the procedures and policies for faculty assessment. This includes criteria for appointment, renewal of appointment, application for tenure and promotion and consideration of merit or bonus pay. This is the area in which the words 'community' or 'communities' are mentioned most frequently in collective agreements. Twenty-three of the 39 universities (59 per cent) use 'community' in some way as part of a faculty member's evaluation. A representative example includes a description of one criterion for tenure at Queen's University, as follows,

> *Tenure as defined in Article 25.2.2.3 shall be granted when there is clear evidence of demonstrated professional growth and the promise of future development as reflected in . . . (c) A record of professional, University or community service which has contributed to the Department, Unit, Faculty, University or broader academic community.* (Article 30.6.3).

The degree to which community engagement plays a role in assessing a faculty member's performance varies considerably among these 23 universities. In some cases, community engagement, more commonly referred to as community service, plays a relatively minor or marginal role in the evaluative process. For example, the priorities for promotion and tenure at Brock University are clearly laid out in the following passage,

> *Although teaching and scholarly activities are the primary criteria for promotion and tenure decisions, evidence of other activities appropriate to the discipline or field and service to the University or Union may be used to strengthen a candidate's case. Such evidence may include, with relative weighting as appropriate . . . v. community service where the individual has made an essentially non-remunerative contribution by virtue of special academic competence . . .* (Article 21.11).

At other universities, language used to guide the evaluation of faculty members incorporates community engagement in a more powerful and prescriptive manner. Cape Breton University's collective agreement includes a good example of this greater degree of significance.

> *Faculty are encouraged and expected to engage in community and professional service (where applicable) . . . Such service includes participating in community activities . . . where the faculty Member's academic and/or research interests and competencies form the basis for such participation.* (Article 18.5).

This quantitative analysis tells us that the notion of community engagement is a part of most collective agreements at Canada's universities. Moreover, it is more commonly found in one of the most critical elements of these Agreements, the criteria for evaluation of faculty. In the more extreme cases, the institutional culture is reflected in community engagement or service as a requirement for appointment and promotion. The next section of the analysis focuses on a few of these outliers; in other words, several Canadian universities where 'community' is either absent or represented in multiple ways and places throughout their respective collective agreements. Examining these outliers (i.e. Toronto, Acadia, Nipissing and Brandon) may allow us to better understand the relationship between university context and community engagement.

By most accounts, the University of Toronto is the most research-intensive university in Canada. It is ranked first in Canada in numbers of publications and citations as well as in the amount of research funding awarded to its researchers and counts almost 250 Canada Research Chairs among its faculty complement (University of Toronto, 2008). Despite these accomplishments, and the existence of a Centre for Community Partnerships, the presence of community engagement and community service is notably absent in public documents and in the Faculty Agreement. The installation address of President David Naylor makes no mention of the current or future role of the university in local or regional community service or engagement. Nor is community engagement or service stated in the university purpose and objectives. The Memorandum of Agreement between the Governing Council of the University of Toronto and the Faculty Association includes the word 'community' only once, in reference to the 'community of scholars'. Service is a part of the responsibilities of faculty members but only as it applies to the institutions and departments of the university itself.

Acadia University, located approximately 100 kilometres from Halifax, Nova Scotia in the small community of Wolfville (2006 population of approximately 3,800), is a small, primarily undergraduate liberal arts university of 3,500 students. The word 'community' in the context of community engagement is found in the collective agreement in sections on academic responsibilities and workload, as part of a list of eight academic freedoms (i.e., 'Freedom to engage in service to the institution and the community') and in a section on the criteria for renewal, tenure and promotion. More specifically, under Article 17 (Academic Responsibilities and Working Conditions) the Agreement states that 'Full-time Employees are encouraged by the Parties to engage in community service.' Language describing the criteria of community service for purposes of renewal, tenure, and promotion is detailed and specific, (i.e., 'Service to the wider community includes active participation in a wide variety of governmental, societal and community institutions, programmes and services, where such participation is based on the candidate's academic or professional expertise.')

Nipissing University is located in the northern Ontario resource community of North Bay (2006 population of approximately 54,000), about 300 kilometres from the major metropolises of Toronto and Ottawa. With approximately 4,750 students in 2008, it offers primarily undergraduate degrees in the arts and in professional programmes such as education. The language in Nipissing University's collective agreement is unusual among Canadian universities in that, for faculty evaluation, it places as much emphasis on community service as on teaching and scholarship. Candidates for new positions or vacancies are to be considered on the basis of a set of criteria that includes, '. . . professional and community service record (or potential) . . .' This prominence is also reflected in the preamble (i.e., 'The parties recognize that the goal of the University is the attainment of the highest possible standards of academic excellence in the pursuit and dissemination of knowledge, to be achieved principally through teaching, scholarship/research and community service.') and in the expected workload of faculty members (i.e., 'The normal full-time workload of Members will include teaching, research/scholarly/creative activities, and service to the community . . .').

Brandon University is located in Brandon, Manitoba (2006 population of approximately 45,000), 215 kilometres from the major urban centre of Winnipeg. Almost all of Brandon's 2,900 students are enrolled in liberal or fine arts degree programmes. As is the case at Acadia and Nipissing, the word 'community' appears in a number of places and in a prominent manner in Brandon's collective agreement. In the preamble, to serve the community is listed as one of five bulleted purposes of the University. Service to the community is listed as one of the responsibilities of Brandon faculty and a record of successful service to the university and to the community is required for appointment or promotion to the rank of Assistant Professor and above.

The most obvious characteristics shared by these latter three universities are their small size and undergraduate liberal arts orientation. Although faculty members are engaged in research at these universities, teaching has traditionally been given greater emphasis. As to their external context, they are all located in comparatively small urban centres in relatively rural or isolated geographical settings. All have an exaggerated presence as organizations in the urban communities within which they are located. By no means are these characteristics prerequisites to significant community–university engagement. However, it appears that the historical development of these three universities is intertwined with the fabric of their surrounding communities in such a manner as to have this reflected in multiple ways throughout their collective agreements. In many respects, the role of these universities is similar to that of the land-grant universities in the United States, wherein universities were, 'regionally embedded 'people's universities' based upon widening access to education and service to the community.' (Goddard and Puukka. 2008, p. 17)

In the United States, this distinction between large and small, and research versus teaching-oriented institutions is more visibly represented according to the three-part institutional types of two-year colleges, four-year colleges, and universities. As Antonio *et al.* (2000) suggest in their analysis of community service activities and attitudes of 33,986 faculty members, '. . . faculty at universities conduct, use, and value community service at rates no greater than (and usually substantially less than) those among two-year and four-year college faculty.' (p. 382). The size, relative role in the local community and research-orientation of post-secondary institutions are clearly not the only factors associated with the emphasis and commitment to community service. For example, in this same analysis, the authors concluded that faculty associated with four-year public colleges, religiously affiliated institutions, and those that included a higher proportion of faculty from professional, practice-based disciplines such as social work, health sciences, and education were more likely to be committed to service (Antonio *et al.* 2000). Although not part of their analysis, it would not be surprising to find that these types of institutions are more likely to have community service embedded in multiple ways within their collective agreements.

Collective agreements at universities are the negotiated result of the goals and objectives of management and faculty. One would expect that where there is greater concordance in the symbols and systems associated with community service by both administration, as for example in mission statements and Presidential addresses, and among faculty (e.g., presence in curricula, recognition in departmental assessment), you would be more likely to find these activities formalized in collective agreements. Conversely, where neither or only one of the groups values community service, it is less likely to be found in collective agreements. As Ward (1998) states,

> *Faculty reward structures also signal institutional values. Faculty success at the organizational level, translated as promotion and tenure, requires faculty participation in the tripartite demands of the professoriate: teaching, research and service. These demands on faculty time vary a great deal,*

depending on the particular culture. If a campus values experiential learning and community involvement, it will value professors who utilize service learning; if it recognized and rewarded in promotion and tenure guidelines and reviews, professors will be encouraged to incorporate service learning into their courses. (p. 74)

Conclusion and next steps

Characteristics of engaged universities from many different contexts have been described in detail (e.g., Australian Universities Community Engagement Alliance, 2006; Furco, 2002; Holland, 1997; Tornatzky, 2005; Tornatzky *et al.*, 2002). In almost all cases, there is a high degree of concordance between mission statements, academic plans and the language in their collective agreements. As Ward (1998) states, 'University missions are translated through symbols and systems, particularly the curriculum and faculty reward systems.' (p. 73). Less well understood is the level of concordance within those universities that are not considered engaged with their surrounding communities. In order to truly understand the engaged university, it would be useful to study the linkages between the language within collective agreements and the characteristics of universities along a continuum, from those that are most engaged to those that are least engaged.

Earlier in this paper, it was noted that change in the language of collective agreements is rarely rapid. However, if these documents are indeed barometers of policy change within institutions, one would expect them to change over time to reflect underlying institutional and societal trends. A longitudinal examination of a set of collective agreements from a sample of universities, linked to other community related indicators on these campuses, would be useful to determine how strong and responsive these agreements really are in reflecting institutional and community culture.

Finally, language in collective agreements does not necessarily translate directly into practice. Especially when review committees evaluate faculty colleagues, criteria for tenure, promotion and merit are interpreted through the filters of their own experiences and the cultural values held by the departments and their respective disciplines, including what constitutes intellectual value. Therefore, the issue that remains is the degree to which language in collective agreements really does influence outcomes such as the appointment, tenure and promotion of faculty members.

The purpose of this paper was not to serve as a call for greater representation of community service in the collective agreements at Canadian universities. However, prior research shows that when faculty reward structures mirror institutional priorities, for example through articles associated with tenure and promotion criteria, then you are much more likely to see more extensive and substantive expressions of community service and more likely to find it integrated into scholarship and instruction at the university. The research described above has also shown that the context of the community within which the university is located, as well as the historically embedded relationships between the university and its surrounding community, are likely as important in shaping the language in collective agreements as the concordance between administration aspirations and faculty practices.

References

Antonio, A. L., Astin, H. S. and Cress, C. M. (2000) 'Community service in higher education: A look at the nation's faculty', *The Review of Higher Education*, 23(4), 373–398.

Australian Universities Community Engagement Alliance (2006) *Universities and Community Engagement*. Retrieved 20 May 2009 from http://www.aucea.net.au.

Bender, T. (1988) 'Introduction', in T. Bender (ed.) *The university and the city, from medieval origins to the present*, 3–10. Oxford and New York: Oxford University Press.

Bond, R. and Paterson, L. (2005) 'Coming down from the ivory tower?: Academia's civic and economic engagement with the community', *Oxford Review of Education*, 31(3), 331–351.

Bringle, R. G. and Hatcher, J. A. (2000) 'Institutionalization of service learning in higher education', *The Journal of Higher Education*, (71)3, 273–290.

Chatterton, P. (2000) 'The cultural role of universities in the community: Revisiting the community-university debate', *Environment and Planning A*, 32(1), 165–181.

Duke, C. (2008) 'University engagement: Avoidable confusion and inescapable contradiction', *Higher Education Management and Policy,* (20)2, 87–98.

Furco, A. (2001) 'Advancing service-learning at research universities', *New Directions for Higher Education,* 114, 67–78.

Furco, A. (2002) 'Self-assessment rubric for the institutionalization of service-learning in higher education', A project of the Campus Compact at Brown University.

Furco, A. (2007) 'Institutionalising service-learning in higher education', in L. McIlrath and I. MacLabhrainn (eds.) *Higher education and civic engagement: international perspectives,* 65–82. Aldershot: Ashgate.

Goddard, J. and Puukka, J. (2008) 'The engagement of higher education institutions in regional development: An overview of the opportunities and challenges', *Higher Education Management and Policy,* (20) 2, 11–41.

Holland, B. (1997) 'Analyzing institutional commitment to service: A model of key organizational factors', *Michigan Journal of Community Service Learning,* Fall, 30–41.

Holland, B. and Gelmon, S. (1998) 'The state of the engaged campus: What have we learned about building and sustaining university and community partnerships', *American Association of Higher Education Bulletin,* October, 3–6.

Jackson, G. and Meyers, R. B. (2000) 'Challenges of institutional outreach: A COPC example', *Cityscape: A Journal of Policy Development and Research,* 5(1), 125–140.

Kellogg Commission (1999) Third report on the future of state and land-grant universities, *Returning to our roots: The engaged institution.* Washington DC: National Association of State Universities and Land-Grant Colleges http://www.eric.ed.gov/ > ERIC#ED426676 Accessed 28 September 2010.

Lucas, C.J. (1994) *American higher education: A history.* New York: St Martin's Press.

Mohrman, K., Shi, J., Feinblatt, S. E. and Chow, K. W. (eds.) (2008) *Public universities and regional development* (Chengdu, China: Sichuan University Press) This book is also available from the University Design Consortium at Arizona State University.

Tornatzky, L. (2005) 'Innovation U: New practices, enabling cultures', in G. A. Jones, P. L. McCarney and M. L. Skolnik (eds.) *Creating knowledge, strengthening nations: the changing role of higher education*, 283–94. Toronto: University of Toronto Press.

Tornatzky, L., Waugaman, P. G. and Gray, D. O. (2002) *Innovation U: New university roles in a knowledge economy*. Research Triangle Park, NC: Southern Growth Policies Board.

University of Toronto (2008) 'By the numbers: excellence, innovation, leadership: research at the University of Toronto'. Retrieved 29 April 2010 from http://www.research.utoronto.ca/wp-content/uploads/2008/02/UofT_by_the_numbers_2010.pdf.

Ward, K. (1998) 'Addressing academic culture: Service learning, organizations, and faculty work', *New Directions for Teaching and Learning*, 73 (Spring), 73–80.

Zlotkowski, E. (1996) 'A new voice at the table? Linking service-learning and the academy' *Change*, 28(1), 20–27.

Notes

[1] Limitations of the FBS database for this research included the following: (1) the word community is not the only descriptor for the relationship between a university and its surrounding locality or region, (2) the five collective agreements in the FBS database that are provided only in French were excluded, (3) a number of the Collective Agreements on the database were not current, and (4) this research excluded Agreements with all but the full-time faculty members (e.g., did not include Agreements with librarians, part-time or laboratory instructors and teaching or research assistants).

Chapter 16

Towards a new architecture of knowledge: The Office of Community-Based Research at the University of Victoria

Budd L. Hall and Lise Bérubé

Although researchers are successfully integrating their efforts at a European level and even global level to address the increasing complexity of scientific inquiry, there appears to be a yawning gap between science and society at large.

Rainer Gerold, Science and Society Director,
Research Directorate-General, European Commission

Sometimes the ring road of the University of Victoria appears to those of us in community agencies as a kind of moat . . . keeping the university from reaching us and us from ease of entry into the university.

Victoria Community Agency Member

Community-based research (CBR) offers higher education a distinctive form of engaged scholarship and a transformative approach to teaching and learning.

(Kerry Strand *et al.*, 2003)

Introduction

This chapter reports on the creation of the Office of Community-Based Research in 2006–2007, its key activities and ways of working and challenges that it faces in carrying out its mission. In doing so, we very strongly dissociate our work from any notion of a 'Third Mission'. Community-engaged scholarship is in fact an integrating function that cuts across the older notions of a separation of research, teaching and service. Trying to understand the work taken up by the Office of Community-based Research and the many other emerging university structures through a 'third mission' lens does serious damage to our capacity to understand current global trends in higher education.

Strategic emergence of community-university research partnerships

There is a wind of change sweeping our research communities. There is a pervasive energy for something that is described variously as knowledge mobilization, knowledge exchange, knowledge translation, and knowledge transfer or knowledge application. What most of these concepts are responding to is the notion that significant social, political and economic investments have been made in the creation and/or accumulation of knowledge based in or with universities. In this context, knowledge is understood as a state of understanding, feeling or awareness based on experience or study. Knowledge is the state of knowing. Universities are often seen by society as institutional repositories of knowledge. Scholars, students and faculty are all understood to be creating knowledge through their research activities. The accepted understanding is that the process of research creates knowledge. Scholars or researchers are regarded as the facilitators of these processes and thereby the creators of this knowledge. This kind of knowledge is put into peer-reviewed journals, professional reports, books, CDs, DVDs, podcasts, blogs and other internet-based products. Much of this knowledge remains in the minds of the researchers, on shelves in libraries or in journals that may remain invisible to persons working on the practical side of social, economic, ecological or health challenges in our communities.

The various modifiers associated with the concept of knowledge all have in common an aspiration that the formal research processes facilitated by university-based scholars will produce ideas, concepts, frameworks or even solutions which can be used in the improvement of the lives of people. Knowledge mobilization speaks of an active process of moving knowledge into the hands of those who can use the knowledge. Knowledge translation and transfer recognizes that academic research, in order to engage with community knowledge, needs to be deliberately or intentionally worked with so as to facilitate its use by non-academic groups. Finally, knowledge exchange recognizes that knowledge is created in community, workplace or social movement settings and that there is or could be an exchange of knowledge between those who create knowledge in both formal academic and other settings. All of these contemporary ideas of knowledge have been expressed 30 or 40 years ago by others using terms such as feminist research, participatory research, action research, decolonizing research, indigenous research and so forth. What is exciting about current times is that funding agencies and universities alike are recognizing that research is not complete without acknowledging its application, use, capacity for change, social transformation or some other forms of engagement.

In the 1970s in the Netherlands, a structure called Science Shop was created to link academic research to community needs (http://www.livingknowledge. org). In Tanzania, India, Latin America and elsewhere, a new research approach called 'participatory research', which recognized the knowledge-creating capacities of community, organizations and social movements, was also gaining visibility (Hall, 1975). Flash forward 40 years, and we have the emergence of a second or third wave of research and knowledge-mobilization initiatives that build on the early work of science shops, the participatory research practitioners and others. It is promoted and supported by a new set of networks and structures such as Sciences Citoyennes in France (http://sciencescitoyennes.org); the Living Knowledge Network based in Germany (http://www.scienceshops.org); The Popular Education Network based in Scotland (Crowther *et al*, 1999); Community-Based Research Canada (http://uvic.ca/ocbr); Campus Community Partnerships for Health in the United States (http://depts.washington.edu/ccph/); as well as the National CBR Networking Initiative (http://www.bonner.org/campus/cbr/home.htm) and the University-Community Partnership for Social Action Research Network (http://www.igloo.org/ucpsarnet). Additional networks and structures include the Society for Participatory Research in Asia (http://www.pria.org); the Global University Network for Innovation of Barcelona (http://www.guni-rmies.net); the Sub-Saharan African Participatory Research Network in Senegal; the Developing Research on Citizenship network based at the University of Sussex (http://www.drc-citizenship.org); 'Observatory PASCAL on Place Management, Community

Engagement and Learning Regions' (http://www.obs-pascal.com); the 'Australian Universities Community Engagement Alliance' (Temple *et al.*, 2005); and many other emerging networks. Between August of 2006 and present, representatives from many of these networks have been engaged in conversations about how best to support this emerging theory and practice of higher education community-based research. We now have an emerging space for the systematic sharing of experiences that did not exist in earlier years.

Local communities in Canada face unprecedented challenges to their social, economic, cultural and environmental futures. These challenges range from growing poverty and homelessness in urban centres (Brown *et al.*, 2008, Cowan and Khandor, 2008; Cunningham and Walker, 2008; Mackinnon, 2008; Walsh *et al.*, 2008) to agricultural and rural decline (Neufeld, 2008; Barry *et al.*, 2008) and from climate change impacts on northern communities to declining health in Aboriginal and First Nations communities (Cairo, 2008; Reading and Nowgesic, 2002). Community-based research (CBR) has become a major focus of several groups, including: community groups attempting to advance action on systemic change (Hall 2005) post-secondary institutions concerned to advance knowledge to inform responses to challenges (Barnet, 2008; Holland and Ramaley, 2008), government agencies concerned to develop evidence-based policy (Israel *et al.*, 1998; Shields and Evans, 2008), and philanthropic donors in the private sector concerned about investing in ways that will produce results (Maxwell, 2006). Recognition of the role of CBR in universities at an international level can be seen in the Talloires Network (http://www.tufts.edu/talloiresnetwork), the Global University network for Innovation (http://www.guni-rmies.net) web site, the Living Knowledge Network (http://www.scienceshops.org), the Community University Partnership Programme (http://www.bton.ac.uk/cupp), as well as The Global Alliance on Community-Engaged Research that has recently been launched (http://web.uvic.ca/ocbr/cuexpo/index.html).

What does it mean for universities?

The interest and support for community-based research and knowledge mobilization is an important component of the broader trend of increased attention to community or civic engagement in all Canadian universities. As the current generation of university strategic plans in Canada is released, it is notable that language around community university engagement has become more prominent. The University of Victoria speaks of 'civic engagement';

other universities use a variety of other expressions from 'social responsibility' to 'local and regional engagement'. The notion of a 'third mission' for higher education (teaching, research and community service) with its narrower and separate realm of community service is being replaced by a variety of ways of expressing engagement with the community, which cut across both the research and the teaching functions.

Ted Jackson at Carleton University has conceptualized what he calls the 'CUE (Community University Engagement) Factor' (Jackson, 2008, p.1). He writes of a dynamic interaction of community-university engagement that includes community-based experiential or service learning; community-based research and community-based continuing education. Community-based learning, service learning, experiential learning and community service learning (the preferred term in Canada) all refer to opportunities for students to have placements or engagements with community organizations. Community service learning as a concept often includes an aspect of social change or transformation as part of the intention. Experiential learning is a more neutral concept placing the value on learning through experience, with less emphasis on 'service' or transformation. Community engagement is about the interaction of a variety of forms of engagement both with each other and with the academic mission of the universities. Continuing education is the grandmother of all forms of community engagement and arguably still represents the deepest set of community partnerships. It is as diverse and multi-faceted as the human imagination. Service learning, community service learning or experiential service learning has seen considerable growth across the country over the past ten years. Service learning is experiential learning for students who learn off-campus through action projects with community groups. UBC's Learning Exchange, where undergraduate students have opportunities to work in Vancouver's Downtown Eastside, is one of the better-known programmes, but the Canadian Alliance for Community Service Learning lists 26 service learning programmes in universities and colleges in every region in the country. Jackson calls on universities across Canada to 'increase their CUE factors by deepening and broadening their teaching, research and volunteering activities with the external constituencies that have the greatest need for sustainable solutions to the challenges they face every day' (Jackson, 2008, p. 1).

The late Ernest Boyer at the Carnegie Foundation laid down some of the early conceptual foundations with his development of the concept of 'engaged scholarship' (Boyer, 1996). More recently the Carnegie Foundation has offered what is the most widely adopted definition of engagement:

'Community engagement describes the collaboration between institutions of higher education and their larger communities for the mutually beneficial exchange of knowledge and resources in a context of partnership and reciprocity' (Boyer, 1996). An emphasis can be seen on the concept of reciprocity. The Kellogg Commission on the Future of State and Land-Grant Universities (Kellogg Commission, 1999) shifted the terms research, teaching and serve to the words discovery, learning and engagement. This is a strikingly different approach to the mission of the university as it creates ideas, which are no longer separate realms of knowledge creation. Discovery happens in all aspects of university work, from basic sciences to new approaches to HIV/AIDS. It happens in classrooms, laboratories, and businesses and in not-for-profit organizations. Learning is the same.

What does it mean for communities?

The United Way of Greater Victoria has established a series of 'impact councils' to make informed, research-based and evidence-based recommendations on what kinds of funding interventions show the most promise for permanent impact on issues of poverty, mental health and addiction, family services and other areas of need in the greater Victoria area. The creation of the OCBR facilitated the identification of university scholars who could sit on these impact councils and bring their academic knowledge and experience to the table shared by local business and government partners. The Downtown Business Association of Greater Victoria has initiated a lunchtime speaker's series in collaboration with the Office of Community-Based Research and the Division of Continuing Studies to bring academics with practical and policy and business ideas to the attention of the downtown businesses. The Municipality of Saanich, one of the 13 smaller municipalities that make up the Greater Victoria area approached the OCBR with a request for help with a community mapping and citizen's consultation process for planning urban development. The Halalt First Nations, an Indigenous community about an hour north of Victoria has asked the University of Victoria for help with planning some agricultural initiatives, with legal help regarding threats to the regional aquifer and with documenting their history.

All of these are examples of the new community-university research partnerships that have emerged from the creation of the University of Victoria's Office of Community-Based Research. They illustrate what is happening across our communities in Canada and elsewhere. There is a new relationship between institutions of higher education and their communities being negotiated through practice. The emergence of these new partnership structures is a critical step in providing the capacity for partnership development. Relationships lie at the heart of community-university research partnerships. Neither brilliance, good intentions, need, passion nor charismatic leadership will work to assure success if relations of respectful and mutual understanding are not established early in a research partnership. Many individuals in both the community and the university have been aware of this, what is different is that this kind of thinking is being taken up at an institutional level.

The CBR tradition at the University of Victoria

The first formal step by the University of Victoria in exploring the extent of community-based research as a model of academic practice at the University came in April of 2005 in the form of a university-wide forum on community-based research. The forum was in part stimulated by a Master's project written in Public Administration by Janet Dunnett (Dunnett, 2004) that documented many aspects of community-based research at UVic. The forum addressed the question 'To what extent do University of Victoria scholars identify their work as falling within the broad understanding of community-based research?' It was also designed to solicit opinions from within the university-community on the value of creating a formal organizational support structure for community-based research.

The CBR forum was a success as over 80 academics answered to the description of community-based research. The President of the Social Sciences and Humanities Research Council at the time, Dr Marc Renaud, in his closing remarks, threw out a challenge to the University of Victoria to take up a leadership position in this field as he felt that we were ideally suited to do so. There was strong support from the participants as well as from some 40–50 additional persons who could not attend the forum in person. On the basis of this strong support, Peter Keller, Dean of Social Sciences, Budd Hall, Dean of Education and Kelly Bannister of the POLIS Project (a legal-environmental research centre) were asked to develop a proposal for a structure and to extend the preliminary thoughts through further consultations on campus. We added Maeve Lydon to lead the community consultation phase of the process and Peter Levesque of Knowledge Mobilization Works! as an external consultant. The report was submitted in June 2006 and the President of the University announced the creation of what was to become known as the 'Office' of Community-Based Research' in November of that year, with the formal launching in January 2007.

Mission and objectives of the Office of Community-Based Research

The Office of Community-Based Research at UVic exists to facilitate collaborative community-university research partnerships that enhance the quality of life and the economic, environmental and social well being of communities. It is located administratively within the office of the Vice-President, Research and has a Steering Committee that is co-chaired by the Vice-President, Research and the CEO of the United Way of Greater Victoria. The OCBR is a small unit with a part-time director who is a senior academic, a part-time Associate Director with a community organizing background and a full-time administrative coordinator. It has a working motto that is necessitated by both size and philosophy: it will do nothing that someone else is already doing and it will do nothing on its own. It has two formal functions: (1) The facilitation of community-university research partnerships; and (2) The support and visibility of students and faculty who are engaged in or interested in community-based research. The OCBR carries out a range of activities under each of these objectives.

Facilitating Community-university research partnerships
  • strengthening our systems and tools for brokering;
  • building partnership and CBR skills;
  • supporting community-driven research alliances; and
  • policy development and networking.

Supporting faculty and students
  • increased recognition of excellence in CBR for merit and promotion;
  • support to teaching, learning and curriculum development;
  • enhancing science, engineering and business engagement;
  • mobilization of resources for CBR;
  • enhancing student engagement in CBR;
  • support for indigenous-centered research; and
  • publication support for CBR scholars.

The Vancouver Island Community Research Alliance (VICRA)

The city of Victoria is situated on the southwest corner of Vancouver Island. Vancouver Island is the largest island off the west coast of North America 500 kilometers long and 100 kilometers wide and about the size of Holland. There are about 800,000 people living here, with the bulk of the population in the southern third of the island on the Saanich peninsula and in the city of Nanaimo. The southern communities are for the most part well to do with excellent educational and health services. The coastal communities on the Northern and Western sections of the island have been hard hit by the loss of the commercial fishery (a dramatic decrease in the salmon stocks), a decline in forestry and the global economic slowdown of the 2008–2011 period. There are a large number of First Nations communities and a substantial number of indigenous citizens living in our urban areas. With a decline of the resource industries and the natural tendencies of global capitalism, poverty continues to be produced as we have a growing number of persons who are unhoused living in many parts of the island. Issues of sustainability, food security, health disparities are also of concern up and down the island.

In addition to the University of Victoria, there are four other post-secondary educational institutions on our island: Vancouver Island University in Nanaimo; Royal Roads University (a largely distance university) in Victoria; Camosun College (a community college) in Victoria and North Island College in several of the North Island communities. We have a total of about 60,000 students, 10,000 staff and about $150 million of research/year when we combine the assets of all five of our institutions. A memorandum of understanding was signed between our five campuses to work together to use research partnerships as a way to respond to the aspirations and needs of the communities that we live in. The OCBR provides the organizational base for the work, and the University of Victoria and Vancouver Island University are co-conveners of the network. Vancouver Island is one of the most beautiful places in the world. It has been consistently voted the 'best island in the world' by various travel magazines. The richness of natural life and ecological diversity are almost mind-boggling. We believe that if our higher education institutions can work together more effectively, we can make strong progress on the stubborn and persistent social and economic challenges that hold us back from becoming what we are capable of being.

VICRA is an alliance of the five post-secondary educational institutions located on Vancouver Island united via a Memorandum of Understanding

(MOU) signed by the respective presidents of each of the five institutions. The five campuses include: The University of Victoria, Royal Road's University, Vancouver Island University, Camosun College and North Island College. The MOU calls on the group to: (1) identify priority research issues with an island wide focus; (2) develop and implement a process to identify relevant and available knowledge, information, skills, and capacities both in the parties and in communities; (3) identify and develop research partnerships and share information on best practices that can be shared with others; (4) promote the engagement of the parties' students in action research projects identified by communities/community members; (5) build capacity for community-based research and evidence-based planning among the spectrum of organizations and agencies that work to address the needs of Vancouver Island residents and communities; and (6) build on each other's experiences and expertise, drawing on lessons from local, national and global networks/projects.

During 2008 and 2009, we worked with communities up and down the island to see what common issues there were that our VICRA team might be able to address. Three areas emerged from these consultations: aboriginal health disparities; lack of affordable housing, and concerns about the sustainability and security of our food sources. In June 2010, with a grant from the Canadian Social Science and Humanities Research Council, our VICRA team began work on a Local Food Production and Distribution Action Plan, a project that we proposed calling 'Bringing the Food Home'. VICRA will support the development of five 'Local Food Production and Distribution' tables in various parts of the Island. With student CBR research interns from each of our campuses and research support from a team of distinguished food policy researchers, business people, organic farmers, chefs, food distributors, local government folks and others will sit together to decide how to remove the obstacles to local food production and distribution. Actions envisaged are the creation of a venture capital pool for small-scale farm producers, new solutions to food inspection sites and regulations, support for farm markets, better links to food wholesalers, and more.

Building the curriculum of community-based research within the University of Victoria

Given the large numbers of faculty involved in community-based research at the University of Victoria, it was a natural step for the OCBR to think about how it could strengthen sharing of the experiences amongst these knowledgeable scholars and between them and students in the University. The goal is to make CBR at the University of Victoria the very best anywhere; to build on the commitment and experience of so many at the University of Victoria.

In order to do this, we developed a speaker's series called, 'Promises and Perils of Teaching CBR at the University of Victoria'. It was developed by the OCBR in collaboration with the Learning and Teaching Centre. Dr Catherine Etmanski, a respected CBR scholar working with the Faculties of Education and Public Administration, coordinated the series. The topics covered included: An Introduction to the Growing World of CBR; Indigenous Approaches to Research; Making Community-University Partnerships Work; From Research to Action in CBR; Using the Arts in CBR; Ethics in CBR and Creating Multi-disciplinary Courses for CBR.

The series that was initiated in the 2009–2010 academic year was extremely popular, welcoming about 300 participants attending one or more of the sessions. There were 28 academics and community resource persons that participated in the first year of the series, which also proved to be very popular with graduate students. The idea that the series might have become a space for academics themselves to share amongst each other was less successful. While several faculty members took part in the sessions, most of the professors only turned up at the sessions where they were speaking. This is fairly typical in university life, but remains a challenge when we are striving to deepen the theory and practice of CBR within our University. We have followed up the series with a proposal to produce a collaborative book on teaching CBR in higher education settings with the engagement of many of these same faculty members. We hope that producing this collaborative publication will strengthen the exchange of ideas amongst the authors involved.

An interactive and web-based Moodle site supported the series as it got started and we hope that this will continue to grow as a way of building dialogue, support and learning. Christopher Bowers has been working with the OCBR as its resident 'story catcher'. His specialty is doing short three to four minute interviews of CBR participants to 'catch' the essence of their thinking. Many of the speakers in the CBR teaching series have been caught and can be seen on at http://ocbrinstitute.blip.tv/.

Networking to strengthen local action: National and international spaces

Universities are structured in such similar ways there is really only one global university. In practical terms this means that when we wish to create a new service or new structure within our own universities, it is important that we do two things: take a look at what other universities are already doing along these lines and either get connected with already existing networks or work with others to create a network. This is the approach that we have taken at the University of Victoria. We have taken initiatives regarding the founding of a Vancouver Island Community Research Alliance (VICRA), Community-Based Research Canada (CBRC) and the Global Alliance for Community Engaged Research (GACER).

Community-Based Research Canada (www.communityresearchcanada.ca) is an evolving open and inclusive network of people and organizations engaged in and supporting community-based research. It was born during the Community University Exposition 2008 that was hosted by the City of Victoria. It held its first national seminar in May of 2009 in Ottawa (http://www2. carleton.ca/newsroom/news-releases/recession-to-renewal-new-knowledge-for-new-solutions/) with a focus on how CBR can contribute to the solution of complex economic and social issues. Its first major policy effort was the publication of a report on the funding and development of community-based research in Canada for the Social Sciences and Humanities Research Council of Canada (Hall, 2009). This report made a series of recommendations to the granting councils, the universities and to community research groups. The study and the desire to follow-up with some of the recommendations in this study led to the launching of a national conversation on Knowledge and Society that is framed within the discourse of a new Knowledge Commons (Hall, 2010). The first national summit on the Knowledge Commons was held on 2 June 2010 in Montreal.

At the Global level, the European-based Living Knowledge Network, the Society for Participatory Research in Asia and Community-Based Research Canada have come together with a number of other regional CBR networks to create the Global Alliance on Community-based Research (GACER). GACER has initiated four key activities to date: a launch of the statement of principles; advocacy within the United Nations World Conference on Higher Education; a global study of the potential impact of community-university research partnerships on issues such as poverty and sustainability and the creation of a global communiqué on the role of community university research engagement as a strategic element in the development of higher education everywhere. The GACER website is the best way to keep up with these developments.

Challenges

The OCBR has found remarkably fertile soil for germination. It is located at a university that puts high value on civic engagement and where a substantial number of its faculty members have a preference for conducting this kind of engaged scholarship. At the same time for some good reasons (genuine interest in working with university students and faculty) and political realities (substantial budget cuts to social services in the region) the community interest in making better use of the University for research purposes is high. However, challenges are significant and include: trying to respond to demand; turning partnerships and interest into research projects; getting credit for engaged scholarship for faculty tenure and promotion purposes; becoming a permanent part of the university structures.

Our experiences at the University of Victoria have given us much hope. We can see new ways of understanding knowledge and get some glimpses of what a new architecture of knowledge might look like. The University of Victoria as well as other universities has not yet come to full grips with what this means for the administrative and knowledge mobilization structures of the University. Getting a full return on the public investment in our universities in Canada means paying for the facilitation and brokering services that will make the connections with the substantial needs in our communities, in our country and in our troubled world.

References

Barnet, R. (2008) 'Recovering the civic university', in McIlrath and Mac Labhrainn (eds.) *Higher Education and Civic Engagement: International Perspectives*, 25–36. Burlington, VT: Ashgate.

Barry, M., Anderson, E., Kittredge, K., Messer, L. and Falconer, N. (2008) 'Building community with locally relevant data: the Sooke Community Health Information Project (CHI)', in *Proceedings of the third international community-university exposition (CUExpo08)*, 45–57. Victoria: University of Victoria.

Boyer, E.L. (1996) 'The scholarship of engagement', *Journal of Public Service and Outreach,* 1, 11–20.

Brown, J., Knol, D., Fraehlich, C., Rodger, S. (2008) 'Providing opportunities for adult learning and employment in aboriginal inner-city organizations', in *Proceedings of the third international community-university exposition (CUExpo08)*, 31–35. Victoria: University of Victoria.

Cairo, A. (2008) 'Opo Yeye: Raise Your Spirit: Community-based participatory mental well-being from a non-western cultural perspective', in *Proceedings of the third international community-university exposition (CUExpo08)*, 41–44. Victoria: University of Victoria.

Cowan, L. and Khandor, E. (2008) 'The Street Health Report 2007: Community-based research on the health, health-care access and daily lives of homeless people in Toronto', in *Proceedings of the third international community-university exposition (CUExpo08)*, 65–68. Victoria: University of Victoria.

Crowther, J., Martin, I. and Shaw, M. (1999) *Popular education and social movements in scotland today*. Leicester: NIACE.

Cunningham, L. and Walker, C. (2008) 'Working Together at the margins: research to break the revolving door experience of homeless service users' in *Proceedings of the third international community-university exposition (CUExpo08)*, 45–48. Victoria: University of Victoria.

Dunnet, J. (2004) 'University and community linkages at the university of victoria: towards a new agenda for community based research.' Submitted to the University of Victoria, School of Public Administration in partial fulfillment of a Master's Degree in Public Administration.

Gerold, R. (2005) 'Opening remarks', Science and Society Forum. Retrieved from http://web.uvic.ca:8080/~ocbrdev/.

Hall, B. L. (1975) 'Participatory research: An approach for change', *Convergence*, 8(3), 15–17.

Hall, B. L. (2005) 'In from the cold? Reflections on participatory research 1970–2005', *Convergence*, 38(1), 5–24.

Hall, B. L. (2009) *The Funding and Development of Community Based*

Research in Canada. Ottawa: SSHRC. Retrieved from http://web.uvic. ca/ocbr/.

Hall, B. L. (2010) 'Enhancing a knowledge commons: A national conversation', A discussion paper of Community-Based Research Canada. Retrieved from www.communityresearchcanada.ca.

Holland, B., and Ramaley, J.A. (2008) 'Creating supportive environment for community-university engagement: Conceptual frameworks', in *HERDSA Annual Conference 2008*, 33–47.

Israel, B. A., Schultz, A., Parker, E. A., and Becker, A. B. (1998) 'Review of community-based research: assessing partnership approaches to improve public health', in *Annual Review of Public Health 1998*, (199), 173–202.

Jackson, E. (2008) 'The cue factor: community-university engagement for social innovation', Open source business resource, September 2008: Social Innovation. Retrieved from (http://www.osbr.ca).

Kellogg Commission (1999) Third report on the future of state and land-grant universities, *Returning to our roots: The engaged institution.* Washington DC: National Association of State Universities and Land-Grant Colleges http://www.eric.ed.gov/ > ERIC#ED426676 Accessed 28 September 2010.

MacKinnon, S. (2008) 'Poverty and social exclusion: solving complex issues through comprehensive approaches', in *CCPA REVIW: Economic and Social Trends (September 2008)*, 1–3. Winnipeg: Canadian Centre for Policy Alternatives.

Maxwell, J. (2006) *Strategies for social justice: Place, people and policy.* Montreal: Community Foundations of Canada. Retrieved from http://www.cfc-fcc.ca/documents/pf_4_Maxwell_Strategies.pdf.

Neufeld, D. M. (2008) *Brooding Over the next generations of prairie farmers: making space for our practical-minded youth.* Winnipeg: Canadian Centre for Policy-Alternatives.

Reading, J. and Nowgesic, E. (2002) 'Improving the health of future generations: The Canadian Institutes of Health Research Institute study of aboriginal peoples' health', *American Journal of Public Health*, 28 (9), 1396–1400.

Shields, J. and Evans, B. (2008) *Knowledge mobilization/transfer, research partnerships, and policymaking: some conceptual and practical consider-ations*. CERIS No. 33.

Strand, K., Marullo, S., Cutforth, N., Stoecker, R. and Donohue, P. (2003) 'Principles of best practice for community-based research', *Michigan Journal of Community Service Learning*, (Summer 2003), 5–15.

Temple, J., Story, A. and Delaforce, W. (2005) AUCEA: An emerging collaborative and strategic approach dedicated to university-community engagement in Australia, in *Proceedings of the International Conference on Engaging Communities*, Brisbane Australia.

Walsh, C., Rutherford, G. E., and Kuzmack, N. (2008) Housing and home: making the connections for women who are homeless, in *Proceedings of the third international community-university exposition (CUExpo08)*, 315–318. Victoria: University of Victoria.

Chapter 17

Inter-university partnership for community engagement: A case study of Canada's French-language minority

Harley d'Entremont

Introduction

Much of the literature regarding the third mission or community engagement activities of universities seems to focus on economic issues (see Arbo and Benneworth, 2004; OECD, 2007; Vorley and Nelles, 2008). This is due to a number of factors, not the least of which is that the research tends to be prevalent in areas where the data is more readily available, thus on commercialization-type activities (Molas-Gallart and Castro-Martinez, 2007). However, many higher education institutions have a strong involvement with health and cultural issues, which often include community engagement activities (OECD, 2007). Another characteristic of the literature is that it deals primarily with individual universities and the impact they have on a specific geographical area, or 'their region'. Kitagawa (2004) states that 'in both policy and academic literature a great deal of effort is devoted to create closer links between a university and its region' (p. 57). This study constitutes a departure from those trends as it deals with non-economic community engagement in relation to an identifiable population (official language minority communities) instead of a defined geographical area.

Canada presents an interesting case study of how a group of higher education institutions have developed collaborative structures to respond to the demands and needs of their communities, the French-language minority communities outside Québec. Out of approximately 100 universities in Canada, thirteen consider that they have as part of their mission a responsibility to those minority French-language communities. These universities range in size from less than a 1,000 students to more than 30,000 students, from primarily undergraduate institutions to research intensive universities. Four of these are French-language universities, six are bilingual universities and three are primarily English-language institutions which have a bilingual or French-language unit whose mandate or mission is related to the French-language minority within their region (see Table 17.1).

A number of these universities organized themselves in a loosely-structured association in 1990. This has evolved into a well-structured organization of thirteen (see Table 17.1) French-language or bilingual universities outside Québec, the *Association des universitiés de la francophonie canadienne (AUFC)* (Association of universities of the Canadian Francophonie). Moreover, another association of ten higher education institutions, including colleges, has been created to respond to community needs in the health sector.

This study will examine the relationship between those universities and the minority French-language communities outside Québec. It will also explore the relationship between Canadian public policy and the development of inter-institutional structures to respond to community needs. The literature on this topic has generated a number of generalizations and hypothesis concerning the development of the third mission or community engagement aspect of a university's role. Among the factors associated with the development of the community engagement are institutional leadership, public policy and institutional support.

The universities and French-language minority communities

Although somewhat of a heterogeneous group, the institutions listed in Table 17.1 in large part have a similar approach to community engagement, which is to some extent independent of the linguistic dimension of their mandate. The importance of community engagement in general and engagement in relation to the French-language minority in particular is very evident in the mission statements and strategic plans of those universities, although the extent and the nature of that engagement depend on the specific circumstances of each individual institution. With the exception of the special-purpose Military College of Canada, none of these universities could be said to have exhibited what Goddard and Puukka (2008) describe as the 'denial of space' approach to their mission.

Table 17.1. French language or bilingual university institutions outside Québec

Name of institution	Language(s) of instruction	Number of students (in French-language programmes)
Université Sainte-Anne (Church Point, Nova Scotia)	French	600 (600)
Université de Moncton (Moncton, New Brunswick)	French	5000 (5000)
Saint-Paul University (Ottawa, Ontario)	French and English	800 (300)
University of Ottawa (Ottawa, Ontario)	French and English	38 000 (12 000)
Dominican University College (Ottawa, Ontario)	French and English	100 (60)
Royal Military College (Kingston, Ontario)	French and English	1300 (not available)
Glendon College at York University (Toronto, Ontario)	French and English	2600 (2600)
Laurentian University (Sudbury, Ontario)	French and English	8000 (1500)
University of Sudbury (Sudbury, Ontario)	French and English French and English	Included in Laurentian University's numbers
University of Hearst (Hearst, Ontario)	French	230 (230)
Collège universitaire de Saint-Boniface (Winnipeg, Manitoba)	French	1000 (1000)
Institut Français at the University of Regina (Regina, Saskatchewan)	French	Not available
Campus Saint-Jean at the University of Alberta (Edmonton, Alberta)	French	600 (600)

Source: this table was constructed from data available on the aucc.ca website, as well as information provided to the author from the AUFC secretariat.

For example, Laurentian University (in Sudbury, Ontario) was founded in 1960 with a mission to contribute to the development of northern Ontario, which is reflected very clearly in its mandate to be a bilingual university with a special mission regarding First Nations, as well as contributing to the overall development of the region. Given its location, it is not surprising that it has developed teaching and research strengths in a number of areas of importance to northern Ontario, particularly in relation to the mining sector. It has also created a Faculty of Medicine with a focus on rural and northern health, in partnership with another northern university. The university participates in and contributes to various Francophone cultural and artistic associations in the region, and its students and professors are very active in the Francophone community in northern Ontario, and are responsible for the establishment of a number of cultural groups and even the creation of the Franco-Ontarian flag (Gaudreau, 2005).

The French-language *Université de Moncton* (University of Moncton) is a key player in the social and economic development of south-eastern New Brunswick. The creation of the *Université de Moncton* (University of Moncton) in the early 1960s by the New Brunswick Government was a very deliberate attempt to enhance the socio-economic development of the sizeable French-language population of that province, know as Acadians. That period in New Brunswick also witnessed major changes in provincial-municipal relations and education, referred to as the 'Program of Equal Opportunity' (d'Entremont, 1985). In a study of the role of the universities in Atlantic Canada in regional development for the OECD, Garlick *et al.* (2007) noted the important role of *Université de Moncton* (University of Moncton):

> *The cultural revival and the surprising economic vitality, especially of south-eastern New Brunswick centred in Moncton, has been referred to as the 'Acadian Miracle'. The Université de Moncton has been a central player in this miracle ... a sign both of the University's bond with the community and the attachment of Acadians to the region.* (p. 22).

Along with the *Université Sainte-Anne* (University Sainte-Anne) in Nova Scotia, it maintains direct and sustained connections with the French-language minority communities in the Atlantic Provinces.

The largest university in the group of francophone and bilingual universities outside Québec, the University of Ottawa, is considered one of Canada's leading research-intensive universities and belongs to the G13, a group which represents Canada's largest research-intensive universities. Part of its stated mission is 'the promotion of French culture in Ontario'. Among its stated values are the following: 'a university committed to promoting Francophone communities' and 'a university that builds strong partnerships to fulfill its social responsibilities' (see http://strategicplanning.uottawa.ca/vision2010/mission-vision-and-values.html).

Post-secondary education was (and is) considered extremely important to the minority French-language communities themselves (*Fédération des francophones hors Québec*, 1985). Individually, the leaders of many of the universities which belong to the AUFC participate in activities of the various national and provincial organizations of the French-language minority (or minorities) outside Québec.

It could be argued that much of what did universities do in relation to their communities falls within what Molas-Gallart and Castro-Martinez (2007) would describe as the academic environment of those universities, thus not really part of third mission activities. They define the third mission to refer to activities that are 'outside academic environments'. Others (Vorley and Nelles, 2008) question the distinction between third mission activities and the core functions of the university, namely research and teaching. They argue that

> *[I]t is therefore puzzling that the third stream is often perceived, discussed and even implemented as a separate agenda. The Third Mission is more accurately conceptualised as a thread that has the capacity to weave together teaching and research, while assuming a more economic and societal focus* (Vorley and Nelles, 2008, p. 125).

We prefer this approach to the study of third mission activities. Since the primary functions of the university are teaching and research, it only makes sense that its engagement with the region or community would in many cases be intertwined with those primary functions.

Development of consortia

Given the importance of education for the development of the French-language minority in Canada, it is not surprising that strong links developed between the French-language minority communities and the post-secondary institutions offering academic programmes in French to these communities. This communality of missions and the limited number of universities involved led to informal contacts among these universities regarding the role that they played in the development of the French-language minority communities outside Québec. By January 1990, the need to collaborate in a more formal and structured manner led to a meeting of institutional leaders. By November 1990, what would eventually become the AUFC was officially established, with a very modest (part-time) secretariat. Eventually the Association developed, with the aid of Heritage Canada funding, a more elaborate organizational structure with a secretariat and a full-time executive director.

The initial aims and objectives of this association (AUFC) were of a somewhat limited scope, focusing mostly on collaborations regarding academic issues such as pedagogical materials and the sharing of teaching resources, as well as joint academic programmes. However, the emphasis on community engagement is evident in a recent document published by the Association on the vitality of its member institutions. The document links the vitality of French-language universities outside Québec to the vitality of the French-language communities:

> *All the academic institutions share the mission of providing access to university studies in French, thereby contributing significantly to the social vitality of Francophone communities ... Given their involvement at the heart of Francophone community living, the academic institutions are important partners in the social realm as the following testimonies illustrate.* (Association des universités de la francophonie canadienne, no date)

Over the past few years, the AUFC has begun to utilize its resources to advance a research agenda, focusing primarily on research related to issues of importance to the French-language minority communities, such as education, culture and the relationship between minority-language communities and the majority. Although the principal focus of the AUFC has been on academic and research issues, the link between the enhancement and development of these universities' academic mission and the development of the French-language minority communities is very evident in the AUFC statement on the 'Vitality of universities in the Canadian Francophonie'. Although one could argue whether or not the link between the vitality of the universities and the communities can (or has) been demonstrated, it nevertheless remains that the continued development of those universities is being justified in large part on linkages with their respective communities; community engagement has thus become part of that justification.

During the 1990s, a debate (or crisis) emerged concerning the future of a French-language hospital in Ottawa known as the Montfort Hospital (Cousineau, 1998). This debate highlighted the importance of French-language health services for the Francophone minority outside Quebec and resulted in a constitutional challenge which was eventually decided by the Ontario Court of Appeal. As a result, the hospital was not only spared from closure, its role was enhanced as a centre for the training of French-language health professionals which eventually led the Canadian Government (through Health Canada) to establish a four-year pilot project at the University of Ottawa to provide medical training to Francophone students from outside Québec and Ontario. This project had an outreach component which required the involvement of other French-language or bilingual post-secondary institutions, including the creation of an advisory group to the project.

This initiative proved to be a success and would pave the way for a much more significant initiative on the part of the Canadian Government. By 2003 this initiative had evolved into a national consortium, known by the acronym CNFS, the *Consortium national de formation en santé* (National consortium for health training). This consortium comprised ten institutions; six universities (all members of the AUFC), three colleges as well as a New Brunswick-Québec Agreement for the training of medical practitioners. Compared to the pilot project, the scope of the initiative had changed considerably to include the training of health professionals in many fields, including nursing and social work, as well as programmes at the community college level. The funding was also significant, with the CNFS being allocated approximately Canadian $63,000,000 over five years by Health Canada. Although considered a consortium, with a national secretariat, Health Canada proceeded by way of 11 funding agreements, one for each member institution and one for the national secretariat. Notwithstanding the separate funding agreements, the consortium is the primary intermediary with Health Canada and communicates to the government on behalf of its members. For example, the submission of institutional proposals for the most recent funding phase (2008–2013) was coordinated and vetted by the national secretariat and the CNFS Board of Directors before being submitted to Health Canada.

The CNFS programme is not a stand-alone programme, but rather one of three related programmes which are part of a broader Health Canada initiative designed to improve health services for the Official language minorities in Canada. The other two programmes are direct aid to the provinces for the provision of French-language health services and a network of French-language health professionals. This broader initiative, as well as the CNFS component, was evaluated recently as part of the regular review process mandated by Treasury Board. The results were positive and a third five-year phase was recommended for funding by Health Canada (Health Canada, 2008).

Although the primary focus and objective of the CNFS initiative is the training of French-language health professionals, the CNFS has also pursued a research agenda with the establishment of a Commission on Health Research of Interest for the French-language Community. This commission comprises both university and lay members, including representatives from the health-care sector and participation from government agencies. This Commission on health research has pushed recently for an increase in funding from the granting councils and Health Canada for research on issues and topics of importance for French-language minority communities, particularly relating to the social-economic determinants of health. Moreover, the CNFS has organized a number of national and regional conferences dealing with these issues which have included as participants a considerable number of health-care practitioners as well as community members.

Vorley and Nelles' (2008) concept of 'entrepreneurial architecture' is useful for our discussion here. This entrepreneurial architecture comprises a number of elements, including leadership, which is considered to be of crucial importance. 'This brings to the fore the critical role of university leadership and management in the pursuit of third stream activities . . . while they are not the only determinants of third stream success, are nevertheless critical agents of its integration and design' (Vorley and Nelles, 2008, pp. 130–131). The development of these two organizations (AUFC and CNFS) stems from informal discussions among university presidents whose institutions shared similar or complementary objectives or missions in relation to the French-language minority living outside Québec. Although neither of these two organizations can be described as bureaucratic, and both have maintained a largely informal and consensual style of decision-making, they have nevertheless evolved into more formal structures, including incorporation, a Board of Directors and other committees. University representation on the

Boards of Directors as well as on some of the most important committees is usually at the most senior levels within the university, typically president or vice-president. There is no doubt that university leadership has played a significant role in the creation of these two organizations as well as in the strengthening of the university engagement role of these universities.

Since the issue here is one of community engagement, it is important to comment on the relationship between these two organizations and the community (or communities) they relate to. Both the CNFS and the AUFC are viewed by official minority language national community organizations as constituting part of their communities, much like their constituent members are regarded as significant actors within their local minority language community. An indication of that status is exemplified by the participation of both the CNFS and the AUFC at a national Francophone Summit in 2007, which had over 800 attendees, organized to discuss the state of affairs and future directions for the French-language official minority communities in Canada. Both the CNFS and the AUFC were viewed as key elements within the Summit, and were included as signatories to the official Summit declaration, alongside 21 other organizations representing various facets of life within those communities, at the social, cultural and economic levels.

Public policy considerations

Others have already commented on the importance of public policy considerations in understanding the regional development role of universities. Arbo and Benneworth (2007) have argued that 'we have seen that universities ... are nevertheless nested within national policy frameworks that have strong influences on their overall regional capacity' (p. 56). Vorley and Nelles (2008) note 'that it is therefore important to consider the impact that policy design and implementation have on the incentive structures faced by target universities'(p. 131). Although in a slightly different context, the development of the community engagement role of the French-language universities outside Québec has also been influenced by public policy. Since Canada is officially a bilingual country, the Government of Canada has a constitutional obligation to provide for the development of official language minority communities (English in Québec and French elsewhere) which has led to a number of initiatives or action plans oriented towards that development. These action plans or initiatives have been developed after consultation with representative groups from the official language minority communities. In and of itself, this might (or should) encourage the universities to maintain good relations with their respective communities or regions. However, the public policy objectives were also supported by significant public funding. The availability of this funding has been a factor in the development of the two inter-university associations in question, CNFS and AUFC.

The initial impetus for engagement with their respective communities was clearly mission-driven and the not the result of public policy considerations. The creation of the AUFC in 1990 was also not directly linked to public policy considerations, although by then the Government of Canada had a constitutional obligation to promote the development of official minority language communities. Moreover, universities were beginning to benefit from the Official Languages in Education Program funded through the Secretary of State Department (now Heritage Canada). The establishment of the AUFC would facilitate consultation among the universities in question and enable them to deal more effectively with the Government of Canada. It can thus be argued that public policy considerations were indirectly linked to, or at least were part of, the background considerations which led to the establishment of the AUFC.

The creation of the CNFS in 2003 is an example of the direct influence of public policy considerations. An Action Plan for Official Languages was made public by the Canadian government in March 2003, which contained provisions for the funding of health initiatives. Following-up on reports from community-based consultative committees, Health Canada in June 2003 launched an ambitious initiative entitled 'Contribution Program to Improve Access to Health Services for Official Language Minority Communities'. The objectives of this programme were related to improving access to health services as well as improving health services and thereby the health of people within minority official language communities. It is important to note that none of the objectives was related specifically to university and/or educational issues. Moreover, the funding came from Health Canada and not from Heritage Canada, the federal department responsible for the funding of education through federal-provincial agreements. Notwithstanding the key role that the universities would play in this initiative, the initiative was clearly society/community focused. The role to be played by the universities within this initiative (through the CNFS) can be described as 'helping to improve the quality of life and the effectiveness of public services' (Molas-Gallart and Castro-Martinez, 2007, p. 322).

In the context of third mission indicators, Molas-Gallart and Castro-Martinez (2007) have argued that because of the ambiguity of third mission policy goals, the focus of discussion regarding this mission often revolves around the issue of indicators, resulting in what they refer to as symbolic policy implementation, with no clear policy goals and lack of explicit policy priorities. The situation regarding the third mission activities coordinated by the CNFS is very different from the symbolic implementation described above. In contrast to the case studies analyzed by Molas-Gallart and Castro-Martinez (2007), the evaluation of this initiative as well as the indicators were community-focused and not university-centred. Moreover, the university activities funded by Health Canada were evaluated as part of the broader public policy initiative in which the CNFS was only one of the elements, albeit the most costly one. Among the questions asked by the external evaluators were the following: 'Does the Program continue to be relevant to departmental and government-wide priorities? To what extent has the Program improved the access to health care services of official language minorities?' (Health Canada, 2008). Although the training of health-care professionals was an integral part of the programme, the objectives of the programme dealt with broader health policy issues of importance to the official language minority community.

Analysis and conclusion

It has been noted that in some countries 'higher education institutions have made tentative steps to address the challenge of closer cooperation by establishing regional associations of higher education institutions' (OECD, 2007, p. 187). Canada has a number of these regional associations, representing universities in specific provinces (Ontario, Québec) as well as multiple provinces (the Atlantic Provinces, the Western Provinces). What is different in the case of the AUFC and CNFS is that these two organizations transcend 'regional' boundaries and have been established to encourage closer collaborations among universities which have a community engagement role to play vis-à-vis an identifiable official minority language group throughout a number of regions. Moreover, both of these organizations are focused primarily on cultural or social issues instead of economic issues, although it would be incorrect to qualify these initiatives as 'social outreach' activities as defined by Molas-Gallart and Castro-Martinez (2007) since these activities, particularly those which constitute part of the CNFS initiative, do generate a significant amount of revenue.

It has been argued that the role of the senior leadership of universities is very important in relation to regional engagement and the development of regional economic policy (OECD, 2007; Vorley and Nelles, 2008). Although not dealing with a specific region or economic policy, this study comes to the same conclusion in relation to the community engagement role of the universities in question and the French-language minority in Canada outside Québec. The direct and continuous involvement of senior university officials in community engagement has been instrumental in ensuring that community engagement remains on the university 'radar screen'. The emphasis placed by university leaders on community engagement signals very clearly to other members of the university-community its importance as part of the university's mission. It ensures that the concept of community engagement finds its way in major university documents such as mission statements and strategic plans.

Although it would not be unusual for a university president to have an important role in any decision concerning their institution's adhesion to external associations and/or consortia, the President and other senior officials do not always have to take a direct personal role in those associations after they are established. In the case of both the CNFS and the AUFC, senior official participation was much more than simply giving approval to their university's involvement in these organizations; university presidents and other senior officials were active participants in the creation of both the CNFS and the AUFC and have remained active participants in their operations ever since. Their participation has ensured that both the CNFS and the AUFC remain visible and supported within their respective universities, and indicates a strong commitment to community engagement. Moreover, the importance accorded to these two organizations by the presence of senior university executives signals this engagement to the French-language communities outside Québec, as well as to governments.

Another element of note here are the structures developed to carry out community engagement initiatives. Some have argued that 'for managing the regional interface the higher education institution may need to establish a regional office' (OECD, 2007, p.184). There is no doubt that the development of administrative structures has advanced the goals of both the AUFC and the CNFS, and therefore of the collective community engagement of the member institutions. In the case of the CNFS, the availability of significant funding from the onset has meant that a national secretariat has been in place from the start, as well as enabling the member institutions to hire personnel dedicated to the CNFS's specific objectives. This has enabled the member institutions to ensure that the training programmes were in place, as well as permitting more intense contact with Francophone health-care professionals and the community. As to internal university mechanisms, although there was no creation of the equivalent of a 'regional office', the larger institutions have assigned personnel to oversee these activities. However, in the case of the CNFS initiative, each institution has a number of staff dedicated to the coordination of the activities financed by Health Canada through the CNFS.

The development of these internal administrative structures was due to the important funding received from Health Canada and the multiplicity of programmes and activities undertaken as a result. It would have been extremely difficult to undertake the necessary coordination within the institutions as well as to maintain relations with a number of external stake-holders in the absence of those internal administrative structures. Whether it is a 'regional office' or a special-purpose office dealing with a sub-set of the university's community engagement activities, it appears that the development of internal administrative structures is necessary when there is a significant institutional commitment and related activities to community engagement.

To sum up, this case study involves a number of bilingual or French-language universities who have a history of community engagement in general and in particular engagement with official French-language minority communities. The fact that a number of them have this in common led to the creation of inter-university associations, the AUFC and the CNFS. Strong interest in and commitment to community engagement on the part of the senior leadership, including presidents, has been instrumental in making this engagement an important element on their institutional mission. Public policy, translated into funding, has enabled these institutions to enhance their role in relation to official language minority communities.

References

Arbo, P. and Benneworth, P. (2007) *Understanding the Regional Contribution of Higher Education Institutions: A Literature Review.* OECD Education Working Paper No. 9. Paris: OECD.

Association des universités de la francophonie canadienne (No date) *The Vitality of Universities in the Canadian Francophonie*. Ottawa, Canada: AUFC.

Cousineau, M, (1998) *'L'affaire Montfort, l'article 15 de la Charte et le droit de la communauté franco-ontarienne à ses institutions'* ('The Montfort Affair, Article 15 of the Charter and the Right of the Franco-Ontarian community to its institutions') *Revue de droit d'Ottawa/Ottawa Law Review*. No 29, 369–392.

d'Entremont, H. (1985) 'Provincial restructuring of municipal government: a comparative analysis of New Brunswick and Nova Scotia' (Unpublished doctoral dissertation) University of Western Ontario, London, Ontario, Canada.

Fédération des francophones hors-Québec (1985) *Actes du Colloque national sur l'enseignement postsecondaire en langue française à l'extérieur du Québec* (*Proceedings of the national forum on French-language post-secondary education outside Québec*) Ottawa: FFHQ.

Garlick, G., Davies, G, Polèse, Mario and Kitagawa, F. (2007) *Supporting the contribution of higher education institutions to regional development peer review report: Atlantic Canada*. OECD Programme on Institutional Management in Higher Education. Paris: OECD.

Gaudreau, G. (ed.) (2005) *Le drapeau franco-ontarien* (*The Franco-Ontarian Flag*). Sudbury, Canada: Editions Prise de parole.

Goddard, J. and Puukka, J. (2008) 'The engagement of higher education institutions in regional development: an overview of the opportunities and challenges', *Higher Education Management and Policy*, 20(2), 3–33.

Health Canada (2008) *Contribution program to improve access to health services for official language minority communities: Summative evaluation report*. Ottawa: Health Canada.

Kitagawa, F. (2004) 'Universities and innovation in the knowledge economy: cases from English regions', *Higher Education Management and Policy*, 16(3), 65–89.

Molas-Gallart, J. and Castro-Martinez, E (2007) 'Ambiguity and conflict in the development of 'Third Mission' indicators', *Research Evaluation*, 16(4), 321–330.

OECD (2007) *Higher Education and Regions: Globally Competitive, Locally Engaged.* Paris: OECD.

Vorley, T. and Nelles, J. (2008) '(Re)conceptualising the academy: institutional development of and beyond the third mission', *Higher Education Management and Policy*, 20(3) 119–135.

Chapter 18

The third mission and the laboratory: How translational science engages and serves the community

Janet Atkinson-Grosjean and Conor Douglas

Introduction

In this chapter, we argue that *translational science* is a key component of the university's 'third mission' of community engagement and service. Translational science (TS), as we define it, is a conversation between the university and the communities it serves. We see TS as a dialectical process through which basic academic research ('discovery') moves into different spheres of application and use ('utility') and is, in turn, informed by the needs and expectations of those who use it. Through our studies of large-scale networks of biological scientists, we have identified three critical ways in which translational science helps fulfill the university's third mission. First, TS connects with communities of practice, in the clinic or in industry, where the application of research discoveries leads to improved operational protocols. Second, TS engages with investors and the marketplace through commercial translation, a form of technology transfer, which helps research innovations become marketable products. Third, through practices of civic translation, TS establishes links with the wider community and contributes to the common good. Civic TS is a broad church. Usually understood as 'public engagement' with citizens about the direction, content, ethics, costs, and benefits of scientific research, it also incorporates participation in science governance and policy development, as well as the construction of freely available research tools of benefit to the wider scientific community. Of these three forms of translational science – clinical/practical, commercial, and civic – the first two are well-established in research funding programmes and are beginning to make inroads in university reward and recognition structures. But civic translational science, despite its comprehensive contributions, remains largely unrecognized at every level. This chapter argues that the value of *all* forms of translational science needs to be recognized and fostered as fundamental to the university's third mission. Only then, we argue, will the translational mandates that have been so pervasive in recent science and innovation policy be inclusive enough to capture the diversity of returns that flow from public investments in university research.

Our exploration follows two broad themes. First, concerning the role of measurement, we argue that translational science is insufficiently appreciated and understood within the institutions of science and policy precisely because metrics are lacking. This situation is a frequent explanation for the fact that 'third stream' translational activities in general receive little acknowledgement (Molas-Gallart *et al.*, 2002). Where metrics do exist, they measure only what is amenable to measurement; for example, commercial outcomes (patents, licences, and so on). In contrast, changes in clinical and industrial protocols, or contributions in the civic arena, are more difficult to count and so are *dis*counted. Yet it is clear that in order to be valued, *all* such activities needs to be recognized, fostered, and measured. Second, we contend that the adoption of a broader understanding of translational science would allow policy-makers and university administrators to achieve a more accurate accounting of socio-economic returns on public investments in science and innovation, and witness a greater uptake of these activities on the part of the academic community.

In what follows we outline what we mean by TS; report on our observations about how a particular scientific network 'serves' the wider community through clinical, commercial, and civic translations; and then point to some recommendations for policy-makers and administrators.

Background and overview

Translational activities that contribute to the accomplishment of the university's third mission are those that comprise interactions between the university and society-at-large. More precisely, they involve 'the generation, use, application, and exploitation of knowledge and other university capabilities outside academic environments' (Molas-Gallart, *et al.*, 2002, p. iii). Although for our purposes translational 'streams,' 'missions,' and 'activities' are considered synonymous, Maria Nedeva (2008, p. 86) makes some interesting differentiations. First, while third stream *activities* are long-established, she suggests that framing them as a *mission* sets up a whole new operational imperative. Second, to the extent that the third mission is about 'interactions with society' Nedeva argues the university is re-producing itself in *relational* rather than *functional* terms. If this is the case then, third, she views universities as ranged along a continuum from 'service provider' to 'private, for-profit institution.' While concurring with much of this discussion, Philippe Laredo (2007) examines limitations of many third-stream analyses, pointing out their inability to come to grips with social, cultural, and civic issues; how they overestimate the economic benefits flowing from commercialization activities; how the importance of longstanding relationships is often overlooked in accounting for third-stream 'successes'; and that there are multiple challenges of capturing benefits at the local level.

In terms of *translational science*, we find the ideas of Laredo, Nedeva, and others to be provocative and interesting, but they do not undermine our own arguments. Despite a longstanding history, there is little doubt that current understandings of translational science arise out of a particular science-policy context, initiated in the neo-liberal years, that is preoccupied with maximizing the utility of public investments in research and forging closer links between academic science and the economy (Atkinson-Grosjean, 2006). In contrast to earlier models, the social contract for science now stipulates that publicly funded research must be directly translated into public benefit (ibid.) The assumption that scientific knowledge is beneficial in it own right attracts lip service rather than funding, and there is little willingness to wait for the utility of knowledge to reveal itself over time. As one example, Industry Canada (2002, p. 52) proposes a *quid pro quo*: '[a]n evolving partnership would see universities more aggressively contributing to innovation in Canada, in return for a long-term government commitment to their knowledge infrastructure.' In other words, buy-in to translational science is necessary for universities to protect ongoing funding. Further, while 'public benefit' is couched in socio-economic terms, specifics are almost invariably economic; largely, we suggest, because economic indicators and metrics are more readily devised than social and cultural indicators.

Current metrics: examples

In 2002, the Russell Group of Universities in the U.K. commissioned the Science and Technology Policy Research Unit (SPRU) at the University of Sussex to report on how best to measure the third stream. SPRU delivered a conceptual framework based on measuring activities rather than impacts (Molas Gallart *et al.*, 2002). The report recognized the need to go beyond commercialization indicators, since these measures cannot account for social and educational benefits that are civic in nature. However the proposed framework was highly complex and failed to achieve adoption. The UK's Higher Education Business and Community Interaction Survey has come the closest to developing a range of third mission metrics, though its indicators also tend to focus on commercial aspects, measuring income generated from consulting activities, for example, and from providing access to equipment and facilities. The recent inclusion of 'community' in the survey's title suggests interest in developing indicators that more accurately reflect the socio-cultural and civic realms.

In Canada (and the United States), the Association of University Technology Managers (AUTM) collects annual data on university commercial activities. The UNICO (University Companies Association) survey provides the equivalent in the U.K. The OECD (2007) also collects a set of science and technology indicators that measures national R&D expenditures and some commercialization information. A study for Canada's Advisory Council on Science and Technology (ACST) noted that Canada and the UK 'appear to have 'chosen' to forego the early financial returns from the licensing of technology in favour of a strategy of more patient equity investment in start-up companies' (Riddle, 2004, p. 1). The comment arises from the fact that both countries have focused on programmes to encourage company creation and capacity building (arguably, as much a social benefit as an economic output) rather than licensing-out to existing businesses as is more often the case in the US. Statistics show that Canada has twice as many start-up companies than the United States (and the UK five times as many) per unit of research expenditure. Further, while normalized licensing income is approximately equal in Canada and the UK, both countries produce only a third of the licensing revenue per unit of expenditure as the US. Although this strategy may prove profitable in the long-run the relative imbalance in licensing revenues has been noted by governments in both Canada (by the Advisory Council on Science and Technology) and the UK (where the Lambert Review noted the relatively low licensing revenues).

Recently, a number of Canadian institutions – particularly in the medical research sector – have mobilized to attempt to quantify non-economic translational activities. For example, the Canadian Academy of Health Sciences (2009) and the Michael Smith Foundation for Health Research (2007) have both released reports on the data collection needed for a more expansive understanding of translational activities. Similarly, Genome British Columbia and the Michael Smith Foundation for Health Research are sponsoring efforts to revise reporting requirements in order to capture civic translational data in project reports.

While such initiatives suggest that the need to account for translational science and third mission activities is being taken seriously, obstacles persist – in part because of the opaqueness of some of the concepts at hand.

Conceptualizing translational science

From the literature
The desire to move research into practical applications in order to capture the benefits derived from scientific discovery has long motivated science funding and programme development. Distinctions between *pure* and *applied* science were common in the 'golden age' of basic research in the 1940s and 1950s. However, it is widely recognized that this linear model of innovation – in which pure science is published in the academic literature, then picked-up by industry and developed into useful applications – is simplistic and inaccurate. As a general rule, scientific research contains aspects of *both* basic inquiry (discovery) *and* practical application (utility) and moves back and forth between the two. Louis Pasteur's substantial contribution to *both* the science of microbiology *and* the control of bacterial disease is only one historical example of this relationship (Stokes, 1997). Attempts to classify the types of research that connect discovery and utility have led, over the years, to terms such as 'mission-oriented research', 'directed research', 'use-inspired basic research', and 'strategic research'.

The adjective *translational* (applied to 'science', 'research', and 'medicine') is a relatively recent addition that started gaining popularity in the 1990s in the health sciences but quickly spread into non-health fields. Its adoption (at least in part) can be attributed to the US National Institutes of Health (NIH) and the affiliated National Cancer Institute (NCI). In 1992, the NCI developed the *Specialized Programs of Research Excellence* (SPORE) to encourage the translation of basic research into clinical settings. The Canadian Institutes for Health Research (CIHR), founded in 2000, was mandated by legislation to support translation of the research it funded. In 2003 the NIH released the *Roadmap for Medical Research* with a specific focus on interdisciplinary and translational research, supported by the Clinical and Translational Science Awards programme. In 2004, the CIHR released a strategy entitled *A Roadmap to Ensure Canadian Leadership in Clinical and Translational Research.*

Thus, it took only a decade for the 'translational' adjective to become commonplace. To increase the term's clarity, some schools of thought specified two translational phases: T1 (research discovery to product development) and T2 (product development to product delivery; CIHR's concept of 'knowledge translation' [KT] would fall under T2). Others in medical research break down translational science even further, into a multiphase process that includes the movement of biomedical research into diagnosis or treatment (T1) (Kerner, 2006, p. 73), subsequent development into evidence-based protocols (T2) (ibid.), deployment into clinical practice (T3) (Westfall *et al.*, 2007), and verification and evaluation for 'real world' impacts on health (T4) (Khoury *et al.*, 2007). While definitions are still not settled, the relative speed of adoption of 'translation talk' suggests that *some* terminology was needed to capture the dynamic process of creating social, medical, and economic utility from fundamental discoveries. Despite the varieties of interpretations, all descriptions of translational science recognize its dynamic and iterative nature, the way it moves back and forth between discovery and utility, which is summarized in Figure 18.1.

Figure 18.1 The translational dialectic

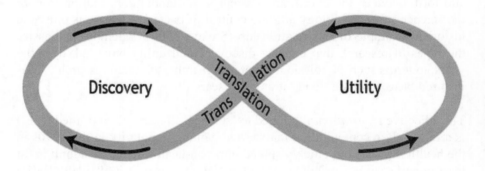

Learned in the field

Within the translational dialectic, our field research identified three distinct, yet related, domains of utility: commercial, clinical/practical, and civic (Figure 18.2). The commercial pathway is characterized by movement between the academic laboratory and, ultimately, the marketplace. Patenting, licensing, company creation, and capitalization are typical features. Variations in the literature include merchant science (Atkinson-Grosjean,

2006) and entrepreneurial science (Etzkowitz, 1998). Public policy directs resources to this pathway in order to promote benefits such as 'knowledge-based' economic growth and high-skills jobs in industries such as biotechnology and pharmaceuticals, and to aid in the development of new therapeutics and/or instrumentation.

The clinical/practical pathway is identified by movement of problems and solutions back and forth between the research laboratory and the context of application, whether the clinic (in biomedical research) or industry (in nonmedical research). This pathway is characterized by the exchange of novel techniques and protocols. Public policy and resources support this type of translational science in order to generate the socio-economic returns associated with healthier populations or more innovative industries.

Figure 18.2 Inclusive model of translational science

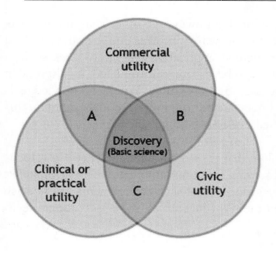

Hybrid Domains
A: Clinical–Commercial
e.g. running clinical trials for new drugs

B: Commercial–Civic
e.g. pharmaceutical philanthropies funding research on 'unprofitable' 3rd world diseases such as malaria

C: Civic–Clinical
e.g. design and implement-ation of new public health modalities

Civic translational science is a multifaceted category involving scientists– in their capacity as citizens of the scientific *polis*– in a variety of roles. Included here is participation in science-policy discussions with governments, public engagement exercises and citizen-to-citizen forums such as Café Scientifique and Minimed Schools. Importantly, civic translational science also includes the creation of freely available research tools such as model organisms and biological databases, for the use and benefit of all. Engagement in civic translational activities is often motivated by communitarian convictions and the belief that scientific knowledge is a social good that should be shared with either the public-at-large or the wider scientific community. While recent decades have seen increasing awareness of the importance of translational engagements in the civic domain – witness public concerns about genetically modified foods and climate change, for example – few policies and resources are directed to supporting these types of activities, especially when compared with the attention devoted to the commercial domain. *Such neglect, we suggest, results in a systematic undercalculation of the social rates of return on public investments in science.*

In the biomedical arena, attention to Figure 18.2 also reveals three 'hybrid' translational pathways: (a) Clinical–Commercial, e.g. running clinical trials for new drugs; (b) commercial–civic, e.g. pharmaceutical philanthropies that fund R&D for 'unprofitable' third-world diseases such as malaria (Novartis; Merck); and (c) civic–clinical, e.g. design and implementation of new public health modalities. These are significant hybrid domains but their exploration lies outside the scope of the current chapter.

The bi-directionality of translational pathways is of crucial importance. While it may seem obvious that basic research informs public policy, clinical and industrial practice, or commercial applications, it rarely does so in a linear fashion. Questions and hypotheses are reformulated to align with knowledge gained in the processes of translation. Whether knowledge is acquired through informal conversations or formal collaborations, this dialectical learning forms the heart of translational science.

While the literature makes it plain that research universities need to refocus their energies on engaging and serving the community (Boyte and Hollander, 1999), our field observations persuade us that such engagements can flourish in academic laboratories, when the right incentives and observational techniques are in place.

Methods and findings

Over the years 2006 through 2009 we conducted an extensive study of a network of academic scientists investigating the pathogenomics of innate immunity ('the PI.2 network'). Members of PI.2 were investigating the underlying genetic functioning of the innate immune system in humans and animals. This system is the first line of immunological defense; it allows us 'to withstand a daily onslaught of tens of thousands of potentially pathogenic microbes in air, food and water, and in our interactions with other people and animals' (PI.2 project website, accessed 17 December 2009). The adaptive immune system is the one more commonly known for its ability to recognize and recall foreign pathogens in order to defend against them; the adaptive immune response underpins medical approaches to immunization/ vaccination. However, with changes in the nature of infectious disease such as the rise of resistant 'superbugs' like MRSA, interest has increased in understanding the fundamental mechanisms of innate immunity.

Our team was integrated into PI.2 as the social science collaborators in this large-scale network. Our task was to examine the nature of translational science and scientists' attitudes towards the translational process. We used a mixed methods approach that incorporated structured face-to-face survey interviews and site visits to network nodes in Canada and the United Kingdom (UK). At the time of the survey, the network comprised 120 members distributed across six network nodes (five in Canada, one in the UK), with individual members in Singapore, Ireland, Sweden, and Hong Kong. We were able to interview 100 of the 120 members. Thus, in our analyses, we treat the data as a full census with 20 missing cases. We also conducted face-to-face survey interviews with a control group comprising members of a non-related network of basic scientists (n=30). Ethnographic fieldwork (participant-observation) and in-depth qualitative interviews (n=42) informed three intensive case studies of the form and function of the translational science found within the network. Qualitative software (ATLAS.ti) was used to explore and extract thematic data from our surveys, interviews, and field notes. A code list was created and evolved during the analysis process as we reflected on the emerging themes. A grounded theory approach (Charmaz, 2006) guided our approach.

To begin the process, we first conducted documentary analysis and pilot interviews to identify the types of translational/ third mission activities scientists engaged in. Based on the pilot-test results, we generated a set of 16 actions which we were able to categorize as either commercial, clinical/practical, or civic translation. Commercial translation involved, for example, filing for intellectual property rights through the University-Industrial Liaison office, conducting consultancy work for a commercial firm, or starting a spin-off company. Clinical/practical translation, on the other hand, included development of clinical applications, engaging in pre-clinical drug development, or even clinical trials. Software development for particular applications was a practical tool also included in this category. The remaining translational activities, while disparate, shared common 'civic' attributes such as consulting to government; giving public talks about science; participating in local outreach activities with high schools and community groups; and writing for non-scientific audiences or otherwise interacting with the media. An important civic element, emphasized by scientists, was the creation of open-access research tools – such as model organisms and bioinformatic databases – freely available to the scientific community.

Table 18.3 shows the 16 translational activities sorted by category. As may be seen, in addition to their basic research and teaching responsibilities, approximately one-third of the scientists in our study have been involved in activities that form part of the university's third mission. What may be surprising, is that they engage in civic translation more often than in commercial or clinical translation. It may be less surprising, however, that

Table 18.3 Translational activities of network scientists (n=100)

Translational Activity	#	% total
Civic		
Public talks on research topics	47	
Local outreach	48	
Science writing for non-scientists	38	
Responding to the media on research topics	31	
Consulting to government	16	
Developing open-access organisms; databases, etc	34	
	213	13.3
Clinical and Practical		
Contract research	44	
Developing clinical applications	38	
Preclinical drug development	24	
Clinical trials	23	
Software development (e.g. bioinformatics)	24	
	163	9.6
Commercial		
Filing for intellectual property	36	
Working in industry	24	
Company start-ups	27	
Consulting to industry	27	
	113	7.1
Other (specify)	19	1.1
'Yes' – translational experience by category	498	31.1
'No' – translational experience by category	1102	68.9
Total possible responses	1600	100

Figure 18.4 Translational experience by role

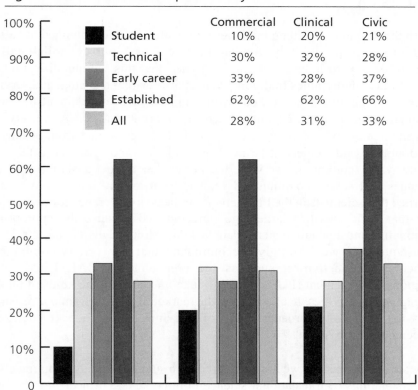

	Commercial	Clinical	Civic
Student	10%	20%	21%
Technical	30%	32%	28%
Early career	33%	28%	37%
Established	62%	62%	66%
All	28%	31%	33%

these 'civic' activities – directed at serving society in a broader and less technical manner – are more often than not undertaken by established academics with the knowledge and freedom to do so (Figure 18.4).

Although these findings are limited to the PI.2 network, they do suggest a significant observation concerning the University's third mission: that much of the work being done to serve the community goes unrecognized. There are many reasons as to why this might be so, such as the absence of evaluative matrices to capture these contributions, and the lack of an institutionalized reward structure that acknowledges and promotes them. However, simply because this work is not properly counted does not mean that it does not count. Adequate recognition would likely surface widespread and diverse engagement in third mission activities across the university-at-large.

Discussion

With the advent of neoliberal policies universities were encouraged to patent and profit from publicly funded research, and pursue collaborative relationships with industry. It can be argued that this 'commodification of universities' undermines traditional values of research, teaching, and service to the community. However, our work indicates that engagement in translational science is rarely motivated by market values. A variety of translational activities move science and technology to and from academic laboratories and society-at-large. While clinics and markets offer two pathways to community service, we argue that civic translation directly engages and serves communities yet has been largely ignored. We have learned that scientists in the PI.2 network indicate a preference for civic work but that such activities largely go unrecognized because the appropriate summative and evaluative metrics are lacking (Molas-Gallart *et al.,* 2002). In consequence, we strongly recommend that university-community benchmarking activities, such as the emergent PASCAL Universities Regional Engagement (PURE) Project, take into account the kinds of public engagement activities that go beyond the market. It is clear from our research that the value of a broader range of activities needs to be recognized, fostered, and measured.

The second theme that we have explored here suggests that by adopting civic understandings of translational science policy-makers, project funders, and university administrators would achieve a more accurate accounting of socio-economic returns on public investments in science and innovation. Such an adoption would in turn work to promote the university's third mission. But such funding and policy frameworks should not only acknowledge non-market translational work, but also provide material and non-material rewards for it. Elsewhere in this volume, the institutionalization of reward structures for community-based research has been explored by Melvin Hill Jr. (2009), and James E. Randall (2009) has examined the evaluation of service and community-based research in faculty tenure and promotion decisions at Canadian universities.

Conclusion

To conclude, despite continuing institutional barriers to the support of third-mission and other translational activities, we are encouraged by the interest in our work on translational science expressed by some funding agencies in

Canada. Genome British Columbia for example – the regional research organization that funds a wide variety of work related to genetics and genomics – is currently modifying project-reporting forms and guidelines to gather information on non-market translational activities of funded scientists; this represents a significant shift given their prior focus on commercialization. Nevertheless, further work is needed to effectively capture the diverse ways in which the laboratory is actively engaging with and serving the wider community. To adequately address the gap, researchers from disparate disciplines must be willing to cross boundaries in pursuit of their common interest in this topic. As STS scholars and sociologists of science, we have endeavored in this chapter to reach out to colleagues in the field of higher education to promote a discourse on 'third mission' activities in the sciences. We look forward to future engagements.

References

Atkinson-Grosjean, J. (2006) *Public science, private interests: cultures and commerce in Canada's networks of centres of excellence*. Toronto: University of Toronto Press.

Boyte, H. and Hollander, E. (1999) 'Wingspread Declaration on renewing the civic mission of the American research university'. *Proceedings from the Wingspread conference,* Michigan, USA.

Canadian Academy of Health Sciences (2009) 'Making an impact: a preferred framework and indicators to measure returns on investment in health research'. *Report of the Panel on the Return on Investments in Health Research*. Retrieved 9 September 2009 from http://www.cahs-acss.ca/e/pdfs/ROI_FullReport.pdf.

Canadian Institutes for Health Research (2004). 'A roadmap to ensure Canadian leadership in clinical and translational research'. Retrieved 9 September 2009 from http://www.cihr-irsc.gc.ca/e/documents/cr_mustreport_e.pdf.

Charmaz, K. (2006). *Constructing grounded theory: A practical guide through qualitative analysis*. Thousand Oaks, CA: Sage Publications.

Etzkowitz, H. (1998). 'The norms of entrepreneurial science: cognitive effects of the new university–industry linkages', *Research Policy*, 27(8), 823–833.

Hill Jr., M. (2009) 'Designing faculty reward systems as a means of promoting the third mission of Universities'. Paper presented at the PASCAL conference, Vancouver, BC. Abstracts accessible from http://chet.educ. ubc.ca/pdf_files/2009/Pascal_Conf%20final%20abstracts_June.pdf.

Industry Canada (2002) *Achieving excellence: Investing in people, knowledge, and opportunity*. Ottawa: Government of Canada.

Kerner, J. F. (2006) 'Knowledge translation versus knowledge integration: A "funder's" perspective', *Journal of Continuing Education in the Health Professions,* 26(1), 72–80.

Khoury, M.J. Gwinn, M. Yoon, P.W. Dowling, N. Moore, C.A. and Bradley, L. (2007) 'The continuum of translation research in genomic medicine: how can we accelerate the appropriate integration of human genome discoveries into health care and disease prevention?' *Genetics in Medicine*, 9(10), 665–674.

Laredo, P. (2007) 'Revisiting the third mission of universities: Toward a renewed categorization of university activities?' *Higher Education Policy*, 20(4), 441–456.

Michael Smith Foundation for Health Research (2007) *Evaluating British Columbia's performance in health research: Technical report 1999–2006*. Retrieved from Michael Smith Foundation for Health Research: http://www.msfhr.org/resources/public/Reports/BC_Health_Research_Tech nical_Report.pdf.

Molas-Gallart, J. Salter, A. Patel, P. Scott, A. and Duran, X. (2002) 'Measuring third stream activities', *Report to the Russell Group universities*. Brighton: SPRU.

National Institutes of Health (2004) *NIH roadmap for medical research*. http://nihroadmap.nih.gov/.

Nedeva, M. (2008) 'New tricks and old dogs? The 'third mission' and the re-production of the university', in D. Epstein, R. Boden, R. Deem, F. Rizvi and S. Wright (eds.), *The World Yearbook of Education 2008: Geographies of knowledge/geometries of power – higher education in the 21st century*, 85–105. New York: Routledge.

OECD (2007) *Main science and technology indicators*, May 2007. Tables 2and3, Pathogenomics of Innate Immunity (PI.2) Project homepage. Retrieved 17 December 2009, from http://www.pathogenomics.ca/.

Randall, J. (2009) 'The role of service and community-based research in tenure and promotion: An analysis of Canadian University Agreements', Paper presented at the PASCAL Conference, Vancouver, BC. Abstract accessible from http://chet.educ.ubc.ca/pdf_files/2009/Pascal_Conf%20final %20abstracts_June.pdf.

Riddle, C. (2004) *Commercialization strategies of Canadian universities and colleges: Challenges at the university/college – industry interface, including intellectual property policies.* Ottawa: Advisory Council on Science and Technology.

Stokes, D.E. (1997) *Pasteur's Quadrant: Basic science and technological innovation.* Washington DC: Brookings Institution Press.

Westfall, J.M. Mold, J. and Fagnan, L. (2007) 'Practice-based research – "blue highways" on the NIH Roadmap', *JAMA*, 297, 403–406.

Notes on contributors

Seth A. Agbo is Associate Professor in the Faculty of Education at Lakehead University where he teaches educational research, educational foundations, and comparative and international education. Prior to his present position, Dr Agbo taught at the State University of New York (SUNY) at Potsdam and at Pacific University of Oregon. He obtained his PhD in educational studies from the University of British Columbia in 1996 and has researched and published extensively on several interest areas including comparative and international education; lifelong learning, educational policy, professional development, teacher effectiveness and community–school relationships.

Janet Atkinson-Grosjean, Translational Genomics Research Group, WM Young Centre for Applied Ethics, University of British Columbia, holds an interdisciplinary PhD in science and technology studies (STS) and science policy (UBC), and an MA in liberal studies with an STS focus, Simon Fraser University. Postdoctoral training was in applied ethics. Her work focuses on large-scale science and ways in which novel institutional and organizational arrangements affect the production and translation of scientific knowledge. The goal is to contribute to a more nuanced understanding within policy guidelines of what constitutes 'translational science.'

Paul Benneworth is a Principal Research Associate at the Center for Higher Education Policy Studies (CHEPS) at the University of Twente, the Netherlands. Paul's research concerns the relationships between universities and society, (the 'social compact'), with a particular focus on reach-out, knowledge exchange and engagement activities (the 'third mission').

Lise Bérubé completed her Masters of Arts in Dispute Resolution from the University of Victoria in 2008. She has worked with the Office of Community Based Research at UVic since 2007, and acted as the Program Coordinator for the European Studies Program from 2008-2010.

Shauna Butterwick is an Associate Professor in the Department of Educational Studies at UBC. She has conducted several community-based research projects, mostly focusing on women's learning experiences within multiple contexts including: the welfare system, advocacy and social movements, and information technology workplaces. Since 2004, she has a faculty researcher with a CURA (Community and University Research) SSHRC grant focusing on economic security. She also engages with art-making processes within her research and teaching.

David Charles is the Dean of Research and Development and professor at the Curtin Business School, Curtin University, Perth, Australia. He has a wide range of research interests, which include innovation management, the role of universities in regional development, regional innovation policy and urban development. He is a visiting professor at Newcastle University in the UK and at the University of Tampere in Finland.

Cheryl Conway was a senior research associate at Newcastle University with research interests in economic development, labour market analysis, science and innovation policy, and gender and work. She has been involved in a number of studies on the role of universities in territorial development, and recently completed an FP6 project on the opportunities and challenges for participation and career advancement of women at the interface between science and the economy. Since then she has been working on a community development project in Guatemala.

Paul Crawford serves as Director of Community College Relations at Northern Illinois University (NIU). Prior to holding this position, he was a Gift and Estate Planning Officer with NIU and Director of Financial Aid at Illinois Valley Community College. He began his career in education as a high school instructor, teaching theology and philosophy, and continues to teach theology courses at Mount Mary College in Milwaukee.

Conor Douglas is a postdoctoral student in the Translational Genomics Research Group, WM Young Centre for Applied Ethics, University of British Columbia, where he works alongside Dr Atkinson-Grosjean exploring the factors that facilitate and constrain scientists engaging in 'translational research'. A social scientist by background, he spent three and a half years as a Research Fellow in the Science and Technology Studies Unit (SATSU) at the University of York (UK) where he is also undertook his PhD, which focused on the changing role of patients in the R&D of new genetic medical technologies.

Chris Duke is the Academic Director PASCAL PURE Project, Chief Executive of the PASCAL International Observatory and Deputy Chair of the Council of the Tavistock Institute in London. He was part-time Director (Higher Education) for NIACE in the UK, and is currently part-time Professor at RMIT University Melbourne, where he was Director, Community and Regional Partnership after being Professor of Lifelong Learning at the University of Auckland. He is an Honorary Professor of Lifelong Learning at the universities of Leicester and Stirling in the UK. He worked at the now University of Greenwich and then at Leeds before becoming Foundation Director of Continuing Education at the Australian National University, then in 1985 Foundation Professor and Director of Continuing Education at the University of Warwick. After serving as Pro-Vice-Chancellor at Warwick he became President of the University of Western Sydney Nepean. He has worked extensively from the 1970s with the OECD and other international organizations mainly on education in relation to development, recurrent education and lifelong learning, also equity and poverty reduction issues, and sustainable development.

Harley d'Entremont is Professor of Political Science at Laurentian University, where he was Academic Vice-President from 2003 until 2008. From 1988 to 2001, he was the President of Université Sainte-Anne. He holds a PhD in political science form the University of Western Ontario. He has served on various boards such as the Atlantic Provinces Economic Council, as well as the Ontario Mineral Industry Cluster Committee. He also participated in many national bodies dealing with French-language post-secondary matters.

Margo Fryer is the founding Director of the UBC Learning Exchange and the UBC-Community Learning Initiative. Margo received her PhD in Interdisciplinary Studies from the University of British Columbia in 2003. Prior to undertaking her PhD program, Fryer worked as a researcher in the health and social service fields, collaborating with community groups, non-profit organizations, and government agencies. This research was concerned with a wide variety of issues, including the health needs of seniors and women, childhood sexual abuse, multicultural service delivery, and the use of community development strategies to improve health.

Robert E. Gleeson is the Director of the Center for Governmental Studies at Northern Illinois University. Prior to that, he served for seven years as associate professor of management and public policy and faculty director of the Institute for Economic Transformation at Duquesne University and also served as the founding executive director and visiting assistant professor at Carnegie Mellon University's Center for Economic Development. Other previous jobs have included director of economic development for the Pittsburgh High Technology Council; senior capital planner for Allegheny County, Pennsylvania; and management consultant in the business strategy services group at the Blue Cross and Blue Shield Association in Chicago. Gleeson earned his doctorate at Carnegie Mellon University in the interdisciplinary field of history and policy. He also holds a Master's degree in public policy from Harvard's John F. Kennedy School of Government. He publishes in the field of regional economic development, most recently authoring a chapter in a Brookings Institution book on metropolitan development patterns and co-authoring the first in an annual series of reports titled *The State of Working Illinois*.

Penny Gurstein is Professor and Director of the School of Community and Regional Planning at the University of British Columbia where she specializes in the socio-cultural aspects of community planning with particular emphasis on those who are the most marginalized in planning processes. Recent research examined the impact of government reduction of social services on single parent families on income assistance in British Columbia. Her current project is focusing on the relationship between climate change, inequality, and housing affordability. Co-authored publications include *Learning Civil Societies: Shifting Contexts for Democratic Planning and Governance*.

Hugo Gutierrez (Ahumada) is Professor, Department of Social Development and Citizenship, Tecnologico de Monterrey, Mexico. Hugo Gutierrez Ahumada is currently studying for his PhD in Social Development (Tecnológico de Monterrey, Campus Monterrey). He serves as Head of Social Programs in the Social Development and Citizenship Department at Tecnologico de Monterrey, and he is a cofounder of Mexico Rural and Mexico Urbano community outreach programs. He is also a Member of the Campus Committee for Social Development, Faculty at the Leadership for Social Development minor and the consulting committee for the Community Learning Centers.

Nora Guzman is the Director, Department of Social Development and Citizenship at the Tecnológico de Monterrey, Mexico. She has a doctorate in Humanities and Arts (University of Zacatecas), and Master in Romance Languages (London University). She has been a professor of literature since 1973 and recipient of the Academic Excellence Award in 1998 and 2003. She belongs to Mexico's National Researchers System and has published on *Society, Development and Citizenship in Mexico* (2008), *Narrative from*

Northern Mexico, Critical Approximation (2008) and *Every Road Leads North* (2009).

Budd L. Hall is currently the Director of the Office of Community-Based Research at the University of Victoria. He was the Convenor of the Task Force on Civic Engagement at the University of Victoria and Co-Convenor of the Task Force on Community-Based Research at The University of Victoria. With a background in adult education and participatory research Dr Hall is a former Dean of Education, former Chair of Adult Education and Community Development at the University of Toronto and was Secretary-General of the International Council for Adult Education for 11 years. He has been involved with the founding of Community Based Research Canada and the Global Alliance for Community Engaged Scholarship. His most recent studies have included a study of Funding-Models and Development of Community-Based Research in Canada and the North American Report for the World Report on Higher Education of 2008. He is also a poet.

Vivian Hermansen is Director, Aboriginal Education, North Island College, Campbell River, British Columbia. Vivian Hermansen (B.Ed, Post-Degree Diploma Special Ed, M.Ed, UBC). She is a member of the Snuneymuxw (Nanaimo) First Nation, and currently the Director of Aboriginal Education at North Island College, Campbell River, British Columbia. Vivian has worked in aboriginal education since 1993 firstly in a district position for School District 69 (Qualicum); the Laichwiltach Family Life Society piloting the Aboriginal Head Start Program, and in the post-secondary system for the last ten years as faculty and then in an administrative position since 2005. Vivian has served on provincial and national committees for Aboriginal post-secondary education and brings 16 years of field experience in Aboriginal education from the pre-school to post-secondary settings.

Melvin B. Hill, Jr. is associated with the University of Georgia, Athens, Georgia. Melvin B. Hill, Jr. is the Robert G. Stephens, Jr., Senior Fellow in Law and Government in the Institute of Higher Education of the University of Georgia. He also served as the editor of the *Journal of Higher Education Outreach and Engagement.* Mr Hill has served as the director of the Carl Vinson Institute of Government of the University of Georgia. Mr Hill holds a BA degree from Bucknell University, and an MPA and a JD degree from Cornell University.

LaVerne Williamson Hill received her PhD in Political Science and Sociology from the University of Georgia in Athens, Georgia in 1982, specializing in Public Law, Public Administration and Criminology. Dr Hill's areas of teaching and research interest at the college level include criminal justice, criminal law, the courts, juvenile delinquency, crime theory, family violence, American government and public policy and public administration.

Lynne Humphrey is a Visiting Fellow at Newcastle University with over 20 years experience of policy-applied research within the academic, public and voluntary sectors. More recently she has focused on contemporary local and regional governance, in particular, the politics and practice of community/ stakeholder engagement. She is currently studying a part-time PhD at Royal Holloway, University of London, researching philosophies of history.

Patricia Inman is a Senior Research Associate with the Center for Governmental Studies at Northern Illinois University and an Associate for PASCAL International. She completed a doctorate in Adult and Continuing Education at Northern Illinois University. Dr Inman's research interests include asset-based community development, engaging educational institutions, adult literacy, regional policy and local food development.

Anne Kaplan is the Vice President for Administration and University Outreach at Northern Illinois University. She is a member of the Advisory and Executive Steering Group of PASCAL International Observatory. Dr Kaplan's involvement with PASCAL allows her to bring an international perspective to her role as the university's representative on two national commissions developing tools for assessing a university's contribution to the economic development of its region and toolkits to help practitioners design, develop, implement and evaluate community and economic development initiatives.

Nirmala Lall is currently a currently a doctoral student in Leadership Studies at the University of Victoria. Her research interest is the area of assessing impact of community-university research partnerships and she is in the initial stages of conducting a case study of the impact of the Office of Community-Based Research at the University of Victoria. Nirmala holds a Master of Education from Harvard University and completed her undergraduate and professional degrees at York University in Toronto. Nirmala has over 20 years of experience working with youth, families, schools, communities and university students to develop a critical understanding of intercultural issues. She has contributed to the design and publication of curriculum, multimedia and resource materials. Nirmala is currently teaching 'Facilitating intercultural relationships', a course offered by the University of Victoria's Intercultural Education Training Program.

Kathryn Mohrman is Director of the University Design Consortium and Professor in the School of Public Affairs at Arizona State University. Her career spans teaching, university leadership and research on public policy issues. Administrative posts include President of Colorado College, Dean for Undergraduate Studies at University of Maryland-College Park, and Associate Dean of the College, Brown University. International activities include Director of the Hopkins–Center and Fulbright Scholar in Japan, Korea, and Hong Kong. She was also a visiting professor at Sichuan University.

James E. Randall, Professor, International Studies Program, University of Northern British Columbia (UNBC) served as Provost (2007–08) and Dean (2003–07) at UNBC. Jim holds a PhD in economic geography (Washington) and an MA and BA from York University. Jim spent 15 years at the University of Saskatchewan as Head of Geography and as Co-Director of a SSHRC-CURA funded 'Community-University Institute for Social Research'. His research is in economic geography, quality-of-life indicators, community economic development and urban/regional planning.

Diana L. Robinson is Associate Director of the Center for Governmental Studies at Northern Illinois University. Her work focuses on effective practice, program evaluation, applied research, and policy studies in workforce development, adult education and workplace literacy, work-based learning, education reform, and knowledge management. In the past 20 years, Ms. Robinson has held leadership positions in public education, workforce and economic development, and business-education partnership programs.

Hans G. Schuetze is Professor emeritus and former Director, Centre for Policy Studies in Higher Education and Training at the University of British Columbia. After studies in law, economics, history and education in Göttingen and Bonn (Germany), Grenoble (France) and Berkeley (University of California), he worked as a lawyer, policy analyst and researcher in Germany, France and has served as the US Honorary Senior Research Fellow at the University of Glasgow, Scotland since 1994. Areas of interest and expertise: comparative higher education, educational policy and legal and economic issues in education.

Bruce Wilson is the Head of the School of Global Studies, Social Sciences and Planning at RMIT University. Professor Wilson teaches in organizational and management studies and research methods, and has research interests in various aspects of social and organizational life, specifically focused on change and learning. In recent years, he has led projects on social inclusion and cohesion, innovation, learning, organizational and work design, and social and economic development, particularly where there is collaboration amongst public, private and community sector organizations. He was project leader of the RMIT team involved with the CRITICAL project, involving collaboration on learning networks in Melbourne and four European cities. Currently, he is Co-Director of PASCAL, and leads the RMIT team involved in PASCAL. On behalf of PASCAL, he has led a number of projects which address the importance of learning in enhancing economic and social benefits from regional development.

Index

Index

Index

Index

337

Index

organizational knowledge creation 90
Ory, J.C. and Braskamp, L. 258
Other, definition of 181
Otherness, definition of 181
outreach, and partnerships 124; projects
148; scholarship 255, 257; work 232, 240,
245

Palmer, P.J. 182
Park, P. 185
participatory action research (PAR) 215,
217
participatory adaptation 192
participatory research 6, 189, 279; definition
184, 185; principles 187; and redefining
the other 183–5
Participatory Research Network 190, 191
partners 154, 155
Parto, S. and Doloreux, D. 58
PASCAL, definition of 1, 2; and social
capital 53–6
PASCAL International 241
PASCAL Observatory 53
patents 72
peer: learning 159; review 76, 226
Penn State Uniscope 255, 256
Percy, S.L. *et al* 147
Perry, B. and Harloe, M. 153
Perry, D.C. and Wiewel, W. 161
place management 1
policy: analysis 122; change 224, **224**, 225;
engagement 218; formation 60; reform 7
politics of, misrecognition 216–18;
recognition 224, 225, 226
pollution 153, 160
Portugal 140, 157
poverty 129, 130, 242, 280, 282, 285, 288;
Mexico 205; reduction 88, 148, 160, 197
power 226; relations 189, 213, 227
private universities, Mexico 203
professional service projects 198
professional social service 198
Progressive Era 131, 134, 135
public engagement 309

public funding 129
public policy 54, 315; Canada 294
public service 128, 146, 251, 252; American
public universities 157
public universities: future of 232; role 243
PURE project (PASCAL Universities and
Region Engagement) 2, 5, 33, 37, 77–80,
242, 243, 320
pure science 313
Puukka, J. and Goddard, J. 158, 159, 271

racism 219
railroad strike (1886) 131
Ramaley, J., Martin, R. and Manning, K. 116
Reagan-Thatcher reforms 4
REAP measurement framework 97, 98
reciprocity 143, 154, 282
region-level public sector partnership 37
regional authorities 40, 42; role 43, 44
regional boundaries 59
regional development 15, 36, 45; case
studies 139, 140–7, 159, 160, 161;
guiding questions 140; and higher
education 158, 159; and policy constraints
158; and public policy 301–3; social
processes 51–66, *61*, *62*, *63*; strategic
priorities 79
Regional Development Agencies (RDAs) 38
regional economic policy 303
regional engagement 4, 16, 159, 241, 304;
of higher education 144; obstacles to 19;
strategic priorities 77
regional infrastructure 79
regional innovation 60, 64–6
regional innovation systems 52, 58; social
processes 64–6
regional issues 104–6
regional policy 3, 103, 104
regional science 58
regional service 231
regional sustainable development 87
regional universities 16, 45
regionalism 103, 104
regions 18, 45, 59, 104; definition 3, 38,

Index

Index